INTERVENTION TO SAVE HONG KONG

INTERVENTION TO SAVE HONG KONG

The Authorities' Counter-Speculation in Financial Markets

CHARLES GOODHART
and
LU DAI

OXFORD
UNIVERSITY PRESS

Great Clarendon Street, Oxford OX2 6DP
Oxford University Press is a department of the University of Oxford.
It furthers the University's objective of excellence in research, scholarship,
and education by publishing worldwide in
Oxford New York
Auckland Bangkok Buenos Aires Cape Town Chennai
Dar es Salaam Delhi Hong Kong Istanbul Karachi Kolkata
Kuala Lumpur Madrid Melbourne Mexico City Mumbai Nairobi
São Paulo Shanghai Taipei Tokyo Toronto

Oxford is a registered trade mark of Oxford University Press
in the UK and in certain other countries

Published in the United States
by Oxford University Press Inc., New York

© Charles Goodhart and Lu Dai, 2003

The moral rights of the author have been asserted
Database right Oxford University Press (maker)

First published 2003

All rights reserved. No part of this publication may be reproduced,
stored in a retrieval system, or transmitted, in any form or by any means,
without the prior permission in writing of Oxford University Press,
or as expressly permitted by law, or under terms agreed with the appropriate
reprographics rights organization. Enquiries concerning reproduction
outside the scope of the above should be sent to the Rights Department,
Oxford University Press, at the address above

You must not circulate this book in any other binding or cover
and you must impose this same condition on any acquirer

British Library Cataloguing in Publication Data

Data available

Library of Congress Cataloging in Publication Data

Data available

ISBN 0-19-926110-5

1 3 5 7 9 10 8 6 4 2

Typeset by Kolam Information Services Pvt, Ltd. Pondicherry, India
Printed by Biddles Ltd., Guildford & King's Lynn

CONTENTS

List of Tables vi
List of Figures ix
Acknowledgements xiii

Chapter 1: Introduction 1
Chapter 2: Background 8
Chapter 3: A Reconstruction of the Intervention 39
Chapter 4: An Assessment of the Effects of the Intervention 97
Chapter 5: Confrontation on the Futures Market 121
Chapter 6: Financing the Intervention 141
Chapter 7: Evaluation of the Intervention 163

Appendix I 191
Appendix II 194
Appendix III 198
References 202
Index 207

LIST OF TABLES

2.1.	Real GDP growth rate of selected Asian countries (1985–2000)	9
2.2.	Exchange rate of selected Asian currencies (Q1 1995–Q4 1999)	11
2.3.	Selected Asian stock market indices (1985–2000)	13
2.4.	Main indicators of Hong Kong (1994–98)	18
2.5.	Hong Kong property price indices (1996–98)	19
2.6.	Hong Kong tourism sector statistics (1990–98)	19
3.1.	Spread sizes in the SEHK	43
3.2.	Price performances during the 'up'-periods	60
3.3.	Mean prices on selected intervention days	62
3.4.	Price changes during the last two intervention days	64
3.5.	Change of the limit order book under a large bid order	68
3.6.	An example of walking up the limit order book	68
3.7.	Definitions of different trading methods under AMS/2 of the SEHK	71
3.8.	Spread and lot size of the intervened stocks	73
3.9.	Estimates of government purchases for each stock	76
3.10.	Summary of intervention values for each stock	79
3.11.	List of intervened stocks dually traded in London	80
3.12.	A comparison of the trading volumes of Hong Kong and London markets	83
3.13.	Average daily trading volumes of Hong Kong stocks on the London market	85
3.14.	Average daily price difference between the Hong Kong and London markets	89
3.15.	Estimation of the government purchase of HSBC shares in both Hong Kong and London	94
3.16.	Intervention estimation from the news	96
4.1.	Aggregate intervention value by each day	98
4.2.	First success (14–19 August)	101
4.3.	Actual market value changes (14–19 August)	102
4.4.	Steady slog (20–26 August)	105
4.5.	Actual market value changes (20–26 August)	106
4.6.	Serious confrontation (27–28 August)	108
4.7.	Actual market value changes (27–28 August)	109
4.8.	Summary of the three phases	110
4.9.	Comparable non-intervened Hong Kong stocks	112

List of Tables vii

4.10.	A comparison of HSBC with other UK banks	119
5.1.	Trading time of the HKFE	124
5.2.	Average amount of gross open interests by month (1998–99)	127
5.3.	Transaction costs for index-futures arbitrages in Hong Kong	135
5.4.	Arbitrage gap after deduction of different transaction costs	136
5.5.	Number of short-sold shares (August–September 1998)	139
5.6.	Correlation between the volume of short-sell turnover and mispricings of the spot/second-month futures	140
6.1.	Illustration of monetary effect of equity market purchase (a–d)	143
6.2.	HKMA foreign currency reserve assets as at 30 June 1998	146
6.3.	Exchange Fund balance sheet as at 30 June 1998	146
6.4.	Month-end foreign currency reserves (June–October 1998)	148
6.5.	Illustration of money market sterilisation of equity market purchase (a–b)	149
6.6.	Money supply of HK (June–October 1998)	150
6.7.	Liabilities of the Exchange Fund	150
6.8.	Hong Kong interbank offered rates (20–30 October 1997)	158
6.9.	Hong Kong interbank offered rates (5–23 January 1998)	159
6.10.	Hong Kong interbank offered rates (8–19 June 1998)	159
6.11.	Currency attacks and HSI performances	160
6.12.	Property price indices by type of premises in Hong Kong (1997–99)	160
6.13.	Hong Kong interbank offered rates (3 August–4 September 1998)	161
6.14.	Month-end 1-month interbank middle rate in Hong Kong and US markets (31 August 1998–31 August 1999)	162
7.1.	Regression results for equation 7.2	167
7.2.	Regression results for equation 7.3	167
7.3.	Regression results for equation 7.1	169
7.4.	Regression results for equation 7.5	169
7.5.	HSI forecast results	170

List of Tables

7.6.	Upper bound for the total profit of all short positions (August contract)	173
7.7.	Upper bound for the total profit of all short positions (September contract)	174
7.8.	Daily trading of August HSI futures contracts (1998)	176
7.9.	Speculators' loss in the August futures contract (1998)	177
7.10.	Price changes of Hang Seng stocks one year after the intervention	181
7.11.	Equity returns in different areas from 31st August 1998 to 31st August 1999	182
A.1.	Regression results of equation (A-2)	193
A.2.	Correlation between different bases and index returns	196
A.3.	Regression results of equation (A-3)	197

LIST OF FIGURES

2.1.	Hong Kong's real GDP growth rate (Q1 1994–Q4 1997)	17
2.2.	The 3-month HIBOR (March–August 1997)	23
2.3.	The HSI and the 3-month HIBOR during the October 1997 attack	24
2.4.	The one-month forward discount of the Hong Kong dollar (December 1997–Febuary 1998)	25
2.5.	The overnight and one-week HIBOR during the June 1998 attack	26
2.6.	The performance of the HSI during 1998	30
3.1.	Price patterns before and after the intervention (Example I)	45
3.2.	Price patterns before and after the intervention (Example II)	46
3.3.	Different patterns during the intervention (Example I)	47
3.4.	Different patterns during the intervention (Example II)	48
3.5.	Unique patterns on 27 August 1998	49
3.6.	Unique patterns on 28 August 1998	50
3.7.	The whole picture of the intervention (Example I)	51
3.8.	The whole picture of the intervention (Example II)	55
3.9.	Histograms of price changes during the 'up' periods	61
3.10.	Histograms of the price movements on 27 & 28 August 1998	65
3.11.	A comparison of the transaction prices and bid prices on 28 August 1998	70
3.12.	Illustration of the estimation process	74
3.13.	Examples of estimations under parallel prices	75
3.14.	London (Hong Kong dollar) trading volume of Hong Kong stocks during August 1998	84
3.15.	Intra-day price performance of Hong Kong stocks on the London market during the intervention	86

x   List of Figures

3.16.	Price comparison between the Hong Kong and London markets	88
3.17.	Comparison of daily average price of HSBC in August 1998	90
3.18.	Intra-day trading of HSBC in London on 27 August 1998	93
3.19.	Intra-day trading of HSBC in London on 28 August 1998	93
4.1.	Performances of intervened and non-intervened Hong Kong stocks (13–31 August 1998)	113
4.2.	Long-term comparison of intervened and non-intervened Hong Kong stocks	115
4.3.	Daily comparison of HSBC with other UK bank shares	118
4.4.	Hourly comparison of HSBC with Standard Chartered Bank	119
5.1.	Percentage of futures trading volume	123
5.2.	Daily gross open interests (January 1998–December 1999)	127
5.3.	Daily trading volume of contracts with different maturities	128
5.4.	Additional open interests for August futures contract	129
5.5.	Additional open interest for September futures contract	129
5.6.	Daily average of HSI spot index and August and September futures	130
5.7.	The basis of spot-month HSI futures (August–October 1998)	131
5.8.	The mispricings of August/September/October 1998 futures contracts	133
6.1.	Day-end spot exchange rate of Hong Kong dollar against US dollar (July–October 1998)	152
6.2.	Week-end 3-month forward discount on the Hong Kong dollar (October 1997–December 1998)	154
6.3.	Day-end 3-month forward discount on the Hong Kong dollar (July–October 1998)	154

6.4. Difference between the notional and actual
Hong Kong 3-month interest rate
(August–September 1998) 156
7.1. HSI and Singapore Straits Times index
(July–December 1998) 165
7.2. Comparison between the actual
and predicted HSI 170
7.3. September futures basis (3 August-28 September 1998) 178
A.1. Price performances of the spot-month
futures on expiration days 195

ACKNOWLEDGEMENTS

Many people have contributed, directly or indirectly, to the production of this book. Our foremost thanks go to Professor Stephen Cheung, who was Dr. Lu Dai's supervisor at the City University of Hong Kong. He has been involved throughout the entire project, supplying the data, helping with the technical analysis, and always offering crucial suggestions.

A debt of gratitude is also owed to Mr. Andrew Sheng (The Securities and Futures Commission of Hong Kong), Mr. Norman Chan (The Hong Kong Monetary Authority), Professor Y. C. Jao (University of Hong Kong), Professor Paul Draper (University of Edinburgh), Professor Gordon Tang (Hong Kong Baptist University) and Dr. Jun Cai (City University of Hong Kong). Their patient reading of this bulky monograph as well as their constructive comments and opinions are much appreciated.

The Hong Kong trading data were kindly provided by the Stock Exchange of Hong Kong and the Hong Kong's Futures Exchange, while the London trading data were prepared by Mr. Stephen Wells (London School of Economics), who also helped a great deal in explaining and analysing the data.

We would also like to thank Anna Maria Reforgiato Recupero (London School of Economics), Marina Emond, as well as many other helpful colleagues from the City University of Hong Kong and the Financial Markets Group at the London School of Economics for their kind assistance in the successful completion of this work. Charles Goodhart thanks the Economic and Social Research Council (ESRC) for financial support for this and other research studies.

Any errors, however, remain our own, and we stress that this exercise involves our own personal and independent interpretation of publicly available information, and does not reflect the views of any other institution with which either author has been associated.

CHAPTER 1

Introduction

'In order to achieve their objectives in undermining the Hong Kong dollar, speculators have deployed a whole host of improper measures which are clear to all.... In order to deter such manipulation, I have exercised my power under the Exchange Fund Ordinance and asked the Hong Kong Monetary Authority (HKMA) to draw upon the resources of the Exchange Fund to mount appropriate counter activities in the stock and futures markets.... Accordingly, the HKMA mounted counter activities earlier today.'
—*Donald Tsang, Financial Secretary of Hong Kong, 14 August 1998*[1]

'The government's Ramboesque intervention in the markets on Friday achieved its short-term goals with spectacular success. It caught speculators by surprise, pushed the Hang Seng Index (HSI) safely over the 7,000 mark at the start of a long weekend when Hong Kong would be dangerously exposed to the whims of the London market.... As such, the authorities mounted a very effective coup. The longer term aims of the operation, however, may be harder to achieve, and may bring considerable risks.'
—South China Morning Post, *16 August 1998*[2]

'Unfortunately, if they're wrong on the fundamentals, all they'll be doing is providing profits for speculators... From our perspective, no matter what they want to do in their

---

[1] 'Statement by FS', http://www.hknews.com.hk, 14 August 1998.
[2] 'Skirmish won: but now for the war', *South China Morning Post*, 16 August 1998.

market, when they wake up on Monday morning they're still going to be in a depression.'
—*Stanley Druckenmiller, Manager, Soros' Quantum Fund*[3]

Hong Kong has usually been described as a shining example of the free market economy operating at its best. In fact, the Heritage Foundation of the United States voted Hong Kong as the world's 'most free economy' for seven consecutive years from 1995 onwards. If there were any single time that Hong Kong's free market image was seriously endangered—then the government's vast purchases of local blue chip stocks in August 1998 would be at the top of the list.

This intervention took place approximately one year after the Asian Financial Crisis began in Thailand in July 1997. During the subsequent year, Hong Kong's economy fell from its peak at the time of the handover to the People's Republic of China, and thereafter contracted in each quarter. On several occasions, intensive market pressures to sell the Hong Kong dollar (HKD) resulted in sharp upward spikes in interest rates, which further dampened the property and equity markets. The Hong Kong government intervention came after the Hang Seng Index (HSI) had reached a low point of 6,660 on 13 August 1998, and the struggle between the authorities and the speculators continued until 28 August 1998, the expiration day of the August futures contracts.

The scale of this intervention in the equity market was the biggest ever, and, relative to the size of the economy, the interventions in both the equity and the foreign exchange markets were unparalleled in size, scope, and intensity.

We consider this whole episode to be a historical event, which deserves an in-depth analysis from several angles. It is important not only for Hong Kong, but also for analysts as a record of capital market behaviour and government intervention.

1.1 *The Significance of the Intervention for Hong Kong*

For Hong Kong, it was the first time ever that the government took such a drastic decision to enter the equity market. If any precedent is to be found, the only one might be when the Hong Kong

---

[3] 'Soros betting on government losing the war', *Hong Kong Standard*, 28 August 1998.

Jockey Club actively bought stocks during the market crises in the 1980s, purchases which were widely believed to have taken place at the government's request.[4] Later, as market prices rose, the Jockey Club slowly reduced its portfolio, and thus made a profit from the exercise. However, those purchases were tiny compared to the intervention in August 1998.

This intervention was especially notable because the Hong Kong government's image has always been that of a government which strongly supports laissez-faire policies. Hong Kong's successful emergence as an international commercial and financial centre has been largely attributed to the 'positive non-intervention' policy adopted by the government. Market forces were allowed to determine the level of prices and of activity in a variety of areas related to public affairs. Following such a massive injection of funds by the government to bolster the stock market, the government had to face the risk of damaging Hong Kong's free-market image. However, despite much criticism both from within Hong Kong and outside, the government action is now widely seen as successful, since the speculators withdrew, and the market recovered, and never subsequently fell back to the pre-intervention level. (Though critics will ascribe that more to good luck than to good judgement).

Moreover, this was the fiercest battle ever waged in Hong Kong to protect its pegged exchange rate under the Currency Board System. The Currency Board System was strengthened, instead of being destroyed as some analysts had predicted. As we now know, except for the Chinese Renminbi (RMB), which was not fully convertible in the capital account, the Hong Kong dollar was the only currency that stood firm during the regional wave of currency depreciations. At the time, however, the Hong Kong dollar's peg to the US dollar was severely criticised, and it became the target of speculative attacks after most of the other currencies in the region had, one after the other, been forced off their pegs. The Hong Kong government had faced several similar attacks before, and almost every time they had responded by forcing interest rates sharply upwards, and then allowing market forces to adjust. But in August 1998 they took the unusual step of entering the equity and foreign exchange markets directly. The event itself, as well as its successful result, needs further study if any policy implications are to be derived.

[4] 'When Donald went to war', *South China Morning Post*, 29 August 1998.

1.2 Importance of the Intervention for Capital Markets

The Hong Kong government's confrontation with the speculators in August 1998 was also an interesting, and perhaps illustrative, experience for capital markets as a whole. Seldom has such direct intervention taken place in equity markets, though it has been more frequently seen in Asia than elsewhere.[5] However, interventions in other financial markets have not been uncommon, with most occurring in the foreign exchange market, with Central Banks buying or selling certain currencies. On the other hand, governments have been seen in the equity market in fewer cases and even when they have intervened, they have usually used indirect means, such as loosening or strengthening certain rules or regulations. Such direct and massive market buying as was done by the Hong Kong government is unusual, perhaps almost unique. Of course it would never become a matter of course. As Hong Kong's Financial Secretary, Donald Tsang, once said, 'We only contemplate intervention in very exceptional circumstances.'[6] However, as capital markets become a more and more globalized, speculative attacks may possibly become a more serious issue in all markets. Whether or not other authorities would have to face the same crisis that the Hong Kong government did, they may benefit from the latter's experience to prepare for any such future eventualities.

Moreover, this event also offers a rare example of waging a successful battle against speculators. In the history of market crises, there have been few such success stories of government intervention. Consider Soros' famous (or infamous) 1992 attack upon the British Pound for instance. On Wednesday, 16 September 1992, now called Black Wednesday, the Bank of England was forced from the Exchange Rate Mechanism (ERM) after spending US$15 billion buying pounds and raising interest rates from 10 per cent to 12 per cent, and then to 15 per cent, in order to try, but failing, to stop the pound's devaluation. After Black Wednesday, the public perceived the central bank as less powerful than they had previously thought. Given that comparatively the Hong Kong government is a much smaller economic power, their achievement is surely remark-

---

[5] For instance, trust funds were set up in Taiwan in the 1990s to keep the market from large falls. In other Asian countries, authorities were reported to have supported the equity markets using quasi-public funds, such as government-owned funds, pension or provident schemes. There are, however, no public records on whether these operations were successful.

[6] 'Statement by FS', http://www.hknews.com.hk, 14 August 1998.

able. Their success could be attributed to an appropriate strategy, or speculation which had driven prices too far away from the fundamentals, or simply good luck. Whatever the reason, we shall try to indicate our views on this; it deserves thorough analysis.

1.3   Other Relevant Studies

The 1998 market intervention is also an event of considerable academic value. It offers an opportunity to examine closely the entire issue of government intervention and how it can sway market developments.

Despite its importance, there have been only a few published studies of this event. Jao's (2001) *The Asian Financial Crisis and the Ordeal of Hong Kong*, although not focused on the government intervention in August 1998, gives a very detailed account of Hong Kong's economic development before, during, and after the Asian Crisis. De Brouwer (2001), on the other hand, traces the interrelationships between the market dynamics and the role of highly leveraged institutions. The author summarized developments in Hong Kong's financial markets in 1998 in three distinguishable stages. In the first stage, the speculators established positions in both currency and equity markets; in the second, the market was seen as highly vulnerable to large one-way movements, and speculative activities became more pronounced and aggressive; and the third stage saw speculators exiting positions. De Brouwer suggested that shorting the Hong Kong markets was initially justified, given the domestic and regional economic fundamentals in 1997 and 1998, but that subsequent concentrated speculative attacks by a group of aggressive highly leveraged institutions (HLIs) may then have caused market prices to overshoot their 'fundamental' value.

There are several other Chinese books, including Li (1999) and Huang and Lin (1999), which offer good chronologies of the intervention process from different viewpoints. The latter is more focused on the stock market, while the former pays more attention to the foreign exchange speculation, and official responses.

As for academic papers, to our knowledge, besides Huque's (1999) analysis of the political issues surrounding the intervention, there is only one published financial paper, by Cheng, Fung and Chan (2000), which is on the dynamic relationships between HSI options and futures. Their data set starts from 1 January 1996 and ends on the next trading day after the intervention, i.e. 31 August 1998. Their article focuses on the impact of the Asian Financial Crisis on Hong Kong's index futures and options markets.[7]

In addition, there are some working papers on the subject. One is by Fung and Draper (2000), which is also on the mispricing of the HSI futures. This paper is based on the relationship between the index futures and the underlying stocks, and the aim of the paper is to identify the mispricing patterns during the crisis and the intervention periods, and to try to find explanations for the patterns. (We cover this subject ourselves in Chapter 5.) A second paper is by Chan (1999), which analyses the volatility of the Hong Kong stock market before, during, and after the intervention. The paper investigates whether the stock market became more volatile after the volume of shares in circulation had been reduced by the official purchases. The results show no subsequent *general* increase in price volatility for either those stocks in the main HSI or those excluded from that Index, after the official intervention. However, for the stocks in which the government bought a *substantial* portion, price volatility increased significantly. Indeed, there was a strong correlation between the additional price volatility in the post-intervention period and the percentage of shares bought by the government. The above papers helped us understand several aspects of the intervention's impact. In our opinion, however, a more complete account of the story is needed in order to understand its full effect. We have made an effort in that respect by reconstructing the whole intervention process, though using only publicly available information. We believe that we have done a good job because the results based on our estimation method are very close to the aggregate data for equity purchases that was announced by the government. In addition, we also give an overall evaluation of the intervention's result based on our calibrations. The spot-futures arbitrage relationship is examined specifically in Chapter 5, because the futures market was an important field of confrontation between the government and the speculator. However, we leave the effect of the intervention on longer-term market volatility and/or bid-ask spreads to future study because, albeit important, they can be completely separable exercises.

---

[7] Both ex-post and ex-ante tests of the Put-Call-Futures Parity are carried out to study the arbitrage relationships between the two derivative products on the HSI. The results show that, during the crisis and the fortnight of government intervention, arbitrage profits and the volatility of such profit, measured by its standard deviations, increased in both ex-post and ex-ante analysis.

The book is organized as follows. Chapter 2 gives some background information on the Hong Kong government's adoption of the intervention strategy. Hong Kong's economic fundamentals, as well as the regional turmoil during the Asian Economic Crisis, are also described. In Chapter 3, we use the transaction data obtained from the Stock Exchange of Hong Kong to reconstruct the intervention process. We estimate the amount that the government purchased for each stock on each day, both the value of the purchase and number of shares purchased, and the results are compared with those announced by the government. In Chapter 4, we assess the government's effort to control the development of the equity market at each different stage, and the behaviour of the intervened stocks is compared with that of the non-intervened stocks, as well as with comparable stocks in London. Chapter 5 endeavours to examine the behaviour of the futures market, with a focus on the spot-futures arbitrage relationship. Chapter 6 examines how the intervention was financed, and, in particular, explores associated developments in the foreign exchange and money markets. We conclude with Chapter 7, which gives an overall evaluation of the government's intervention, together with some concluding remarks.

CHAPTER 2

Background

During the Asian Financial Crisis, Hong Kong was particular not only because of its firm currency peg, but also because of the way in which the government acted to protect the peg. To some, the August 1998 intervention came as a shock since it was totally unexpected of a government which took pride in its non-interventionist stand. The decision was seen as extremely controversial. However, government officials claimed that their only intention was to protect the Hong Kong people's interests and that it was not really a departure from the famous 'positive non-intervention' policy.[1] In order to understand the various arguments for and against such intervention, it is useful to have some background knowledge on the economic conditions both in Hong Kong and in the whole affected Asian area. We will first give a brief account of the Asian Crisis in the following section, before we come to Hong Kong's own story.

2.1   Asia: From Miracle to Crisis

2.1.1   The Asian Miracle

In the decades before 1960, Southeast Asia used to be one of the poorest regions, with one of the highest population densities in the world. However, economists were subsequently amazed by the ability of these countries not only to pick themselves up from such poverty, but also to establish some of the strongest economies in the world. The so-called 'Four Tigers', namely South Korea, Hong Kong, Taiwan, and Singapore, experienced rapid economic

---

[1] 'Intervention true to guiding policy' by Joseph Yam, Chief Executive of the HKMA, *South China Morning Post*, 24 August 1998.

growth, well above the average rate of expansion in the world as a whole. Take Korea for instance, although impoverished after the civil war in 1953, in a span of three decades, from 1960 to 1990, the country recovered to become the world's eleventh largest economy. Other countries, including Japan, Malaysia, Indonesia, and Thailand, also made rapid strides in economic growth in a relatively short period of time (Table 2.1). The economic competitiveness of these countries improved dramatically, and they suddenly became strong competitors even to some well developed countries. For weaker economies, in fact, Southeast Asia offered a vivid example of the possibility of economic takeoff.

One of the most distinctive features of these Asian countries is that the governments have had a strong hand in shaping the marketplace. These countries are looked upon as relationship-based economies. In these economies, the governments promoted certain sectors by giving them favourable treatment, like extending tax credits and subsidies. They strongly believed that, for the economy to take off quickly, they should be closely involved; that investment should be channelled into those industries with high growth potential, but where private sector investment was unlikely due to the risk involved. Other policies included the use of tariffs and other measures to protect their domestic

TABLE 2.1. *Real GDP growth rate of selected Asian countries (1985–2000)*

Country	Hong Kong	Taiwan	Singapore	Korea	Malaysia	Thailand	Indonesia	Philippines
1985	0.2	5.0	3.9	6.9	−1.1	4.6	2.5	6.3
1986	10.8	26.1	4.6	12.4	1.2	5.5	5.9	3.4
1987	13.0	12.7	4.0	10.8	5.4	9.5	4.9	4.3
1988	8.0	7.8	5.1	11.4	9.9	13.3	5.8	6.7
1989	2.6	8.2	−1.4	10.5	9.1	12.2	7.5	6.1
1990	3.4	5.4	3.9	7.5	9.0	11.2	7.2	3.2
1991	5.1	7.6	−0.4	9.2	9.5	8.6	6.9	−0.7
1992	6.3	7.5	2.2	5.4	8.9	8.1	6.5	0.3
1993	6.1	7.0	−2.2	5.5	9.9	8.4	6.5	2.1
1994	5.4	7.1	2.9	8.3	9.2	9.0	7.5	4.4
1995	3.9	6.4	4.7	8.9	9.8	9.3	8.2	4.8
1996	4.5	6.1	5.2	6.8	10.0	5.9	7.8	5.7
1997	5.0	6.7	5.0	5.0	7.3	−1.4	4.7	5.2
1998	−5.3	4.6	5.7	−6.7	−7.4	−10.8	−13.0	−0.6
1999	3.1	5.7	5.0	10.7	5.6	4.2	0.3	3.3
2000	10.5	6.5	5.5	7.6	8.4	4.8	4.7	3.6

Source: Datastream.

industries from international competition. Rather than let the market determine the winners, the governments picked sectors or even individual businesses. Such a policy gave rise to some super-large corporations that became top competitors in the world market. However, the relationships built up between the government, the banking sector, and the industrial sector drew much criticism from some economists and commentators who closely observe the region's development. They argued that this kind of close relationship embodied serious dangers, especially if there was a lack of supervision and if corruption became rife.[2] But initially such expressions of doubt received little attention; that is, as long as the Southeast regional economy remained robust.

2.1.2 Asian Financial Turmoil in 1997

The immediate trigger for the Asian Financial Crisis was the devaluation of currencies in the region. In July 1997, Thailand's central bank de-pegged its currency, the baht. This was, perhaps, inevitable given the decline in the central bank's reserves and the underlying pressure in the market on the currency. The purpose was obvious: the price of Thai goods in dollar terms would be lowered and its competitiveness restored in foreign markets. It was hoped that, as a result, Thailand could attract new investment. Nevertheless, this action was, later on, seen as the starting point for the financial turmoil in the region.

Like many currencies in the region, the baht's value had been pegged to the US dollar, partly to provide stability. In part due to the appreciation of the dollar, the baht as well as other currencies pegged to the dollar were then increasingly seen as overvalued. Foreign investors started to worry about a possible sudden decline in the baht's value, and a sell-off gained momentum. The central bank tried to defend the peg by pumping billions of dollars into the foreign exchange market (mostly covertly in the futures market), and later on even imposed currency controls by limiting access to baht for currency traders. But as confidence in the baht weakened, more and more foreign companies and banks tried to get out of the country, and available foreign reserves dropped dramatically. Finally, the government was forced to devalue the currency, hoping thereby to restore confidence.

---

[2] See, for example, McKinnon and Pill (1996) and Krugman (1998).

However, the devaluation had an additional effect, which turned out to be devastating to the domestic economy. According to an article in *The Economist*,[3] out of Thailand's $90 billion foreign debt, $70 billion was owed by the private sector, mostly financial institutions. These foreign debts, denominated in terms of dollars, became more expensive to repay when the home currency devalued, and thus unleashed a flurry of loan defaults by ultimate borrowers. This, in turn, pushed the banking sector into a dangerous situation. When the government recognized this and wanted to help, it found that its ability to save the banking system had also been much weakened by the devaluation of its currency, since it could not provide the needed foreign currency. Finally, the Thai government turned to international institutions for help and an IMF bailout package was implemented.

Other countries, such as Malaysia, Indonesia, and South Korea, were also badly hit, and their currencies suffered a huge decline in value as well (Table 2.2). It is now accepted that this disturbing result

TABLE 2.2. *Exchange rate of selected Asian currencies (Q1 1995–Q4 1999)*

Country	Taiwan New Dollar	Singapore Dollar	Thailand Baht	Malaysia Ringgit	South Korea Won	Hong Kong Dollar
Q1 95	26.36	1.45	24.94	2.55	788.45	7.73
Q2 95	25.81	1.39	24.74	2.46	761.15	7.73
Q3 95	27.46	1.42	25.04	2.50	776.85	7.74
Q4 95	27.30	1.42	25.14	2.54	765.75	7.73
Q1 96	27.48	1.40	25.23	2.55	779.70	7.73
Q2 96	27.37	1.41	25.31	2.49	781.45	7.74
Q3 96	27.50	1.41	25.31	2.49	818.15	7.73
Q4 96	27.50	1.40	25.42	2.52	828.35	7.73
Q1 97	27.58	1.42	25.94	2.48	857.10	7.75
Q2 97	27.83	1.43	25.51	2.50	890.85	7.74
Q3 97	28.73	1.50	33.65	2.77	899.75	7.75
Q4 97	32.15	1.59	38.85	3.41	1053.00	7.73
Q1 98	32.91	1.65	44.65	3.85	1661.50	7.75
Q2 98	33.54	1.64	39.32	3.80	1382.50	7.75
Q3 98	34.64	1.77	41.60	4.23	1300.00	7.75
Q4 98	32.43	1.64	36.16	3.80	1245.30	7.74
Q1 99	33.09	1.72	37.58	3.80	1211.50	7.75
Q2 99	32.79	1.72	37.02	3.80	1194.30	7.75
Q3 99	31.85	1.68	38.30	3.80	1197.50	7.76
Q4 99	31.73	1.67	38.75	3.80	1169.50	7.77

Source: Datastream.

[3] 'Feeling the heat', *The Economist*, 17 May 1997.

was largely due to over-optimistic domestic investment. Believing that high growth could be sustained for a longer time, companies in the region kept borrowing money and, when the investment turned out to be unprofitable, they simply borrowed more to cover the loss. Banks were encouraged to make risky loans under pressure either from the government or their owners. These large debts, however, then led to a series of bankruptcies, and badly damaged the confidence of both local and overseas investors. No financial institution wanted to extend more loans to the region; indeed, foreign banks tried to withdraw their existing involvement. So, without any back-up, the currencies of these countries fell drastically.

The Asian Miracle had finally ended, with a whimper, in the Asian Crisis. The devastating effects on the regional economy were clear enough. Throughout the region, there was a sharp loss of wealth. Massive withdrawals of capital from the region not only dragged down the value of the currencies but also sent the stock market into a nosedive reaching lows of almost ten years previously (Table 2.3).

2.1.3 From Financial Crisis to Social Crisis

Besides threatening currency and banking stability, the Crisis had serious macroeconomic consequences, which, in turn, led to social instabilities. For example, the corporate crisis and the credit squeeze caused lay-offs, weak demand for new labour market entrants, and also real wage declines. According to a World Bank report (1998),[4] unemployment increased in Thailand by 50 per cent from the start of the Crisis to February 1998. In Korea, unemployment reached 7.0 per cent in June 1998, and in the Philippines one million additional people became jobless between April 1997 and April 1998. The poor were hit the hardest since there was no demand for their labour, while the prices of commodities rose sharply. To make things worse, governments could not offer any help, and even had to cut spending on social services. When confidence in the economy collapsed, social order completely broke down, and domestic crime and violence increased. Indonesia faced the most serious situation. Friendly neighbourhoods turned to fighting each other. Food riots and ethnic pressures made people feel unsafe. Children had no choice but to drop out of school, and seek work. Government officials reported that the enrolment rate

---

[4] 'East Asia: The road to recovery', The World Bank, 1998.

TABLE 2.3. *Selected Asian stock market indices (1985–2000)*

Country	Hong Kong	Singapore	Malaysia	Philippines	Korea	Thailand	Taiwan
Index (Year End)	Hang Seng	Strait Times	Kuala Lumpur Composite	Philippines SE Composite	Korea SE Composite	Bangkok S.E.T	Taiwan SE Weighted
1985	1668.5	502.3	192.5	163.2	184.8	137.3	968.0
1986	2798.6	927.2	333.7	472.3	350.5	213.3	1288.1
1987	2472.3	775.0	276.6	788.7	615.9	376.1	3306.1
1988	3058.9	926.8	390.5	933.1	921.5	429.1	7190.9
1989	2933.2	1230.8	599.7	1023.8	857.5	804.4	11462.1
1990	3647.3	1201.8	596.2	967.2	676.3	803.2	4487.8
1991	4908.8	1171.0	590.9	1118.8	626.0	807.6	4988.0
1992	6502.8	1304.4	638.3	1543.1	615.5	898.7	4731.8
1993	9918.1	1868.2	1064.3	2606.8	896.5	1359.2	5672.8
1994	8093.9	1746.7	953.4	2456.5	933.4	1235.7	6474.9
1995	11378.7	2119.2	1136.1	2918.8	851.0	1318.2	4725.8
1996	13416.3	2046.2	1249.8	3279.8	678.1	676.6	8081.0
1997	10919.5	1430.3	690.3	2181.9	522.5	508.0	8847.6
1998	10241.1	1449.6	516.8	2013.4	538.1	336.2	6383.0
1999	17758.7	2119.9	940.4	1738.3	909.3	379.2	9367.9
2000	14321.0	1900.0	706.0	1611.4	568.1	299.8	5635.0

Source: Datastream.

was down from 78 per cent to 54 per cent. Other countries faced very similar problems. In Thailand, farmers protested; in Korea, workers refused to accept the economic policies and resulting conditions. Starting as a currency crisis, the conjuncture escalated into a much more painful social turmoil, vitiating the entire social fabric.

2.1.4 Summary

In East Asia, some 370 million people had escaped poverty during the two decades prior to 1995.[5] Yet this achievement was nullified by the recession which followed the Crisis. What was seen in the region, though to different degrees, was a sharp loss of wealth, a sudden capital flight, asset price collapses, currency devaluation, and banking instability. Besides the fundamental aspects of the local economies, the group most accused of instigating this collapse was the hedge funds. They were charged with manipulating the markets in search of profit, and hence throwing these vulnerable economies into collapse. Even relatively well-regulated economies, such as Hong Kong and Singapore, did not escape such attacks, and suffered grievously from the sudden economic downturn; though Taiwan came out less scathed than the others. Hong Kong's adjustment was painful, particularly because of the property price collapse and salary reduction. Yet the Hong Kong dollar currency peg remained intact amongst the disturbances of regional currency depreciation. This achievement was, at least partly, attributed to the government's unconventional market intervention and the subsequent policy measures to strengthen the financial system. In the following section, we give an introduction to Hong Kong's experience during the Asian Crisis.

2.2 An Overview of Hong Kong's Economy

Hong Kong is one of the most important markets in Asia. Among all its neighbours, Hong Kong's economy did not initially appear to have suffered as much from the regional Crisis. However, due to close linkages with other economies in the region, Hong Kong was actually under considerable stress. At the worst, there was roughly

---

[5] 'East Asia: The road to recovery', The World Bank, 1998.

a 50 per cent decline in prices in the property and stock markets. Indeed, the whole economy experienced a severe setback in 1998. In constant price terms, GDP contracted by around 5.1 per cent, while the seasonally adjusted unemployment rate rose sharply from 2.5 per cent in the fourth quarter of 1997 to 5.7 per cent in the fourth quarter of 1998.

2.2.1 A Brief Note on Hong Kong's Policy Framework

After being a British colony for 155 years, Hong Kong became a Special Administrative Region (SAR) of the People's Republic of China on 1 July 1997. Despite various anxieties and suspicions, this transfer of sovereignty was accomplished smoothly and successfully, and the new government of the Hong Kong SAR continues to pursue its famous free-market policies with a high degree of autonomy.

On the fiscal policy side, Hong Kong has always tried to foster a flexible and competitive private sector, and to retain its small government posture. To achieve that, Hong Kong maintains a simple and stable tax system with low tax rates, keeps current account expenditure in line with GDP growth, and tries to maintain an adequate level of fiscal reserves. Before 1998, the budget was in deficit only once during the previous fifteen years. Indeed, the Basic Law, which sets the constitutional basis for the SAR, provides for the continuation of the previous revenue and expenditure policies. The Law also insists that the SAR retains its independent fiscal policies; that its financial resources are not transferred to the Central People's Government; and that the Central People's Government does not levy taxes in the SAR.

On the monetary policy side, a pegged exchange rate system was adopted in Hong Kong in 1983, with the Hong Kong dollar linked to the US dollar at HK $7.8 to US $1. The Basic Law, apart from requiring that the Hong Kong dollar be fully backed by the reserve fund, provides for an independent monetary policy in Hong Kong. The Hong Kong Monetary Authority (HKMA), under a modern version of the currency board arrangement,[6] is responsible for implementing monetary policy and administering the exchange rate system. In order to preserve the exchange rate peg, the HKMA can use various tools to smooth out serious volatility in interbank

---

[6] A more detailed account of the Hong Kong currency board arrangement is given in section 2.3.1.

interest rates, such as selling/buying foreign currencies, shifting government deposits between commercial banks and the Exchange Fund, open market operations, and the extension of credit through the Liquidity Adjustment Facility (LAF). The LAF was provided in 1992 to banks that have surpluses or deficits in their clearing accounts. It allowed banks to make late adjustments (after the close of daily interbank trading) to their liquidity positions. The Exchange Fund could absorb or provide liquidity at the LAF bid or offered rate, and these two rates set the floor and the ceiling of the overnight interbank interest rate. However, this facility was accused of certain defects, potentially contributing to interest rate volatility, and was abolished later in September 1998. The discount window took its place to continue the function of supplying liquidity to banks.[7]

2.2.2 Hong Kong's Economic Position at the Time of the Crisis

Recovering from a cyclical downturn in 1995, Hong Kong's economy began gradually to improve during 1996 and the first two quarters of 1997. In real terms, Hong Kong's GDP growth increased steadily from under 3 per cent in late 1995 to over 6 per cent in early 1997 (Figure 2.1). An early impetus to this recovery came from a revival in asset markets. In the residential property market, too, sentiment turned around in early 1996. Good results were seen in primary sales, and trading in the secondary market was also active. By the end of 1996, the prices of private residential flats had increased by almost 20 per cent over the 1995 average level. The main reasons for this upturn included: a cut in the lending rates following a reduction in US interest rates; stronger end-user demand for housing from an inflow of returnees, expatriates and Chinese immigrants; a continuous increase in household income, etc.

In contrast with domestic demand, export sector performance was slack during 1996. Growth in total exports of goods moderated significantly to 5 per cent in real terms from 12 per cent in 1995. From mid-1995 to end-1996, the real effective exchange rate (REER) of the Hong Kong dollar appreciated by 12.5 per cent, in

---

[7] A more detailed explanation can be found in 'Strengthening of Currency Board Arrangement in Hong Kong', *Quarterly Bulletin of the HKMA*, November 1998.

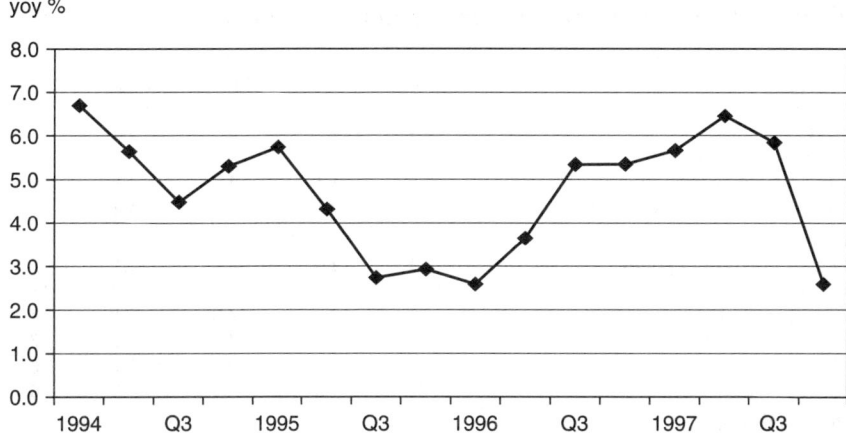

FIG. 2.1. Hong Kong's real GDP growth rate (Q1 1994–Q4 1997).
Source: CE1C.

line with the stronger US dollar.[8] This coincided with slack external demand in several major markets, which in 1996 affected most Asian economies. Mainland China's weakened demand had an immediate impact on Hong Kong's re-exports and its growth rate halved to 7.5 per cent. Nevertheless, the slowdown in exports was matched by an even greater deceleration in imports. In 1996, import growth slowed down substantially from 14 per cent in 1995 to 4 per cent in real terms (Table 2.4).

The recovery gained greater momentum during the first half of 1997. This was partly because of steady progress in resolving transition issues; and the encouraging economic situation in Mainland China boosted private investment and consumption. Real GDP growth accelerated to 6.8 per cent year-on-year in the second quarter (Figure 2.1). Inflation remained in check, as import prices fell and wages rose only moderately. However, inflation of property prices spilled over into the rental market, and pushed up the Consumer Price Index (CPI) inflation rate. Export performance in 1997 was slightly better than in 1996. In particular, domestic exports saw a notable recovery. Overall investment spending, as well as consumer spending, remained robust up to the third quarter.

[8] 'People's Republic of China-Hong Kong Special Administrative Region: Recent Economic Developments', IMF Staff Country Report No. 98/41, April 1998.

TABLE 2.4. *Main indicators of Hong Kong (1994–98)*

Yoy %	1994	1995	1996	1997	1998
GDP	5.4	4.7	4.5	5.3	−5.1
Private consumption	6.7	0.8	4.7	6.7	−6.7
Government consumption	3.9	4.4	4.0	2.4	0.6
Gross domestic fixed capital formation	15.7	9.6	10.8	15.6	−6.4
External Sector					
Domestic export of goods	−2.3	2.0	−8.4	2.1	−7.9
Re-export of goods	13.8	14.3	7.5	6.8	−3.7
Total export of goods	10.4	12.0	4.8	6.1	−4.3
Import of goods	14.0	13.8	4.3	7.2	−7.2
Export of services	6.5	11.3	9.7	−1.1	−6.6
Import of services	8.8	5.8	4.9	−3.6	−0.6
Price indicator					
GDP deflator	6.9	2.4	5.9	7.2	0.9
Consumer Price Index	8.1	8.7	6.3	5.8	2.8

Source: *Economic Background* (editions from 1996 to 1999), Economic Analysis Division, Financial Services Bureau, HKSAR

During the summer of 1997, the Crisis in the area began to affect Hong Kong's economy. Growth slowed down in the third quarter, with a 5.7 per cent expansion over a year earlier, and then declined dramatically to 2.9 per cent in the fourth quarter (Figure 2.1). Market sentiment took a distinct negative turn after late October, when a speculative attack on the Hong Kong dollar led to a rise in the overnight interbank interest rate almost as high as 300 per cent.[9] Asset markets, including both the stock market and the property market, fell sharply.

Following a sharp rise in prices of residential flats in the first half of 1997, activity in the residential property market began to taper off in the third quarter, though in part due to the government's announced commitment to increase flat supply substantially in the longer term. The downturn started to accelerate in the fourth quarter after the currency attack. Towards the end of the year, trading in the secondary market shrunk sharply as the impact of the Asian financial turmoil quickly spread to the local economy (see Table 2.5).

The tourism sector also saw an immediate impact. The total number of visitor arrivals fell in the third quarter by 27 per cent and the hotel room occupancy rate fell to 65 per cent from a near 90 per cent average previously (Table 2.6).

---

[9] The currency attack in October 1997 will be described in more detail later in section 2.3.2.

TABLE 2.5. *Hong Kong property price indices (1996–98)*

Year	Quarter	Residential flats	Office space	Shopping space	Factory space
		(1995 = 100)	(1989 = 100)	(1989 = 100)	(1989 = 100)
1996	Q1	99	182	281	149
	Q2	107	183	283	143
	Q3	109	174	285	138
	Q4	119	196	297	140
1997	Q1	140	214	340	147
	Q2	161	217	379	145
	Q3	165	202	413	141
	Q4	155	191	395	135
1998	Q1	126	159	342	123
	Q2	112	145	294	118
	Q3	90	110	241	108
	Q4	88	105	220	95

Source: Datastream.

TABLE 2.6. *Hong Kong tourism sector statistics (1990–98)*

Year		Visitor arrivals	Hotel room occupancy rate
		(yoy %)	(%)
1990		10	79
1991		3	75
1992		18	82
1993		12	87
1994		4	85
1995		14	85
1996		15	88
1997	Q1	9	86
	Q2	2	81
	Q3	−27	65
	Q4	−23	73
1998	Q1	−25	70
	Q2	−16	75
	Q3	10	77
	Q4	5	81

Source: Hong Kong Tourism Association.

The downtrend in the Hong Kong economy continued and deepened throughout 1998. Market confidence suffered from this exceptional economic setback. At the same time, the US dollar strengthened further due to the robust performance of the US economy, in contrast to the financial instability in East Asia. This put more pressure on Hong Kong, because of the Hong Kong dollar's peg to the US dollar. Obviously, if the currency value could not change freely, then other prices have to make the adjustment: by the end of 1998, property prices declined almost 50 per cent from the pre-crisis level (Table 2.5); office and flat rentals fell sharply; wages and salaries eased. Consumer prices receded quickly towards the end of the year. This drastic economic adjustment led to an increase in the unemployment rate to 5.5 per cent. Moreover, as we will describe, further speculative attacks were to occur in 1998.

2.3   Currency Attacks and Intervention

2.3.1   The Currency Board Arrangement and Auto-pilot Mechanism

The Hong Kong dollar has been pegged to the US dollar at a rate of HK $7.8 per US dollar ever since 1983, and the associated currency board arrangement adopted under this Linked Exchange Rate System. First introduced in the British colony of Mauritius in 1894, a currency board system is a rule-based monetary institution. It is different from a standard central bank system in the sense that a currency board cannot perform some of a central bank's functions. For instance, under a currency board system, the monetary authorities have no power to change the money supply at their own will simply by printing more money. Instead, a monetary rule has to be observed, which requires any change in the monetary base to be brought about only by a corresponding change in foreign reserves in a specified foreign currency at a fixed exchange rate. The primary objective of this monetary regime is to stabilize the exchange rate.

However, Hong Kong's monetary system has not operated within the classical definitions of a currency board arrangement. The HKMA, under the linked exchange rate system, has carried out certain functions of a central bank and this role has been strengthened and developed during recent years. As we know, one difference between a central bank and a pure currency board is that the central bank is allowed to hold, and to undertake, open market operations in domestic assets such as government bonds. In Hong

Kong, the Exchange Fund issues Exchange Fund Bills and Notes for this purpose. This note/bill issuing programme was introduced in March 1990, and the maturity profile extends from three months to ten years. These notes and bills give the monetary authority some flexibility for performing open market operations, and may be used to stabilize the exchange rate.[10]

Another distinct feature of Hong Kong's exchange rate system has been that only transactions conducted for note-issuing purposes between the Exchange Fund and the note-issuing banks are carried out at the linked exchange rate, whereas foreign exchange transactions between the public and the banks, as well as all interbank transactions, are conducted at market-determined rates.

Due to the above features, the market exchange rate of the Hong Kong dollar *can* actually float within a limited range. But there are two distinct arbitrage mechanisms to keep the exchange rate stable. The first one is Currency Notes arbitrage: convertibility between the local currency and the anchor currency can help to prevent any large deviation under normal conditions and, therefore, keeps the exchange rate close to the linked level. The second and more effective adjustment mechanism is via interest rates. When there is a significant market development that creates an interest rate differential, interest rate arbitrage opportunities will attract an offsetting capital movement, and thus help to stabilize the exchange rate level. However, interest rate fluctuation can hurt the economy, and sometimes the distress can be sharp and prolonged under a severe attack on the local currency, which was exactly the case for Hong Kong during the Asian Financial Crisis.

From late 1997 to early 1998, regional currencies came under a series of attacks, and Hong Kong's currency was no exception. According to Joseph Yam, the Chief Executive of the HKMA, 'Hong Kong became a target because of the transparency of its financial systems: we were singled out for our efficiency and predictability rather than for any fundamental flaws'.[11] Under the basic rule of a currency board system, any change in the Hong Kong dollar reserves must be strictly matched by a corresponding change in the amount of monetary base. This is an *autopilot mechanism*, and the currency board can only act passively to the change in external flows. When there is outflow (inflow) of funds over the

---

[10] See http://www.info.gov.hk/hkma for more information on the Exchange Fund and its Notes and Bills.

[11] 'Coping with financial turmoil', speech by Joseph Yam on 'Inside Asia Lecture 1998', Sydney, 23 November 1998.

foreign exchange market, the HKMA has to sell (buy) US dollars in return for Hong Kong dollars, thereby reducing (increasing) the monetary base. These flows then debit (credit) the clearing accounts of the banks. The aggregate balance[12] that commercial banks maintain in their clearing accounts with the HKMA is, indeed, the crucial element in the monetary base influencing the rise and fall of interest rates. Usually banks in Hong Kong have held a low level of balances in these clearing accounts because of the efficient financial infrastructure, such as the real-time interbank payment system. Therefore, when the attacks came, it was, perhaps, predictable that the consequential effects on the aggregate balance would then lead to sharp fluctuations in domestic interbank interest rates.

Starting from late 1997, large capital flows were seen at times, and the local economy was seriously affected by the high interest rate, in some large part brought about by the autopilot mechanism under the currency board system. In fact, the severity of the currency and stock market turmoil seen in Hong Kong in late October 1997 shocked both the government and market participants. The government believed that the ultimate purpose of the speculators was to attack the currency peg and thereby to gain a large profit at the expense of the local economy. In the following sections, we give more details about these speculative attacks.

2.3.2 The October 1997 Attack

During the first three months of the Asian Financial Crisis, Hong Kong seemed to be relatively untouched by external pressures. However, in spite of the stability of the spot exchange rate, forward foreign exchange rate spreads on the Hong Kong dollar began to widen in May 1997. Speculative pressure picked up by late July and mounted again in mid-August. The government adopted a strategy of intervening in the foreign exchange market at, or around, the exchange rate of US $1 = HK $7.75. This strategy initially worked quite well, and the spot exchange rate remained roughly unchanged during this period. However, the interbank interest rate rose steadily. As can be seen from Figure 2.2, the three-month HIBOR rose

---

[12] Aggregate balance usually refers to the sum of balances in the clearing accounts and reserve accounts maintained by commercial banks with the central bank. In Hong Kong, this refers to the sum of the balances in the clearing accounts maintained by the licensed banks with the HKMA for settling interbank payments, and payments between banks and the HKMA. It represents the level of interbank liquidity.

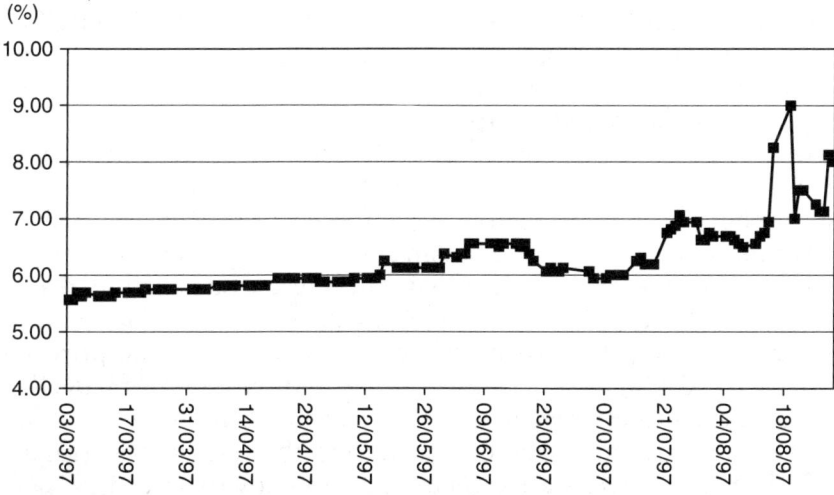

FIG. 2.2. The 3-month HIBOR (March–August 1997).

from around 5.5 per cent in March 1997 to over 8 per cent by August 1997.

After August 1997, speculative pressure on the Hong Kong dollar eased for a while, but the situation deteriorated again in mid-October, when the central bank of Taiwan suddenly, and without prior notice or any serious attempts at intervention, abandoned its own dollar peg in the face of an apparently quite mild speculative attack. The New Taiwan dollar was floated on 18 October 1997. By that time, the Hong Kong dollar and the Chinese RMB were the only two major currencies in the region that had not depreciated against the US dollar. Since the RMB was still not freely convertible in its capital account, the Hong Kong dollar became the next target for international speculators. Market confidence in the sustainability of the Hong Kong dollar peg weakened, and pressures against it intensified. Large sales of Hong Kong dollars were apparently (according to the authorities) seen in the market both from some hedge funds selling the currency short, or forward, and from hedging activities by overseas investors.

As mentioned earlier, banks in Hong Kong usually held a low level of balances in their clearing accounts. Any bank short of Hong Kong dollars would have to approach the LAF for assistance. On 23 October, the HKMA warned that banks' repeated recourse to the LAF would be subject to penal interest rates. Although the penalties were never imposed, the attack activated the autopilot mechanisms under the currency board and, as a result, the HIBOR rose overnight to 100 per cent (closing high), and interbank rates increased to as high as 280 per cent during the day. On 25 October, the HKMA also raised the spread between the LAF's bid and offer rates to 3 percentage points (from 4.25 per cent and 6.35 per cent to 4 per cent and 7 per cent). The foreign exchange market strengthened, and speculators were forced to unwind their short position in the Hong Kong dollar, and probably incurred losses.

The exchange rate peg survived, but interest rates had increased sharply and the suffering imposed on the community was severe. On 23 October, the HSI nosedived from 13,601 on the previous Friday to 10,426, a 23 per cent drop. The three-month HIBOR, a benchmark interest rate, also surged to 25 per cent on the same day, and remained around 10 per cent during the rest of 1997 (Figure 2.3). Property prices started their long-term downward adjustment and the unemployment rate picked up gradually.

2.3.3 Early Attacks in 1998

Speculative attacks continued in early 1998. In January, confidence was further shaken by the failure of two securities investment companies (the Peregrine Group and C. A. Pacific) and by the deterioration of the Japanese economy. On 12 January, the HIBOR went up from 8.5 per cent to 12 per cent and then on 15 January it was driven up to 10 per cent again. The stock market

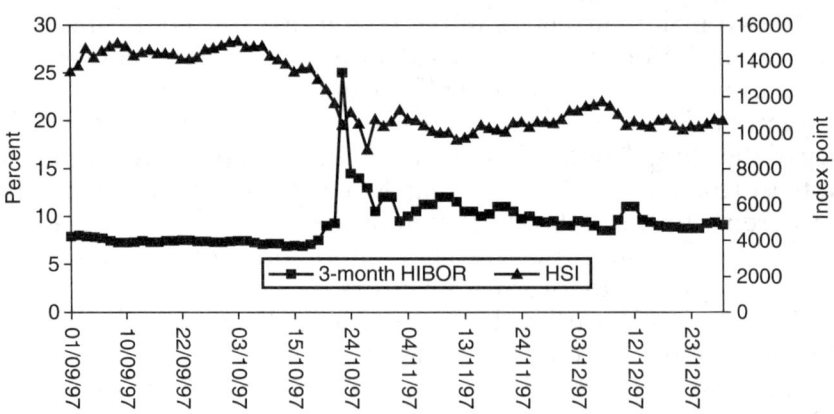

FIG. 2.3. The HSI and the 3-month HIBOR during the October 1997 attack.

was also volatile; the HSI fell to 8121 from 10681 on 2 January, the first trading day in 1998. On the money market, the attack was even clearer. Although the spot rate was kept quite stable, the forward exchange rate of the Hong Kong dollar was under pressure, due to large sales of the currency in the forward market. The one-month and three-month forward discounts on the Hong Kong dollar reached 950 and 2,050 basis points respectively on 12 January. Figure 2.4 depicts the behaviour of the one-month forward exchange rate of the Hong Kong dollar around the time of the January attack.

The following months saw a rapid deterioration in both the domestic economic situation and the external environment. At the end of May 1998, the government announced that real GDP growth rate in the first quarter had turned negative—which was worse than expected. Moreover, the unemployment rate for June 1998 reached a record high for the past 15 years of 4.3 per cent. Externally, political strikes and economic turmoil in Indonesia, as well as the heightened recession in Japan, were also indications of weakness. Foreign investment kept declining, and funds were withdrawn from the market. There were worries that, with the devaluation of the Japanese yen, other currencies would suffer additional pressure, and that massive devaluation would result.

In early June, the Japanese yen dropped abruptly to a new record low of 146.55 JPY/USD, and some commentators feared that this

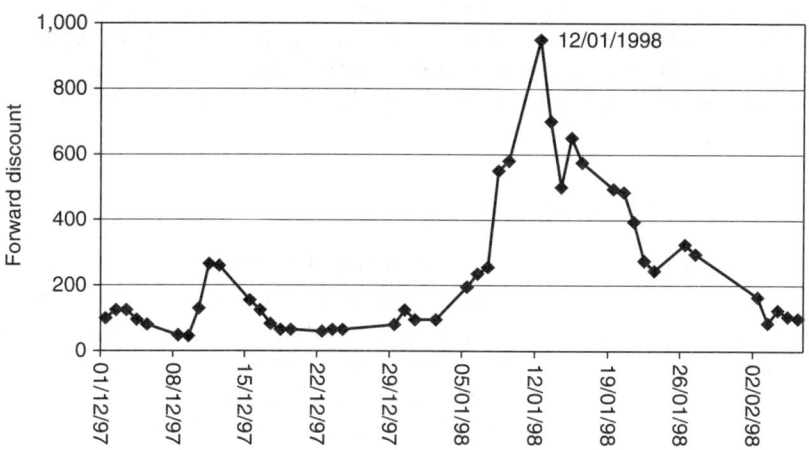

FIG. 2.4. The one-month forward discount of the Hong Kong dollar (December 1997–February 1998).

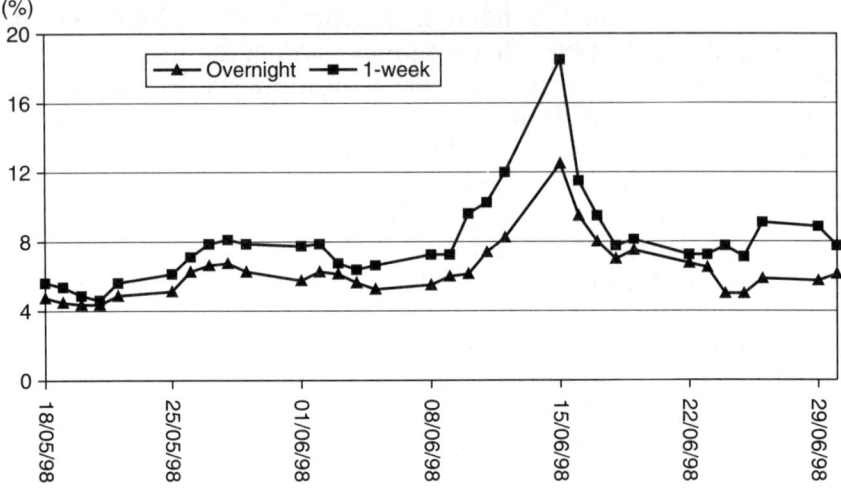

FIG. 2.5. The overnight and one-week HIBOR during the June 1998 attack.

would initiate another wave of currency turmoil. All stock markets in the Asian countries fell accordingly: with a 3.5 per cent drop in Singapore, a 4.2 per cent drop in Malaysia and a 5.7 per cent drop in Thailand. Hong Kong was among the worst affected: the HSI dropped 452 points (−5.7 per cent) to 7463. Again the HIBOR was pulled up: 12.5 per cent for overnight and 18 per cent for one week (Figure 2.5). Although the HSI rebounded 470 points after the US intervened on the night of 17 June by spending US $2 billion, market sentiment was still very weak, the common opinion being that Hong Kong was going into recession. This weakness in confidence was later probed by the speculators in the August 1998 attack.

2.3.4 Speculators' Double Play

In August 1998, speculators were accused of carrying out a 'Double Market Play'. The government believed that: 'In August...speculators launched coordinated and well-planned attacks across our financial markets.... By pressuring the currency and selling stocks short, they could realize a profit on stock index futures contracts, even if they could not break the exchange rate link.'[13]

---

[13] 'Causes of, and solutions to, the recent financial turmoil in the Asian region', speech by Joseph Yam, http://www.info.gov.hk/hkma, 5 January 1999.

Ever since early 1998, hedge funds were observed (by the authorities) to be borrowing a large amount of Hong Kong dollars. As Joseph Yam said in one of his speeches,[14] 'From the beginning of this year (1998) to the middle of August, over HK $30 billion of one- and two-year money were raised through the issue of debt paper in Hong Kong.' The government believed that, although there were various issuers, the money was swapped from US dollars into Hong Kong dollars by some large hedge funds dealing with these multilateral issuers. Joseph Yam estimated that 'the cost of running a HK $30 billion position, with an interest rate premium over the US dollar that had been driven up to about 5 percentage points, is over HK $4 million a day.' Meanwhile, activity in the index futures market seemed to have risen sharply. 'With an estimated 80,000 short contracts held amongst these hedge funds, for every thousand-point drop in the stock market index, they stood to profit $4 billion.' The relative profits and losses now become rather clear. Say, if the speculators could push down the index by 1,000 points within 100 days, the cost would be HK $400 million and the (net) profit would be HK $3.6 billion.

The strategy of the 'Double Market Play' can be roughly summarized as follows. The speculators simultaneously sold short Hong Kong dollars, both spot and forward, on the foreign exchange market and shorted Hong Kong stocks on both the spot and futures markets. Such massive selling of Hong Kong dollars squeezed the liquidity of the Hong Kong banking system, leading to a sharp increase in the HIBOR. The stock and futures markets were then under great pressure to fall. Moreover, if under such pressures the HKMA were to give up the Hong Kong dollar peg, the speculators could reap enormous profits from the foreign exchange and, perhaps, also the securities markets. The Hong Kong residents, on the other hand, would have to suffer the collapse of their asset markets, and with banks facing serious difficulties, maybe even a banking crisis, which was exactly what had happened in other Asian countries.

In fact, August 1998 provided a good opportunity for speculators. Market sentiment was clearly unfavourable in July and during the first half of August. Rumours abounded about a possible devaluation of the Chinese yuan, and doubts about the stability

---

[14] 'Defending Hong Kong's monetary stability', speech by Joseph Yam, http://www.info.gov.hk/hkma, 14 October 1998.

of the Hong Kong dollar peg were ramifying. The stock market steadily plummeted down, and turnover shrunk to about a third of its normal level, which made it more vulnerable to manipulation. It was estimated by the government that speculators sold short US $6.2 billion in Hong Kong dollars in Hong Kong, New York, Sydney, and London markets in the first two weeks of August.[15] Other estimates were even higher: the Financial Stability Forum Working Group on HLIs reported that the short position held by HLIs against the Hong Kong dollar may have amounted to over US $10 billion at the peak in August 1998.[16] Had it not been for the unexpected intervention by the HKMA, those hedge funds might have gathered huge profits. Given the laissez-faire tradition in Hong Kong, it was doubtful whether the speculators had fully anticipated the likelihood of this intervention.

2.3.5 Government Intervention

2.3.5.1 An Overview

On 14 August 1998, a Friday, the HKMA entered the equity market, drawing on official reserves to purchase stocks with the aim of ensuring that the speculators did not profit. According to Joseph Yam, the government did the unexpected in order to prevent their predictable and transparent system from falling prey to manipulation.[17]

Prior to the intervention, the stock market had fallen from 10,563 on 1 May 1998 to 6,660 on 13 August 1998—a 40 per cent decline! Moreover, in the first half of August, the government revised Hong Kong's GDP growth for the first quarter down to 2.8 per cent; the Yen fell to over 147 against the US dollar, and the Dow Jones Industrial Average Index had fallen nearly 300 points since the beginning of August. There was a danger of a breakdown of confidence in the Hong Kong dollar peg, and of panic reactions in other asset markets. Fearing that the speculators would probably launch another strong attack at the approach of the long weekend in the middle of August, (Monday, 17 August being a holiday in Hong

---

[15] 'Intervention averted disaster, claims Tsang', *South China Morning Post*, 8 September 1998.
[16] 'Report of Working Group on Highly Leveraged Institutions', Financial Stability Forum, 5 April 2000.
[17] 'Defending Hong Kong's monetary stability', speech by Joseph Yam, http://www.info.gov.hk/hkma, 14 October 1998.

Kong), the HKMA intervened in the stock and futures markets on 14 August.

The HSI was successfully pushed up to 7,224 at the close of day on 14 August, with the estimated amount of stock purchase amounting to HK $3 billion (see Chapter 3). The government stock purchases lasted until 28 August—altogether ten working days. As disclosed by the government in late October,[18] the HKMA spent HK $118.13 billion overall in the process of acquiring shares in the 33 HSI constituent stocks, representing about 7.3 per cent of such stocks. The biggest stakes were in three companies: Swire Pacific (12.28 per cent), New World Development (11.91 per cent) and Cheung Kong (10.34 per cent). The largest amount invested was in HSBC Holdings (HK $40.77 billion).

Figure 2.6 shows the change in the HSI and the market turnover in shares traded from July to September 1998. Note that the index turned down again after the intervention ceased on 28 August. But on that last day of the intervention, the government firmly supported the index in the face of massive selling, and daily turnover reached a record high (a total of 3.5 billion shares traded for 33 HSI constituent stocks and the total market turnover reached HK $7,189.8 billion).

After the August futures contract expired on 28 August, the stock index fell back immediately on the following Monday (31 August 1998) in conjunction with a global downturn. The HSI went down from 7,829 to 7,275, while the Dow Jones Industrial Average also dropped over 500 points. However, the HSI still stood more than 600 points higher than the lowest level before the intervention without any further support of buying from the government. Starting from mid-September, the outside environment, as well as increased stability in local financial markets, encouraged funds back to the market, and the HSI increased from below 8,000 in September to above 10,000 around the end of October.

The amount of government purchases in the futures and options markets did not become known to the public until early December 1998. In replying to a Legislative Council member's enquiries, Rafael Hui, the Secretary for Financial Services, revealed that the government purchased 36,935 August HSI futures contracts, 1,100 August HSI options contracts, and 10,176 September HSI futures contracts, but neither the HSI futures nor the options contracts for

---

[18] HKMA's press release, http://www/info.gov.hk/hkma, 26 October 1998.

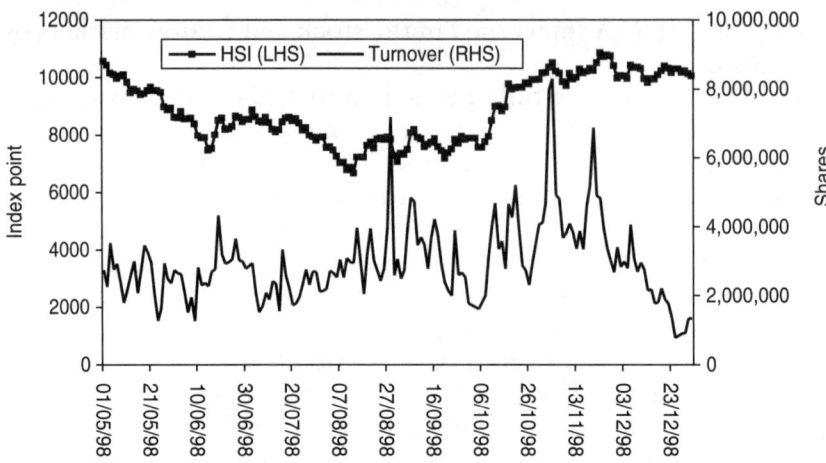

FIG. 2.6. The performance of the HSI during 1998.

October; and that the net profit generated from these transactions was about HK $50 million.[19]

The money market did not experience as much fluctuation in the HIBOR as speculators might have expected and hoped. This could have been, in part, because of the HKMA's active buying for the Treasury. Previously, the HKMA had rarely used the Exchange Fund fiscal reserves instead of the aggregate balance in the LAF, to settle the speculators' selling orders in the local currency. Government officials claimed that the summer months of July and August are normally 'dry' months for the Treasury. The government then asked the HKMA to convert part of its fiscal reserve from US dollars back into Hong Kong dollars to finance its anticipated HK $21.4 billion budget deficit for the year.[20] So, the massive sale of Hong Kong dollars by the speculators did not lead to a reduction in the banking system's clearing balance, thereby preventing any sharp escalation of money market rates. 'The amount of Hong Kong dollars absorbed in this manner was large, exceeding the HK $30 billion accumulated by the hedge funds.'[21]

[19] 'Government's trading in the futures market', http://www.hknew.com.hk, 2 December 1998.
[20] 'Money market trade jumps while HKMA acts and dollar fears rise', *South China Morning Post*, 6 August 1998.
[21] 'Defending Hong Kong's monetary stability', speech by Joseph Yam, http://www.info.gov.hk/hkma, 14 October 1998.

Although the government revealed some of its operations in August 1998, no further technical details about the intervention were disclosed by any official or non-official sources. (In later chapters, we try to use a combination of transaction data and bid-ask data, as well as other public information to reconstruct artificially the operations of the Authorities.)

2.3.5.2 Reasons for the Intervention

Why would the Hong Kong government choose to risk its reputation of having one of the freest markets in the world, and intervene directly in the financial markets? The Financial Secretary of Hong Kong, Donald Tsang, once offered a more detailed glimpse of why the government took the difficult decision when addressing legislators at a key meeting of the Financial Affairs Panel.[22] He said that the government believed that, if it had not intervened, the stock market would have fallen between 2,000 and 3,000 points, and interest rates would have risen by 50 per cent. He believed that this was far below the fundamental value of the market. Hong Kong's whole economy might have been put in danger by such falls in asset values. These worries were not unfounded. In other Asian countries, speculators' activities had triggered serious reactions by other investors, and sent local economies quickly into recession.

Domestic market sentiment was also very fragile during August: the Japanese yen was dangerously weak, and Russia was approaching default. Speculation was widespread that Mainland China could not sustain the economic pressure for long, and would devalue the yuan to improve export competitiveness. 'China, which has denied reports that it plans to devalue the yuan, is expected to let the yuan lose its value within this year to make up for sluggish exports and cover flood damage. Currency experts project that the yuan will be devalued from the 8-yuan level to the dollar to the 9-yuan level.'[23] If the yuan had been devalued, it may have pulled the rug out from under the Hong Kong dollar, and it was felt that in all likelihood, 'the (Hong Kong) peg to the US dollar will, in due course, go as Hong Kong falls victim to a retail panic.'[24]

---

[22] 'Intervention averted disaster, claims Tsang', *South China Morning Post*, 8 September 1998.
[23] 'Government Prepares for Impending Devaluation of Yuan', *Korea Herald*, 9 August 1998.
[24] 'Devaluation fears dominate', *Waikato Times*, 10 August 1998.

As mentioned earlier, during the first two weeks in August 1998, the HKMA, the de facto central bank of Hong Kong, was buying Hong Kong dollars on behalf of the government to finance the budget deficit. This helped to keep interest rates quite stable.[25] However, such buying could hardly continue once the government's needs had been met. Meanwhile, the stock and futures markets saw no cessation of the downtrend, and new lows were seen almost every day. The government felt the need to do something else to save the market, and their choice was direct market intervention. It was an unusual choice, but one cannot say that it was an unwise one. By making direct purchases in the equity market, the government could actually achieve two goals. One was to stop the stock market from nosediving and restore public confidence; the other was to ensure greater manoeuvrability for the HKMA to buy Hong Kong dollars from the speculators in the foreign exchange market, so that the interest rate would not jump. We may call this entire exercise a 'double counter-play' strategy of the government. (The interactions between the foreign exchange, money and equity markets are discussed further in Chapter 6.)

2.3.6 *An Additional Note on Highly Leveraged Institutions (HLIs)*

2.3.6.1 The Presence of HLIs in Hong Kong

Besides the publicized intervention by the Hong Kong government, another issue that has aroused much controversy in the wake of the Asian Financial Crisis, among both government regulators and market participants, is the role played by hedge funds in the Crisis. Hong Kong's experience suggested that the series of aggressive attacks in late 1997 and 1998 had been more than simply general market players taking advantage of expected changes in asset prices, but rather specific speculators trying to force the markets to move in a direction favourable to themselves. However, in contrast to their big size and market power, very little data on hedge funds' positions in financial markets are publicly available, thus making it even harder to monitor their activities.

---

[25] 'Money market trade jumps while HKMA acts and dollar fears rise', *South China Morning Post*, 6 August 1998.

In February 1999, the Financial Stability Forum (FSF) was established by the G7 Ministers of Finance and Central Bank Governors, with the objective of promoting international financial stability through enhanced information exchange and international cooperation among authorities responsible for financial stability. One of the three working groups of the Forum, the Working Group on HLIs, was set up with the task of assessing the challenges posed by HLIs and to achieve a consensus on how to minimize their destabilizing potential. One of the conclusions that their Report[26] draws is that in unsettled and fragile conditions, large and concentrated HLIs' positions have the potential to influence market dynamics.

In the case of Hong Kong, their Report (p.130) shows that the speculative attacks were well planned on several fronts, with concentrated short positions established in the equity and currency markets, in both spot and futures trading.[27] With respect to equity futures trading, their Report suggests that hedge funds accounted for around 40 per cent of total short open positions in HSI futures as of early August prior to the HKMA intervention. Some hedge funds continued to add to their positions during the intervention period, with four hedge funds ending up with 49 per cent of total open positions and one in particular holding about one-third (p.131).

There is, of course, nothing wrong with selling, *per se*. Hong Kong, with its renowned free and open financial markets, has certainly often seen large waves of sales in financial derivatives on other occasions. The Securities and Futures Commission of Hong Kong (HKSFC) had previously examined the active trading in HSI futures market in 1997. Since the finding then was that the bulk of short positions was evenly spread and not concentrated among just a few players, the Hong Kong government concluded at that time that there was no evidence of manipulation in the futures market, or of any collusion between currency speculators and futures market participants.

---

[26] 'Report of Working Group on Highly Leveraged Institutions', Financial Stability Forum, 5 April 2000.

[27] For a more detailed description of the role played by HLIs in the gyrations of the Hong Kong financial markets from late 1997 to 1998, please refer to De Brouwer (2001).

34 *Intervention to Save Hong Kong*

However, in the second half of 1998, the accumulation of futures and option positions was much more concentrated, coinciding with a steady build-up of selling pressure in the foreign exchange market.[28] It was under these circumstances, with market integrity being threatened by the hedge funds' aggressive behaviour and financial prices being exposed to distortion, that the Hong Kong government decided to take direct action to 'correct' the market.

2.3.6.2 The Near-collapse of LTCM Brought Global Attention to HLIs

On 23 September 1998, the president of the Federal Reserve Bank of New York, William J. McDonough, helped to organize a rescue of the hedgefund, Long Term Capital Management (LTCM). In a matter of only a few hours, fifteen or so, American and European institutions came up with US $3.5 billion in return for a 90 per cent share in the fund. In his Congressional testimony, Federal Reserve Chairman Alan Greenspan explained that the rescue was 'not to protect LTCM's investors, creditors, managers from loss, but to avoid the distortions to market processes caused by a fire-sale liquidation and the consequent spreading of those distortions through contagion.'[29] The near-collapse of this flagship hedge fund revealed massive positions that few previously had suspected.

Analysts estimated that LTCM's US $100 billion-worth position was supported by a capital of only $500 million in mid-September.[30] The high leverage used by LTCM was later confirmed by a leaked report by the North American credit-control department of the Union Bank of Switzerland (UBS). This internal credit appraisal on LTCM, dated December 1996, indicted that 'Leverage was very high: on balance sheet 27.2 times, off balance sheet not disclosed but we assume total leverage is at least 250 times.'[31] With an estimated capital base of $4.8 billion at the

---

[28] 'HK Financial Secretary expects more attacks on HK dollar', Reuters, 8 August 1998.
[29] 'Text-Fed chairman Greenspan to house banking committee', *Market News International*, 1 October 1998.
[30] 'Hedge funds—the high rollers of the markets', Reuters, 24 September 1998.
[31] 'UBS ignored own policy on LTCM–UBS document', Reuters, 10 October 1998.

start of 1998,[32] this implies assets under management of more than $130 billion, and a potential exposure of 1.2 trillion dollars!

Not all hedge funds have had such a high leverage, but considering the total capital base of hedge funds as a whole, one can only guess at the scale of funds they can summon with leverage, and how destabilizing it could be when they place bets in any markets, let alone small ones, as in Asia.

Given the considerable risk of trying to oppose such powerful speculators, Hong Kong had a most successful experience. Following the HKMA intervention, market pressures eased gradually from early September, with positions in futures contracts by the large hedge funds mostly unwound by late September to early October.

2.3.7 The Aftermath of the Intervention

2.3.7.1 Measures to Strengthen the Monetary and Financial Systems

Donald Tsang stated at the time of the intervention that, 'We did not mount the market operations announced a fortnight ago in haste. They were part of an overall strategy to strengthen our financial markets.'[33] Other parts of his 'overall strategy' included various policy measures announced immediately after the government stopped its buying in the stock and futures market. These measures were aimed both to strengthen public confidence in the currency peg and also to prevent future attacks. Some of the major points are discussed below.

After several currency attacks, the authorities realized that jacking up interest rates in response could be a double-edged weapon, and it should not be the *only* choice for defence. To facilitate this change of strategy, on 5 September 1998, the Hong Kong government announced seven measures to strengthen the Hong Kong dollar's peg to the US dollar, as well as to stabilize the interest rate in the face of shocks to liquidity, for example, in the form of flows over the foreign exchange. In announcing this

---

[32] 'Long-term capital near collapse—seeks bank rescue', Reuters, 23 September 1998.

[33] 'FS's statement at press stand-up session part II', http://www.hknews.com.hk, 28 August 1998.

package of technical measures, the HKMA emphasized that this was to purify the currency board system, while the government would continue to be fully committed to its free economy policy and there would be no foreign exchange controls. The package is briefly summarized as follows:[34]

- First, to boost confidence in the linked exchange rate system, the HKMA gave a 'clear undertaking' to all licensed banks that it would convert Hong Kong dollars in the clearing account at a fixed rate of HK $7.75/US$. The HK $7.75 rate was chosen since it was around this point that the HKMA intervention was triggered when the currency was under attack. When the Hong Kong dollar subsequently strengthened, the conversion rate was moved, in tiny pre-announced steps, to HK $7.8—the formal value of the pegged rate.
- A discount window replaced the LAF with a base rate to be determined from time to time by the HKMA. The HKMA also introduced a schedule of discount rates applicable for different percentage thresholds of holdings of Exchange Fund paper by the licensed banks. As contrasted with the LAF, the discount window would not receive surplus funds from banks, and this would prevent them from holding on to their surplus funds until the end of the day, thus artificially raising interest rates.
- Together with the abolition of the LAF, restrictions on repeated borrowing were removed in respect of the provision of overnight liquidity through repo agreements using Exchange Fund Bills and Notes. However, the HKMA retained such restrictions should the repo transactions involve debt securities other than Exchange Fund paper.
- New Exchange Fund paper would be issued only when there was an inflow of funds, which had the effect of including Exchange Fund Notes and Bills into the monetary base, thus making interest rates less sensitive to the change in the aggregate balance that licensed banks hold in their clearing accounts with the HKMA.

These measures were one element in the restoration of public confidence. A test of their effectiveness would be to examine

---

[34] More details of the seven technical measures can be found in the HKMA's press release on 5 September 1998, 'Strengthening of Currency Board Arrangements in Hong Kong', http://www.info.gov.hk/hkma/eng/press/index.htm.

whether interest rate *volatility*, both inter- and intra-day, subsequently declined. This, however, is beyond the scope of this study.

Almost at the same time, the government unveiled a 30-point package on 7 September 1998 to tighten up controls in the securities and futures markets.[35] These announced measures mainly dealt with the regulation and enforcement on short selling, enhanced risk management, and more rigorous enforcement of the T+2 settlement rules. In August 1998, short selling peaked at nearly three times the average trading volume of previous months in 1998. Certainly, short selling by itself is not illegal, provided that stocks have been borrowed in advance. The form of short selling that would be illegal refers to 'naked short-selling', where no stocks are available for delivery. The package called for heavier penalties on breach of these laws and regulations. According to Donald Tsang, this package, together with the seven measures mentioned above, would form a comprehensive plan to improve the ability of Hong Kong's monetary and financial systems to withstand cross-market manipulation by market players.[36]

2.3.7.2 Later Market Developments

After the intervention ended on 28 August 1998, the HSI closed at 7,830, nearly 18 per cent higher than the monthly low of 6,660 on 13 August. While some smaller speculators could not sustain the financial cost of holding onto their positions, some stronger ones rolled over their futures positions into September. However, the HSI then rose to over 7,880 on the settlement date of the September contract and over 10,150 by the October settlement day. This was largely due to a fortunate turn-around in external economic conditions. The speculators lost money both from having to bear the cost of financing their positions and from the capital losses incurred in the futures market.

In the event, the government thoroughly defeated the 'double market play'. The next question facing them was how to dispose of the large number of shares. In June 1999, the Exchange Fund Investment Ltd., set up by the government to take over the management and custody of the acquired shares, decided in principle to

---

[35] 'Measures taken to strengthen securities and futures markets', *South China Morning Post*, 8 August 1998.
[36] 'Measures to tighten up securities and futures markets', http://www.hknews.com.hk, 7 September 1998.

dispose of its portfolio gradually through the creation of a unit trust. This unit trust was later named TraHK, and its initial market issue was announced in October 1999, with a total value of HK $10 billion, representing about 16 per cent of the original portfolio. The government wanted to signal that the August intervention was a one-off event, and not a permanent departure from its traditional 'positive non-intervention' policy.

CHAPTER 3

A Reconstruction of the Intervention

3.1 Introduction

As already noted in Chapter 1, the government's intervention was not only important for Hong Kong's financial markets, but perhaps also instructive for any future analysis of capital markets. In the foreign exchange market, central bank interventions are a fairly regular phenomenon, but, in equity markets, an intervention on such a large scale has seldom, if ever, been seen before. Moreover, it was unusually successful by most criteria (as demonstrated subsequently in Chapter 7).

The few previous studies of this event have focused on one aspect or the other of the intervention's impact. But this study sought a comprehensive understanding of the entire event during the intervention. For any in-depth analysis, more complete information on the intervention was required. Throughout the whole intervention period, the government remained silent about the technical details of the operation, no doubt partly because they did not want speculators and other market operators to perceive their strategy. But even today—four years after the event—relatively little has been disclosed to the public, except for the total amount of each stock purchased. The story had, however, received fairly good press coverage, with reports including estimates made by either market participants or observers. However, those guesses and comments were occasional and far from complete.

In this chapter, what we aim to do is to use publicly available data to reconstruct the intervention story as far as possible. A comparison of our results with both the reported news and available government announcements is also included in order to show the robustness of our effort.

3.1.1 A Description of the Trading Mechanism of the Stock Exchange of Hong Kong

Before we can go into details of the trading, it is first necessary to know the institutional structures, as well as the trading mechanism of the Stock Exchange of Hong Kong (SEHK). Briefly, the SEHK is an automated *order-driven* market, which has no market-making system. This is similar to the Paris Bourse and, to a lesser extent, to the Tokyo Stock Exchange as well.

Order-driven means that only orders from investors, (or sometimes from brokers trading as investors on their own account), are entered into the trading system and the price is set by the execution of such orders against one another. In the SEHK, there is no market-maker in the market. The member brokers act mainly as agents, buying and selling securities not for themselves but on behalf of the investors. For a pure order-driven system like that of Hong Kong, the market is very transparent. The order queues are visible to the whole market and execution is on an objective and independent basis, in accordance with price and time priority.

In contrast to this kind of system, in a *quote-driven* market (e.g. the London Stock Exchange) or an order-driven market with market-makers (e.g. the New York Stock Exchange), dealers (or specialists) provide all or part of the liquidity to the market by displaying quotations at which they are willing to participate in a transaction. In spite of the differences between these trading systems, they also have similarities. For instance, in a continuous auction system, public limit order traders provide liquidity to the market and in fact have a function similar to market-makers. To see this, note that an unexecuted sell limit order can be characterized by the quantity that is to be sold at a stated price (*the limit*) or any higher price; and a buy limit order can be characterized by the quantity that is to be bought at the stated price or any lower price. In this sense, a limit order is comparable to the quote of a market-maker standing ready to sell at his ask quote or to buy at his bid quote.

The SEHK has two main trading sessions for each trading day. The morning session is from 10:00 to 12:30 hrs. The afternoon session is from 14:30 to 16:00 hrs.[1] The market operates under the *continuous auction* method, which allows investors to place their orders in the computerized market through brokers continuously

---

[1] There is no afternoon session on the eves of Christmas, New Year, and Lunar New Year.

for execution against one another. All brokers are directly connected to the current Automatic Order Matching and Execution System (AMS), which during the period under our study was a pure order-driven system, accepting only limit orders.[2]

Effectively from 3 March 1997, all securities listed on the Exchange have been registered for automatching through AMS. Under AMS/2, only firm orders for a specific quantity of stock at a specific price can be entered into the system. By committing himself to a definite price and quantity, i.e. the posting of a limit order under the AMS/2 mechanism, the investor effectively grants a free option to the rest of the market to trade against him at that price. Orders are executed on a *strict price priority and time priority*. An order entered into the system at an earlier time must be executed in full before an order at the same price entered at a later time is executed. Ask orders priced lower than the current best bid price are not allowed to enter the system. The same applies to bid orders priced higher than the current best ask price. Investors can input an order with a price equal to the best opposite orders and this has the effect of a 'market order', which will be executed immediately. *However, if the order is too large, any excess that cannot be executed at that price remains as a quote at that price rather than being executed against less favourable prices by walking up or down the limit order book.* This feature could affect investors' order-submission strategies to a certain extent (later we also found that the price patterns during the intervention period were closely related to this feature). Similar arrangements can also be found on the Paris Bourse.

Although all the stocks traded on the SEHK were registered for automatching through the AMS, they can also be traded manually. For automatching, one or more transactions are struck automatically based on the small-order FIFO (first in, first out) method. Alternatively a transaction may be struck upon the completion of negotiation. Each *selling* broker has to input into the system details of any transaction *not* automatically struck by the AMS within 15 minutes after the conclusion of the transaction, but not later than 12:30 for the morning session and 15:55 for the afternoon session.

---

[2] The AMS kept being enhanced ever since its introduction in 1993. AMS/2 was launched in January 1996 and the current AMS/3 took its place on 23 October 2000. AMS/3 could provide more functionality in various areas, including market model, trading method, market access, etc. For instance, in addition to the present automatching method, single price auction and market making are also allowed in the system. For more details, refer to the SEHK's website: http://www.sehk.com.hk.

However, these transactions through non-automatching methods represent only a very small fraction of the market. According to Ahn and Cheung (1999), the automatched trades account for 97.7 per cent of all trades, 88.9 per cent and 85.9 per cent of all shares traded and dollar volumes respectively.

As for the size of the order, the maximum order for automatching today is 400 board lots,[3] while the number of orders in each order queue is limited to 1,000. Outstanding orders carried on from the morning session may be cancelled before the opening of the afternoon session, between 14:15 and 14:30 hrs. At the end of the trading day, all orders are removed from the system.

For order submission, brokers have to observe the Operational Trading Rules set by the SEHK.[4] The first bid or ask order entered into the trading system on each trading day is governed by the rules of Opening Quotations. The first order, if it is a bid (ask), must be higher (lower) or equal to the previous closing price minus (plus) four spreads (a spread or a tick-size is assigned for each stock based on its price). The first order, whether it is a bid or ask, shall not deviate by nine ticks or more from the previous closing price. Intraday quotations other than the opening bid or ask are governed by the Rules of Quotations. Basically, for an automatched stock, a buy order may be quoted:

(1) within four spreads below the current best bid price when there are existing bid prices quoted on the primary queue;
(2) within four spreads below whichever is the lowest of the current ask price, the previous closing price, and the lowest transacted price of the day when there are no existing bid prices quoted on the primary queue.

On the SEHK, the spread is a step function of share price, which ranges from Hong Kong dollar 0.001 for stocks priced lower than Hong Kong dollar 0.25, to Hong Kong dollar 2.5 for those priced over Hong Kong dollar 1,000. This range is detailed in Table 3.1.

3.1.2 The Data Sets

Before starting the analysis, we should reiterate that only publicly available data has been accessed, and no insider information has

---

[3] The board lot means the generally accepted unit of trading on the exchange. On the SEHK, the lot size can be chosen by the individual firm and, therefore, is not uniform for every stock.

[4] See Rules of the Exchange (SEHK, 2000), Rules 503–510.

been taken into account. This has both advantages and disadvantages. For example, there could be some missing links in our estimation and evaluation process, but we shall aim to expose our guesses or assumptions wherever appropriate.

In this section, the scope of the analysis will be confined to the 33 HSI constituent stocks, covering the trading in both the Hong Kong and London markets. The reason that we want to examine both markets is that 28 of the 33 intervened stocks are dually traded in London, and it appeared necessary to look into both markets in order to have a complete picture. In later chapters, we will also extend our analysis to other comparable stocks from both the Hong Kong and London markets. The data sets included in this exercise cover the following.

- Transaction data and bid-ask data of Hong Kong stocks retrieved separately from the trade record CD-ROMs and bid-ask record CD-ROMs provided by the SHEK. The Trade record is time-stamped tick-by-tick data, which provides information with regard to the price, volume, and type for each transaction. The bid-ask record, however, is taken at 30-second snapshots, which provides the prices and volumes of the best five bids and offers.
- For information on London transactions, the data were originally retrieved from the London Stock Exchange trading record, which is also time-stamped.[5]

TABLE 3.1. *Spread sizes in the SEHK*

Price range (HK$)	Spread (HK $)*
0.01–0.25	0.001
>0.25–0.50	0.005
>0.50–2.00	0.010
>2.00–5.00	0.025
>5.00–30.00	0.050
>30.00–50.00	0.100
>50.00–100.00	0.250
>100.00–200.00	0.500
>100.00–1000.00	1.000
>1000.00–9995.00	2.500

*The minimum price changes for all securities other than debt in the SEHK.

[5] The dataset was acquired from Mr. Stephen Wells of the London School of Economics, who retrieved the data originally from the London Stock Exchange trading record.

3.2 The Intervention Process

3.2.1 Special Market Behaviour

3.2.1.1 Unusual Intra-day Patterns

When plotting out price movements during August 1998, the long periods of peculiar patterns of price movements were noteworthy. We plotted the intra-day movements for all the 33 intervened stocks from 13 to 31 August, i.e. from one trading day before the intervention through to one trading day after it. Most, if not all, stocks displayed some downward movement on these two days outside the intervention period. Figures 3.1 and 3.2 give two examples of the price patterns before and after the intervention.

However, once the intervention commenced, the market price pattern changed and there were many episodes during the ten days when the prices of almost all stocks remained nearly constant with only small occasional variations around a central price. Figures 3.3 and 3.4 display the price patterns on two intervention days for two other randomly selected stocks.

As can be seen, the two sample stocks exhibited very similar movements on both days. Indeed, such a similarity can be observed with regard to most of the intervened stocks for a larger part of the intervention period, implying that the government probably applied a similar buying strategy to most of the 33 constituent stocks simultaneously. The most spectacular moments during the intervention period were in the last two days. As shown in Figures 3.5 and 3.6, prices were either kept at one level or moved a few steps up or down. Though there were some pop-ups at certain moments, the price floor could easily be identified.

In order to give an overall view of the whole period, 12 intra-day price movements of two stocks from 13 to 31 August are charted in Figures 3.7 and 3.8. HSBC was specifically chosen because it was the top stock during that period in terms of market value. To change market behaviour, HSBC should be on the top of the government's

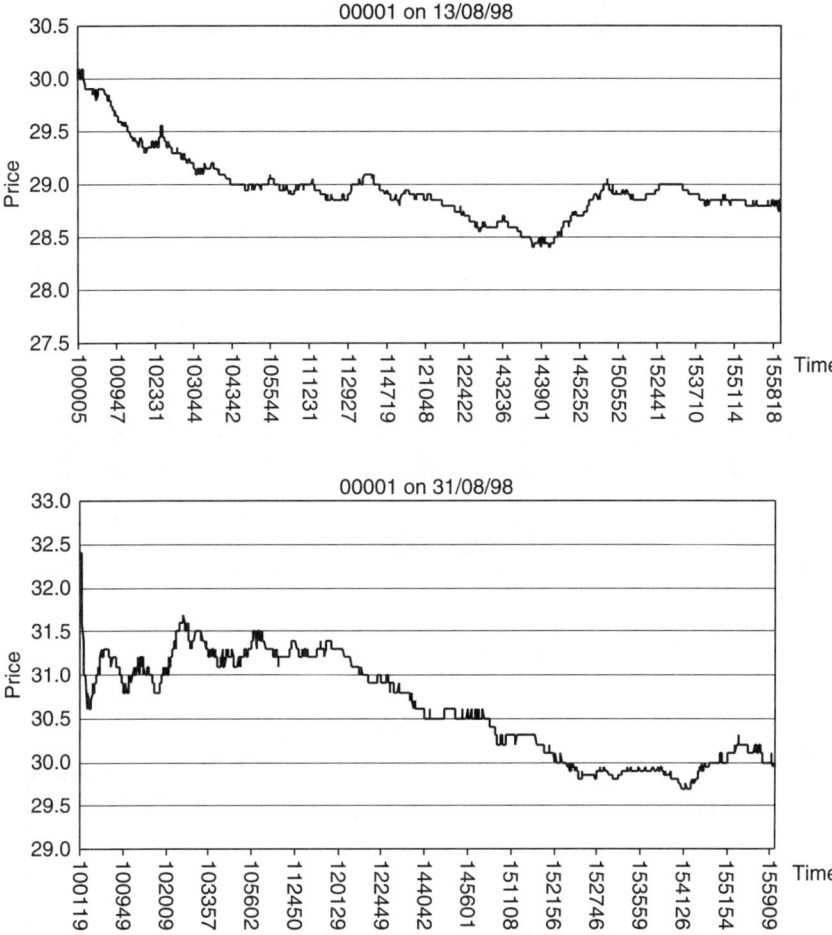

FIG. 3.1. Price patterns before and after the intervention (Example I) Cheung Kong Holding (00001)

intervention list, and its price movement is a definitive example for study.

The two sample stocks, Hutchison Whampoa and HSBC, exhibited very similar price behaviour. To cite a few instances, besides 27 and 28 August, both stocks had a long period of price holding on 18 August; the prices for both went up on 24 August after 12:00 noon and an abrupt drop occurred in both cases on 26 August around 15:10 hrs.

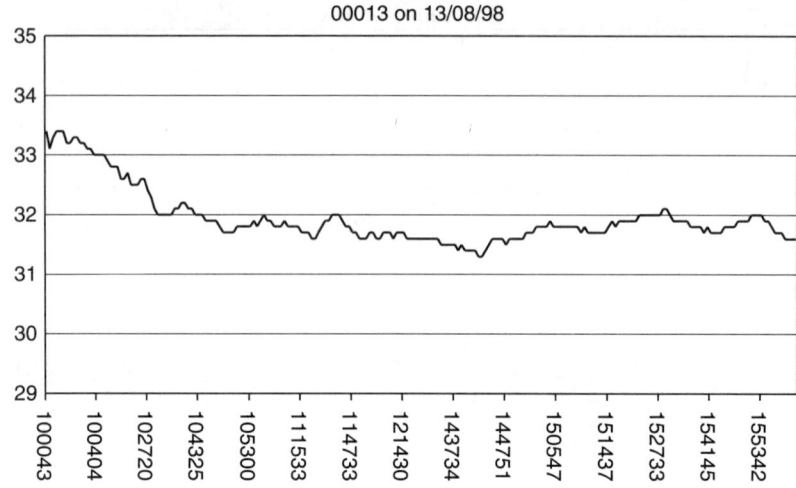

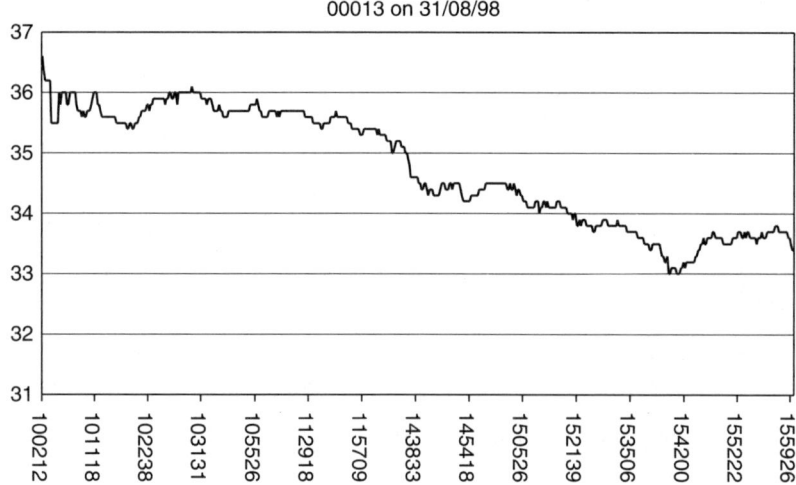

FIG. 3.2. Price patterns before and after the intervention
Example II: Hutchison Whampoa Ltd (00013)

3.2.1.2 Three Kinds of Price Movements

Such patterns of price movements provided the basis for our later analyses. Our hypothesis was that, based on these patterns, we could describe the intervention process in detail. Having examined the price patterns, the price behaviours of all the intervened stocks during the ten days of the intervention were grouped into

A Reconstruction of the Intervention 47

three categories. Figures 3.3 and 3.4 can be used to identify the following three types of price movements:

(1) periods when the prices were driven up, such as at the market opening on 14 and 19 August;
(2) relatively long periods when the prices were held, for example, in the half-hour after the earlier pushups on 19 August; and

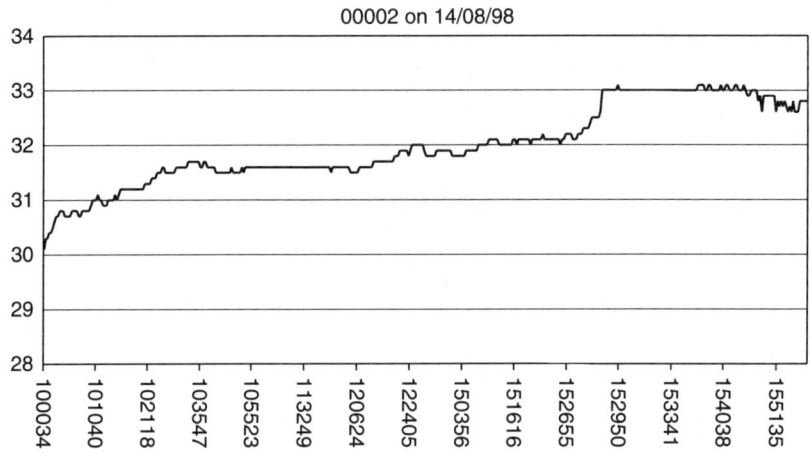

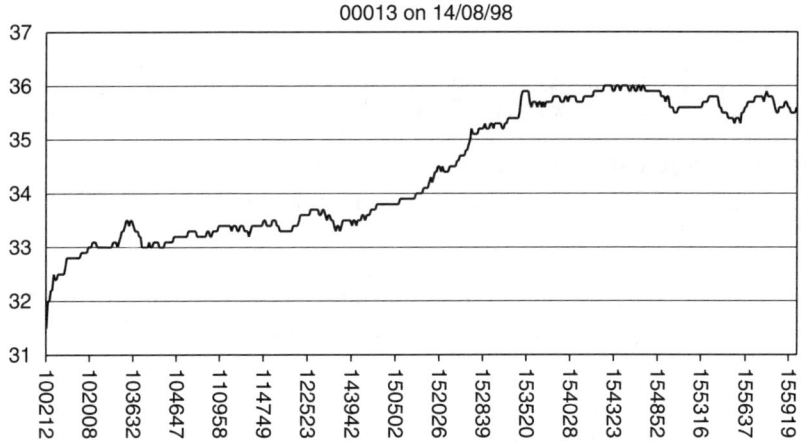

FIG. 3.3. Different patterns during the intervention
Example I: CLP Holdings (00002) and Hutchison Whampoa (00013) on 14 August 1998.

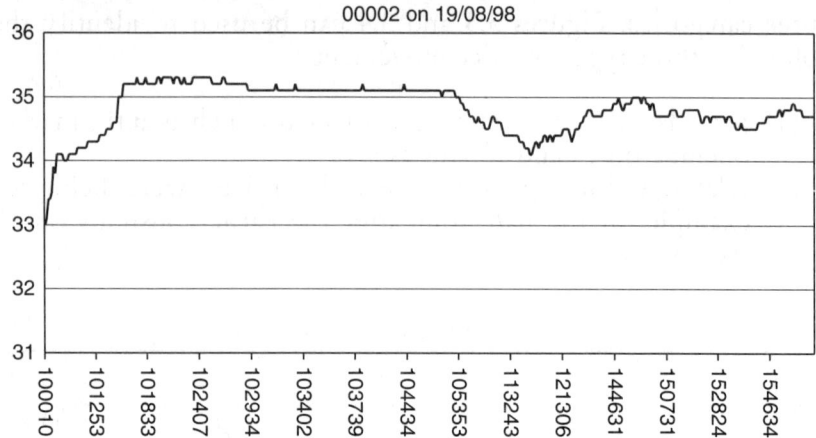

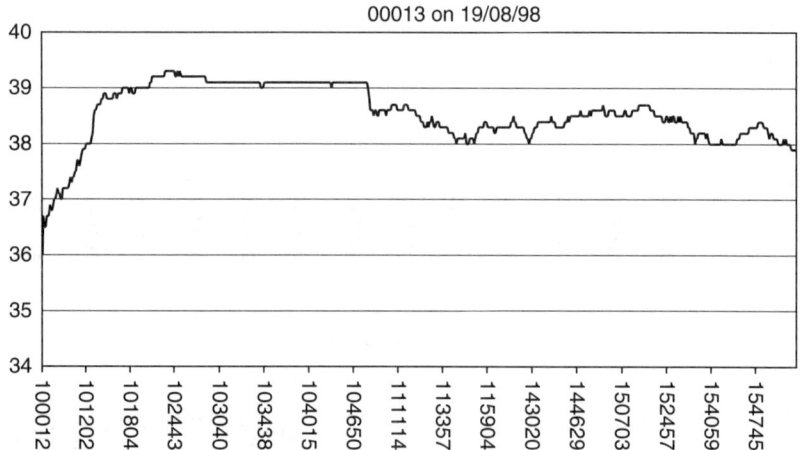

FIG. 3.4. Different patterns during the intervention
Example II: CLP Holdings (00002) and Hutchison Whampoa (00013) on 19 August 1998.

(3) some periods when the market seemed to be allowed to fluctuate freely, for example, in the afternoon trading session on 19 August.

3.2.2 Intervention in Terms of Prices

Before the stock market intervention, the HKMA had already intervened in the foreign exchange (currency) market by actively buying a large amount of Hong Kong dollars that were being sold short by the speculators. They did so by converting the fiscal reserves from US dollars to Hong Kong dollars, a process that had little or no effect on the aggregate balance of the banking system. This action prevented interest rates from escalating sharply, as in October 1997. However, the stock market continued to drop at that time due to two factors: (i) continuing rumours of a forthcoming devaluation of the RMB and the Hong Kong dollar;

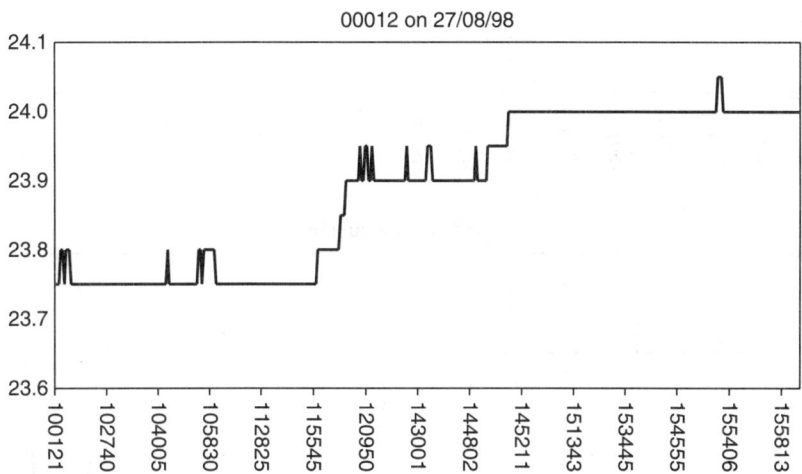

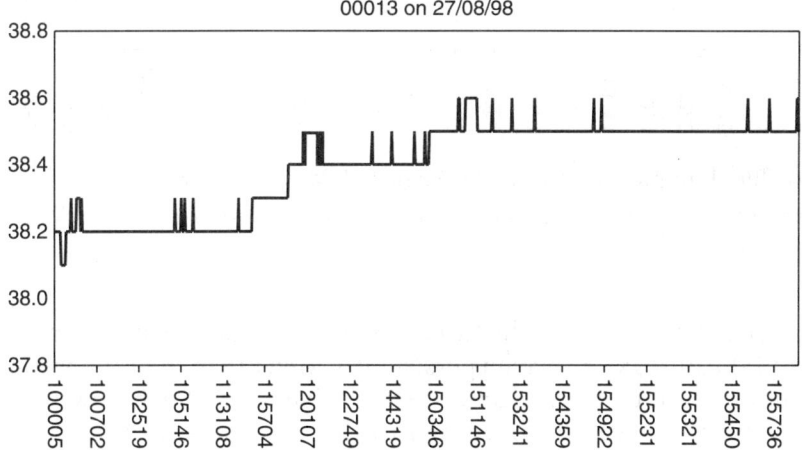

FIG. 3.5. Unique patterns on 27 August 1998.
Examples: Henderson Land Development (00012) and Hutchison Whampoa (00013).

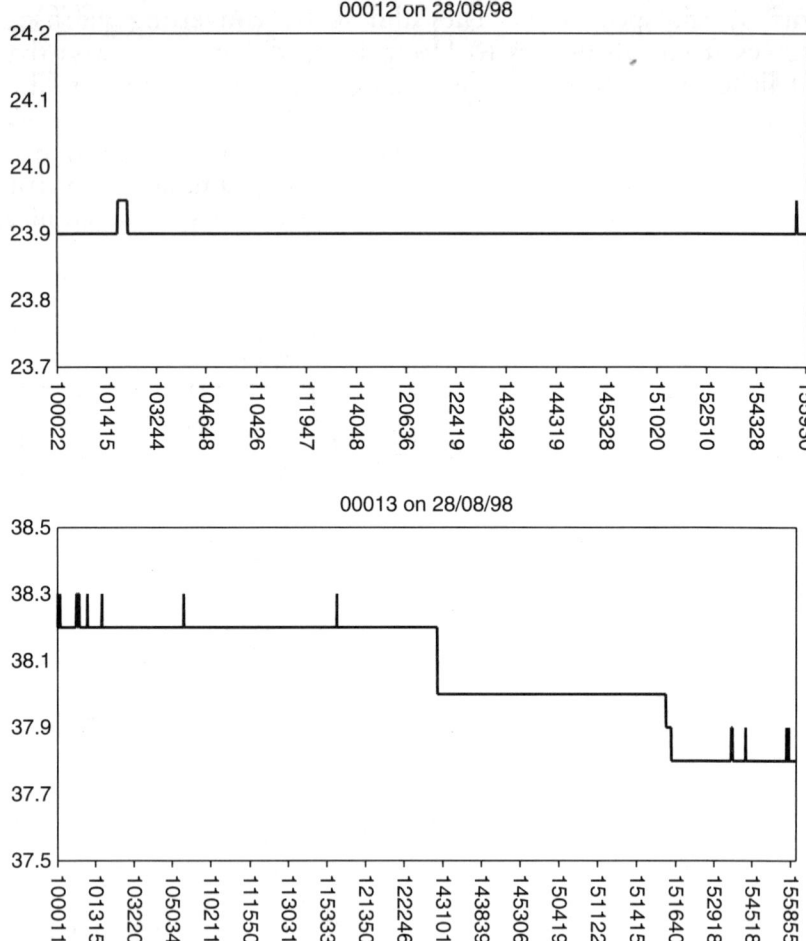

FIG. 3.6. Unique patterns on 28 August 1998.
Examples: Henderson Land Development (00012) and Hutchison Whampoa (00013).

(ii) speculators' play in the futures market. Before the intervention, the HSI futures were driven persistently lower than their theoretical prices (as will be further described in Chapter 5). Such downward pressure is normally transmitted to the spot market through two channels, namely, a psychological effect and an arbitrage mechanism. If the market believes that the futures contract prices indicate the direction of spot price changes, market sentiment could be easily depressed. Further, by creating a negative arbitrage gap, speculators

A Reconstruction of the Intervention 51

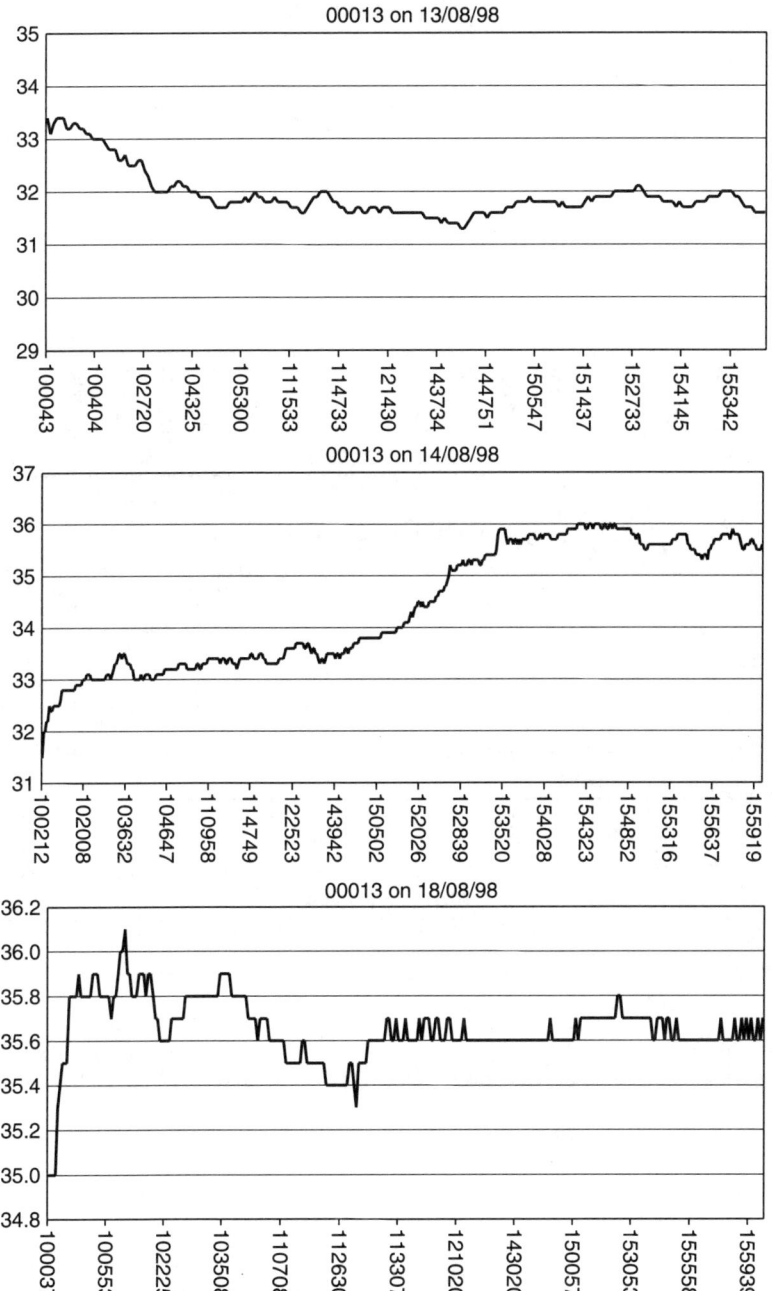

FIG. 3.7. The whole picture of the intervention
Example I: Hutchison Whampoa (00013). (*continued*)

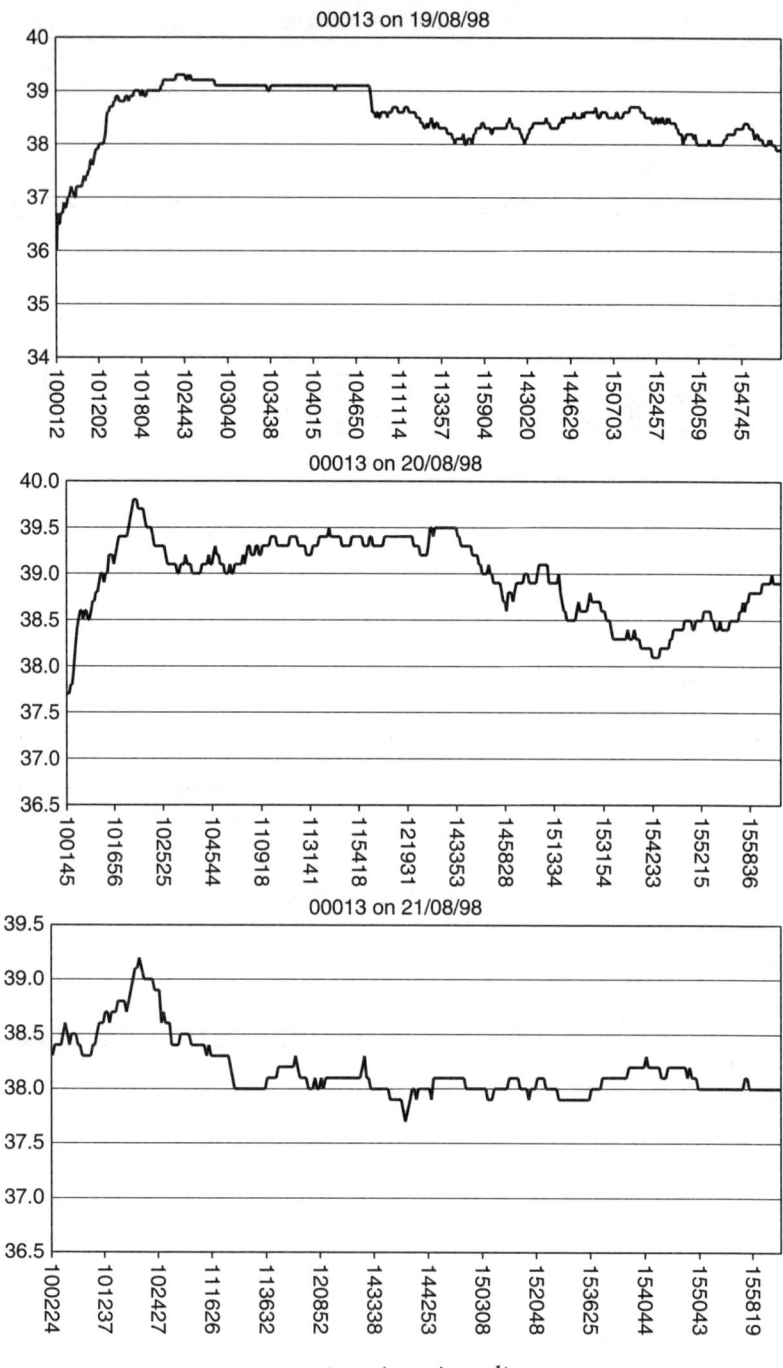

FIG. 3.7. (*continued*)

A Reconstruction of the Intervention 53

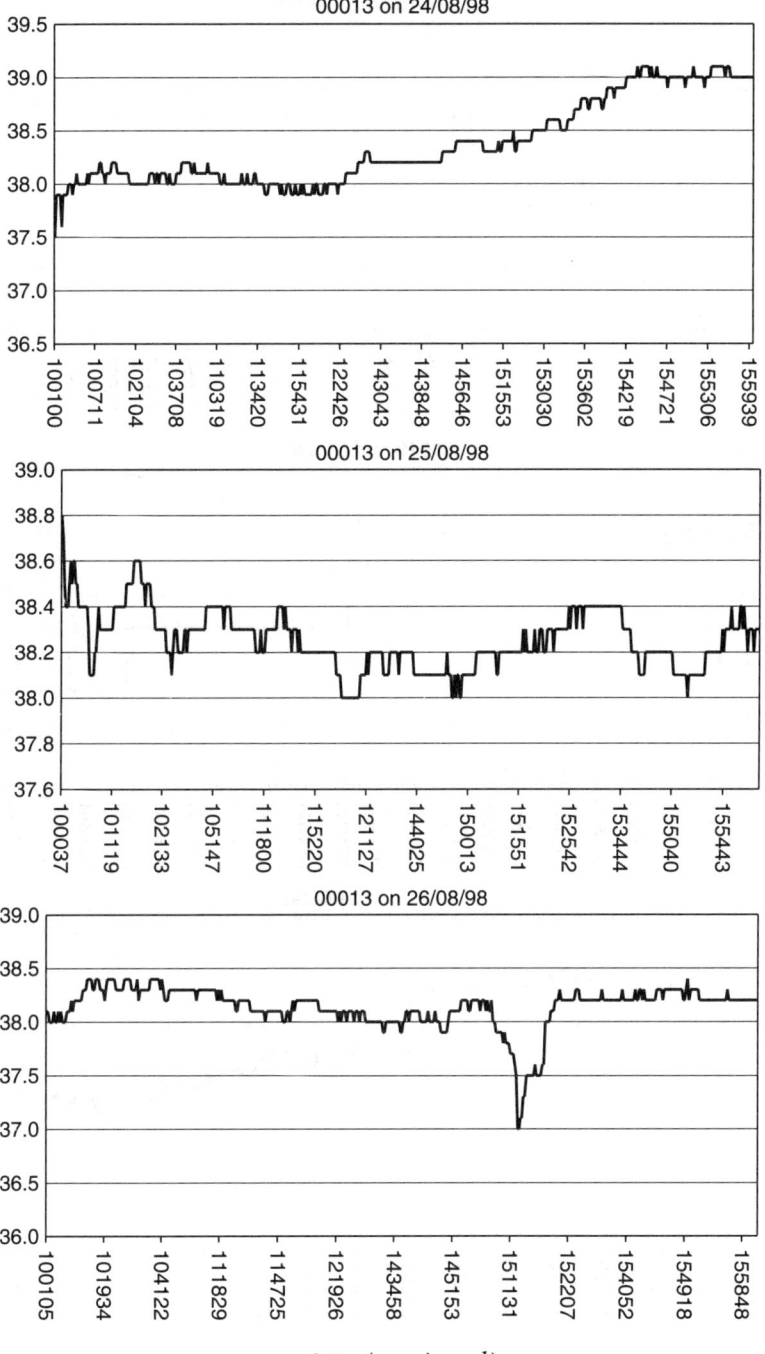

FIG. 3.7. (*continued*)

54 *Intervention to Save Hong Kong*

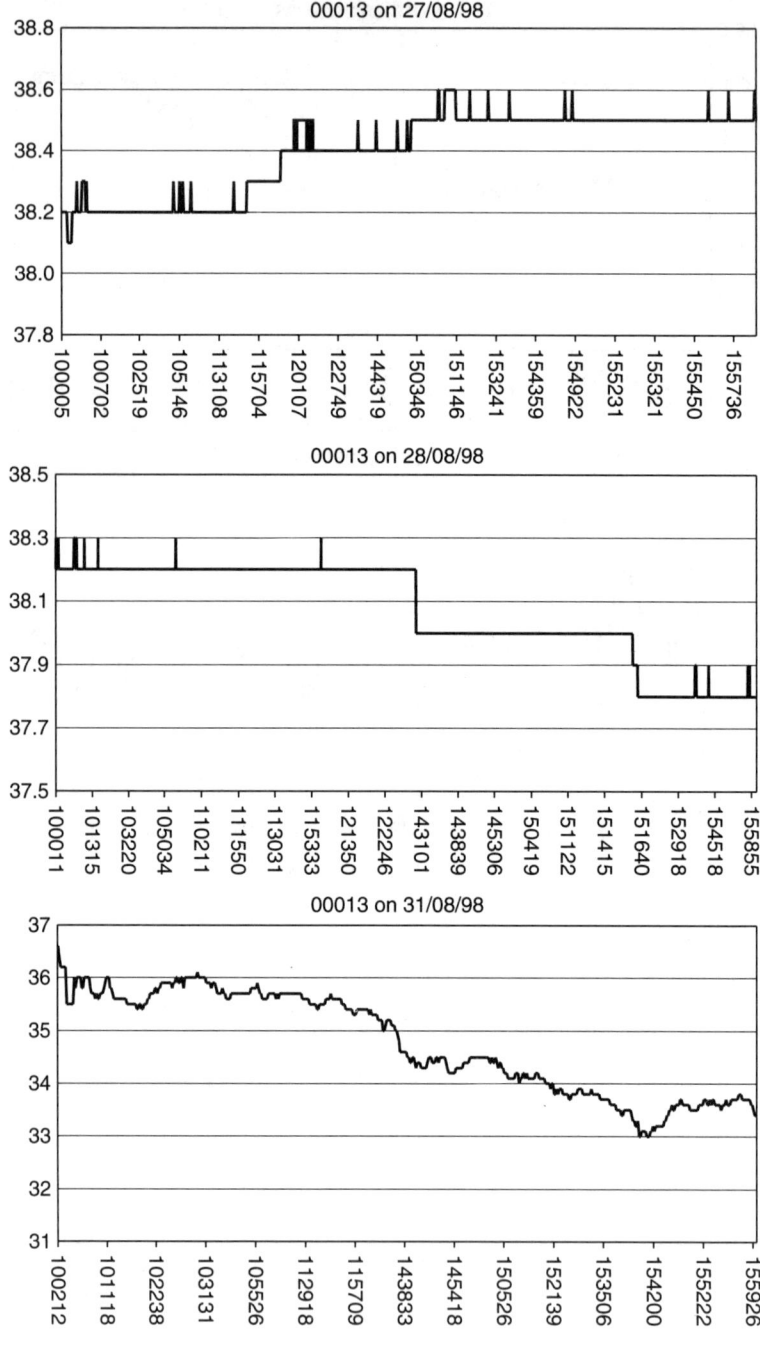

FIG. 3.7. (*continued*)

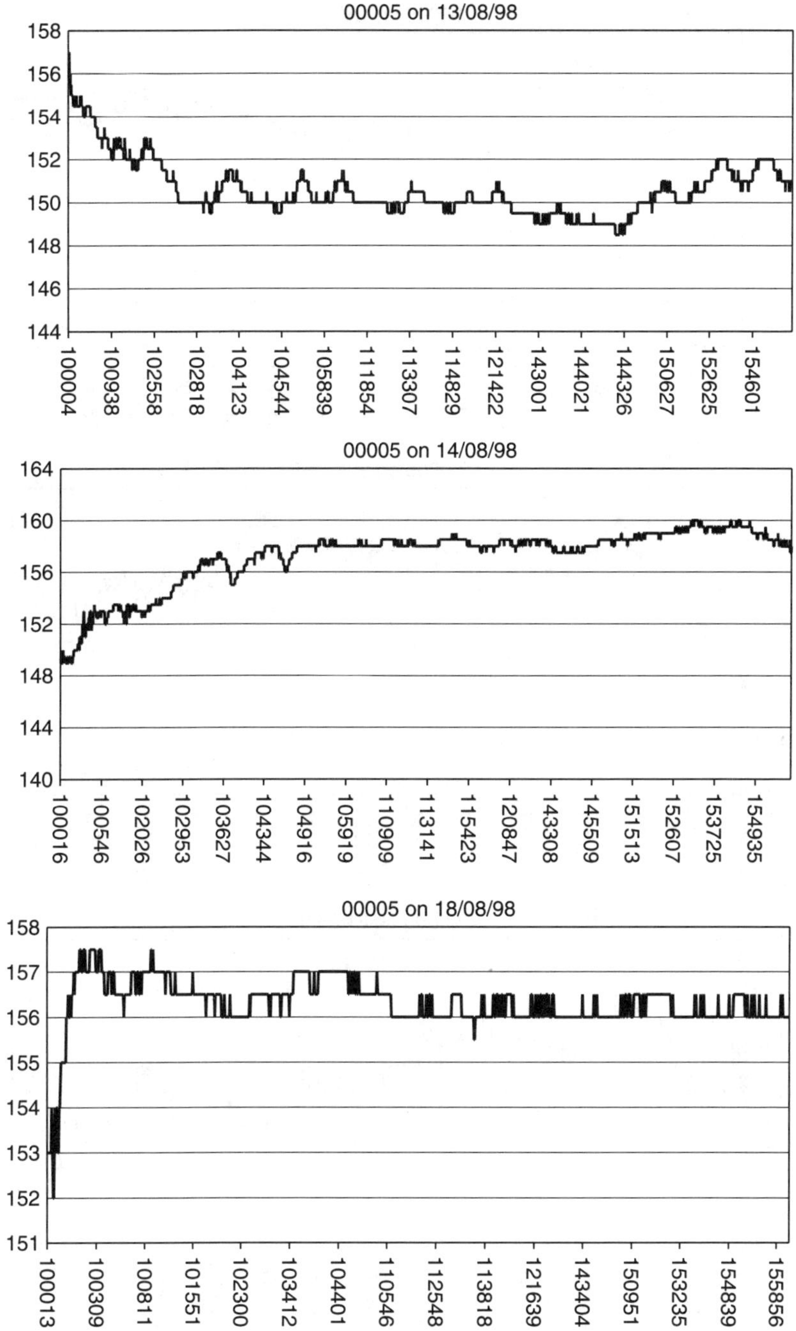

A Reconstruction of the Intervention 55

FIG. 3.8. The whole picture of the intervention
Example II: HSBC (00005). (*continued*)

56 *Intervention to Save Hong Kong*

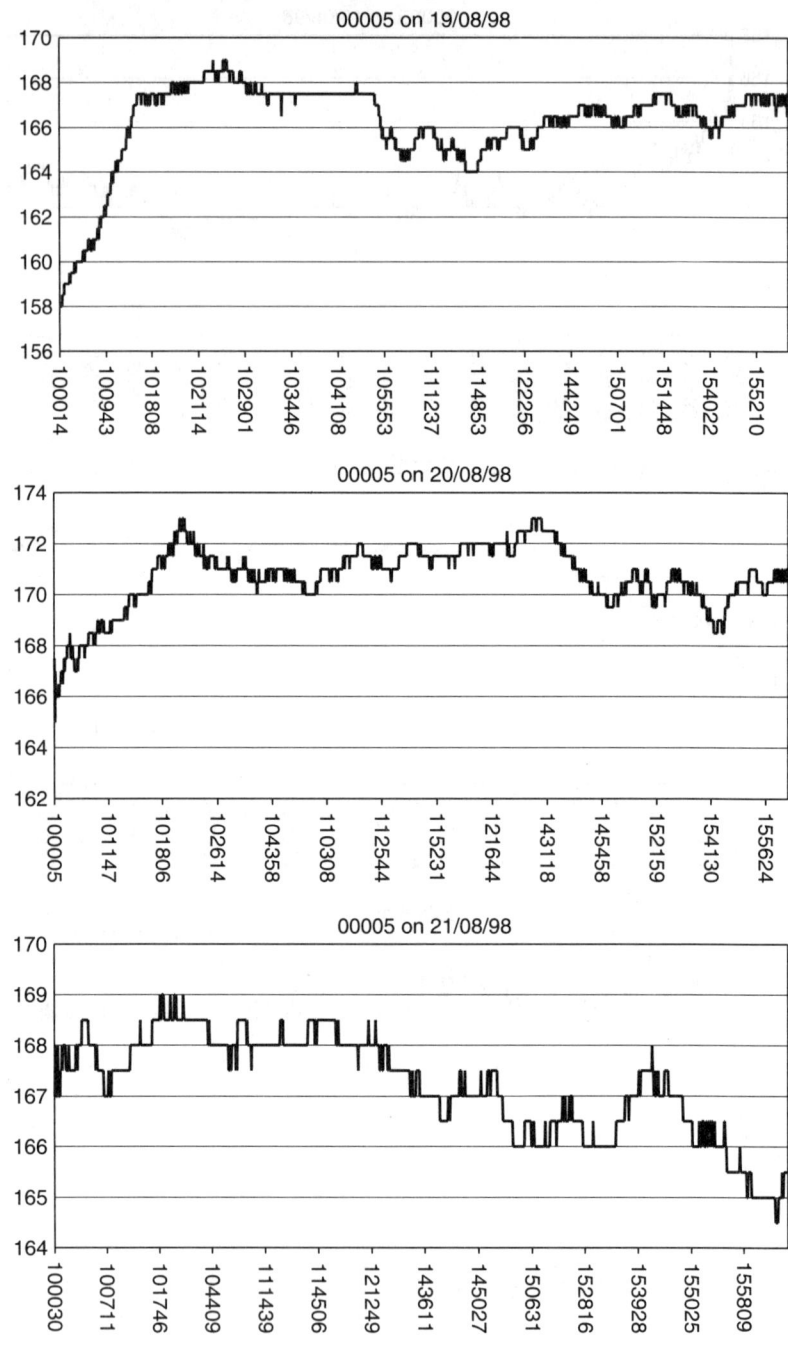

FIG. 3.8. (*continued*)

A Reconstruction of the Intervention 57

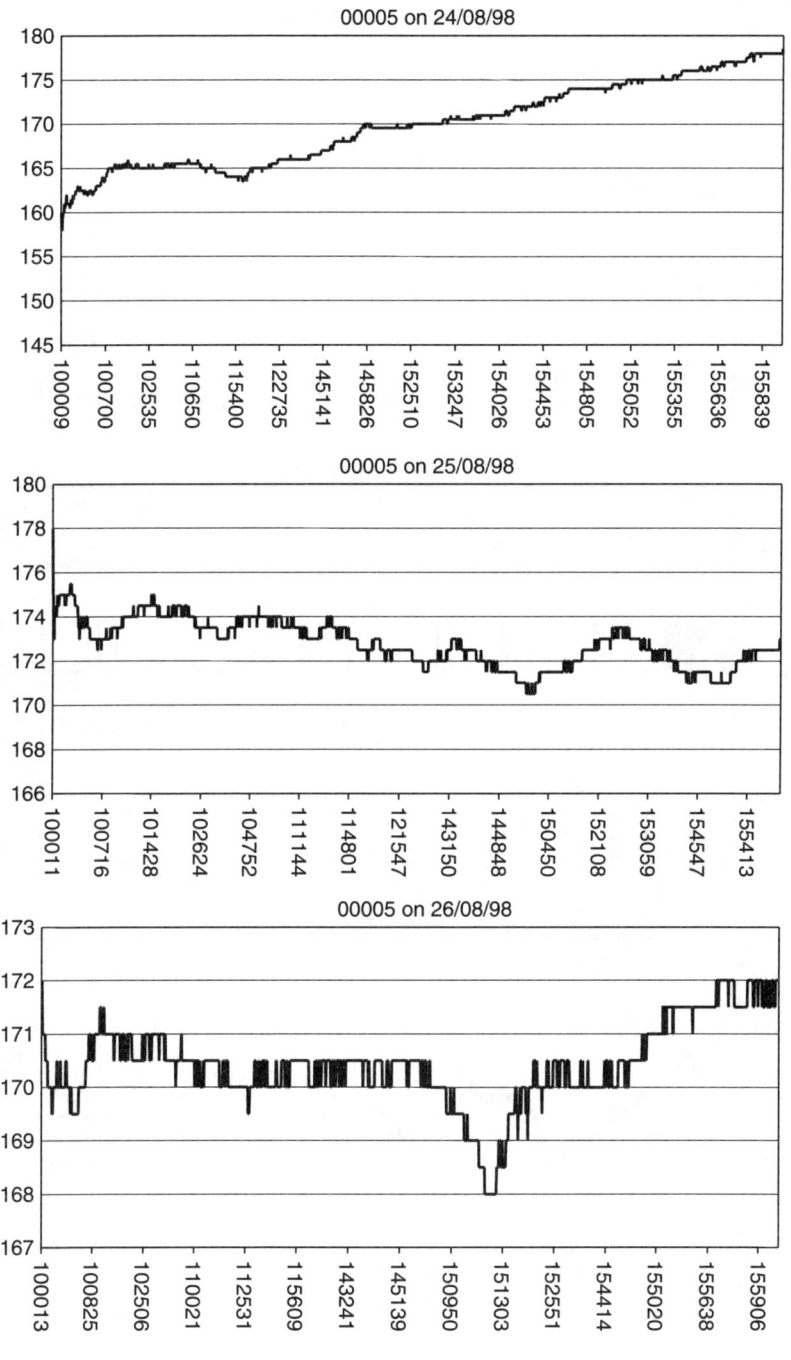

FIG. 3.8. (*continued*)

58 Intervention to Save Hong Kong

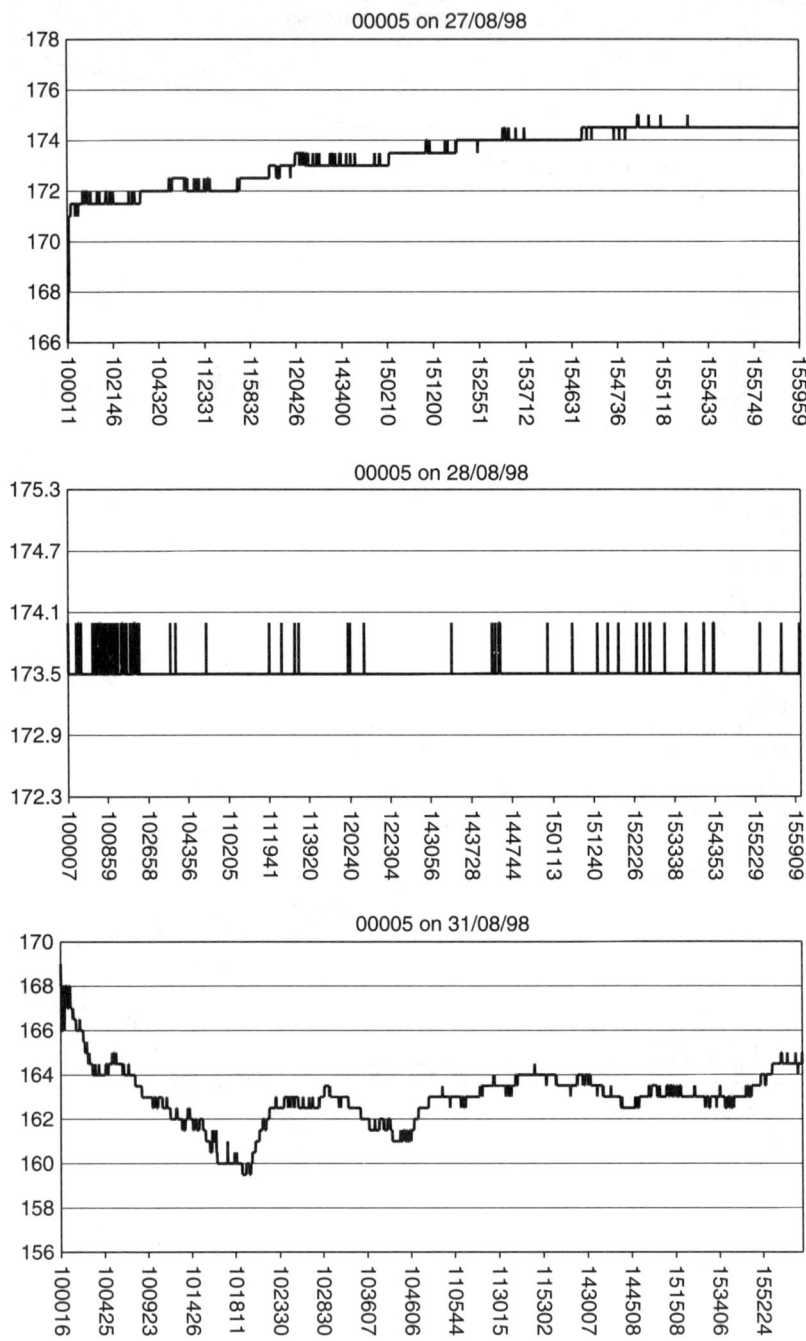

FIG. 3.8. (*continued*)

can attract inter-market arbitrageurs to buy the futures and sell the index stocks, thus pushing the spot market down.

The government had observed this pressure. In order to frustrate the speculators' double-play plan, they decided to adopt a 'double-counter-play' strategy. In the money market, the HKMA deliberately kept a relatively high interbank rate by delaying lending overnight funds; the purpose of this was believed to be to raise the cost of borrowing funds for speculators to settle their Hong Kong dollar short positions. In the stock market, the government bought up the 33 Hang Seng constituent stocks in order to support the Index level. In this section, we focus on the intervention process in terms of the consequent price level. For convenience, we group the first five days from 14 to 21 August as the 'first week' of the intervention and the next five days from 24 to 28 August as the 'second week'.

3.2.2.1 Episodes to Drive up Prices

During the intervention, there were several episodes of prices being driven up. For example, the market showed a unanimous rise on several morning open sessions, notably on 14 and 19 August. There were also similar common rising periods during some trading days. Consider 24 August for instance. Before 12:00 noon, the performances of the 33 stocks varied. Some remained steady, but others showed random fluctuation. However, nearly all the 33 stocks started to climb after 12:00 noon. Table 3.2 shows the performance of each stock during the four chosen 'up' periods.

As shown in Table 3.2, the average price increases were as high as 3.4 per cent, 4.4 per cent, 4.7 per cent and 5.2 per cent respectively. However, the individual stocks did not behave identically. On the morning of 14 August between the opening and 11 AM, the most uniformity can be observed, with a standard deviation of only 1.5 per cent. The most disparate performances occurred on the afternoon of 24 August, showing a standard deviation of 3.5 per cent. If we attribute all these surges to government intervention, which should be a reasonable assumption, as shown in the later section on quantity estimation, then the figures can give us some insights into the government's strategy during the intervention period. It seemed that, although the government may have been simultaneously buying into each stock, they did not have a set target for each of them. For example, on the morning of 19 August, the highest price

TABLE 3.2. *Price performances during the 'up' periods*

Stock code	% change on 14th push <= 11:00am	>= 2:30pm	% change on 19th push <= 10:30am	% change on 24th push >= 12:00am
00001	6.14	4.92	3.94	0.61
00002	5.00	3.13	6.06	0.29
00003	3.70	1.19	5.29	1.19
00004	4.07	3.94	5.19	7.49
00005	5.33	1.27	6.01	8.23
00006	2.33	2.22	4.76	0.42
00008	5.60	4.55	4.96	8.00
00010	2.75	7.02	−2.33	2.46
00011	5.48	3.90	3.78	7.41
00012	1.91	4.61	3.04	2.22
00013	4.76	7.46	6.85	2.63
00014	2.13	3.03	4.08	7.29
00016	4.65	4.35	5.31	1.79
00017	3.80	6.02	5.49	6.17
00019	5.00	2.38	2.67	7.24
00020	2.24	2.19	4.79	13.14
00023	1.37	2.65	3.23	3.90
00041	1.87	1.77	−1.57	4.13
00045	3.12	12.12	8.16	5.26
00054	1.56	4.62	4.05	2.60
00069	3.62	14.29	18.07	10.11
00083	2.50	5.95	2.17	4.35
00097	0.00	2.14	5.33	1.29
00101	3.12	5.30	3.45	3.62
00142	1.96	1.98	3.70	11.96
00267	4.30	8.00	5.05	7.34
00270	2.56	2.46	6.56	7.94
00291	3.30	3.14	3.72	11.11
00293	2.94	2.86	6.90	2.59
00363	3.41	3.93	3.70	8.25
00511	2.00	1.30	3.27	4.00
00941	5.38	7.00	5.99	2.90
01038	3.18	2.61	3.15	1.92
Average	3.37	4.37	4.69	5.15
Standard deviation	1.46	2.95	3.19	3.52

changes were as much as 18.07 per cent for Shangri-La (00069), while the lowest was 2.33 per cent for Hang Lung (00010). Also, on different days, the government might have focused on a different set of stocks, pushing them relatively higher than others. However, the histograms for each of the four periods, as given in Figure 3.9, revealed that a large number of the stocks fell into the range of 2 per cent to 4 per cent.

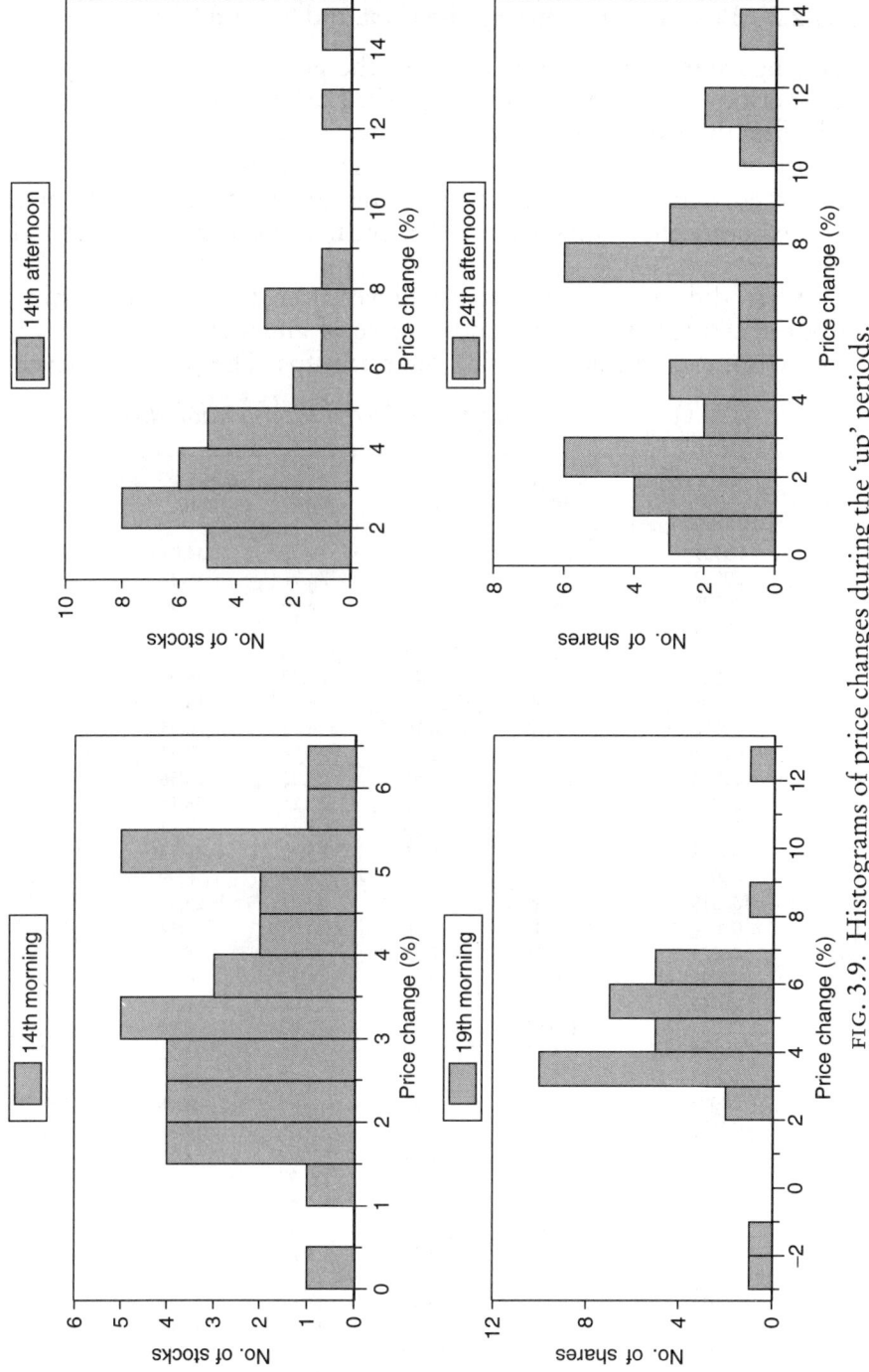

FIG. 3.9. Histograms of price changes during the 'up' periods.

3.2.2.2 Price Ranges During the First and Second Week

Having examined the price changes, the next step was to separate the periods in which prices were pushed up into two sub-sections. The first three days from 14 to 19 August were grouped as the initial effort and the afternoon of 24 August as the second phase effort. We observed that, after the first push, the government relaxed for a while before they launched another push at the start of the second week.

What did the government achieve after these two pushing efforts? Table 3.3 gives the mean price of all stocks on four days, two from each week following the push-ups. The prices achieved

TABLE 3.3. *Mean prices on selected intervention days*

Stock code	Mean price		Mean price	
	20th	21st	25th	26th
00001	34.13	33.19	34.07	34.04
00002	35.08	34.15	34.91	35.02
00003	8.96	8.54	8.76	9.00
00004	7.37	7.28	7.13	7.49
00005	170.63	167.18	172.75	170.37
00006	24.73	23.74	24.37	25.00
00008	14.93	14.81	15.77	15.50
00010	6.22	6.19	6.45	6.53
00011	40.78	40.50	43.84	43.62
00012	23.09	22.52	23.23	23.56
00013	39.00	38.21	38.25	38.15
00014	5.15	5.15	5.25	5.34
00016	25.54	25.05	25.71	26.15
00017	9.55	9.10	8.79	8.99
00019	23.60	22.72	23.77	23.98
00020	3.85	3.86	4.01	4.17
00023	8.08	7.90	8.10	8.25
00041	6.26	6.21	6.34	6.51
00045	3.97	3.81	4.07	4.11
00054	0.78	0.77	0.80	0.82
00069	5.02	4.99	5.26	5.32
00083	2.36	2.33	2.48	2.58
00097	3.95	3.96	4.05	4.18
00101	3.65	3.57	3.66	3.77
00142	2.70	2.60	2.60	2.59
00267	10.87	9.98	9.97	10.24
00270	1.40	1.38	1.40	1.42
00291	5.84	5.67	5.66	5.81
00293	6.57	6.23	6.24	6.27
00363	11.47	10.84	10.66	10.96
00511	15.13	15.41	16.50	17.55
00941	11.41	10.75	10.92	10.86
01038	13.73	13.88	13.93	14.38

after each pushing effort were very close, probably in the range that the government desired. After the initial push-up when they achieved this level, they relaxed and let market forces take control most of the time during the next two days. On 21 August, prices even slid down a bit. There was an episode on this day that needs to be mentioned. The HSI shed 215 points, but most of the drop happened during a very short period just before the market closed. The government was quite relaxed during the day and some big players might have taken advantage of this low-key involvement to fight back right before the market closed for the weekend. The August futures contract also experienced a sudden fall during the last few minutes of the same day, with a 137-point discount to the cash market at the close.

The second week opened at a much lower level. This was probably due to the drop in the Dow Jones Industrial Average on the previous Friday, the acute situation in Russia, and a weaker yen. So the government made another effort to push prices back up again, and prices were pushed back to almost the same level on 25 August as on the 20th. This time the government was more careful to maintain the level.

3.2.2.3   Common Lowering of Prices on 28 August

As mentioned earlier, the last two days of intervention were the most spectacular. Prices of all the 33 stocks were held tightly by the government. Table 3.4 shows the price changes on the last two days and Figure 3.10 gives the histograms of the changes. On each of these last two days, prices were held flat for many stocks. On 27 August, 12 out of the 33 stocks had no price change during the day and the government managed to drive 20 stocks up a bit, the highest being for China Telecom (00941)—a rise of 3.3 per cent. The only drop was for Swire A (00019). Compared with 27 August, however, the opening prices on 28 August of all the 33 stocks were lower than the previous closing prices. Then on 28 August, prices of 27 stocks were kept at one level during the day, while the other 6 stocks showed small price falls. This lowering of prices, we believe, was to release some of the pressure on the government.

3.2.3   Intervention in Terms of Quantities

In Section 3.2.2, we examined the intervention process in terms of price levels, which is basically a summarized description of what

TABLE 3.4. *Price changes during the last two intervention days*

Stock code	Price changes on 27th			Price changes on 28th			Per cent change of price from 27th to 28th	
	Open	Close	Per cent change	Open	Close	Per cent change	From Close27 to Open28	From Close27 to Close28
00001	34.00	34.00	0.00	33.80	33.20	−1.78	−0.59	−2.35
00002	35.10	35.40	0.85	35.20	35.20	0.00	−0.56	−0.56
00003	9.10	9.10	0.00	9.00	9.00	0.00	−1.10	−1.10
00004	7.60	7.80	2.63	7.65	7.55	−1.31	−1.92	−3.21
00005	171.50	174.50	1.75	173.50	173.50	0.00	−0.57	−0.57
00006	25.10	25.25	0.60	25.15	25.15	0.00	−0.40	−0.40
00008	15.50	15.50	0.00	15.25	15.10	−0.98	−1.61	−2.58
00010	6.65	6.75	1.50	6.70	6.70	0.00	−0.74	−0.74
00011	44.00	44.40	0.91	44.30	44.30	0.00	−0.23	−0.23
00012	23.75	24.00	1.05	23.90	23.90	0.00	−0.42	−0.42
00013	38.20	38.50	0.79	38.20	37.80	−1.05	−0.78	−1.82
00014	5.35	5.35	0.00	5.25	5.25	0.00	−1.87	−1.87
00016	26.20	26.20	0.00	25.90	25.70	−0.77	−1.15	−1.91
00017	9.05	9.05	0.00	8.95	8.85	−1.12	−1.10	−2.21
00019	25.25	24.35	−3.56	24.00	24.00	0.00	−1.44	−1.44
00020	4.20	4.25	1.19	4.23	4.23	0.00	−0.59	−0.59
00023	8.45	8.60	1.78	8.50	8.50	0.00	−1.16	−1.16
00041	6.55	6.65	1.53	6.60	6.60	0.00	−0.75	−0.75
00045	4.20	4.25	1.19	4.20	4.20	0.00	−1.18	−1.18
00054	0.83	0.84	1.20	0.83	0.83	0.00	−1.19	−1.19
00069	4.90	4.90	0.00	4.80	4.80	0.00	−2.04	−2.04
00083	2.63	2.63	0.00	2.60	2.60	0.00	−0.95	−0.95
00097	4.25	4.28	0.59	4.25	4.25	0.00	−0.58	−0.58
00101	3.85	3.95	2.60	3.93	3.93	0.00	−0.63	−0.63
00142	2.63	2.63	0.00	2.58	2.58	0.00	−1.90	−1.90
00267	10.35	10.55	1.93	10.40	10.40	0.00	−1.42	−1.42
00270	1.43	1.43	0.00	1.42	1.42	0.00	−0.70	−0.70
00291	5.85	5.85	0.00	5.75	5.75	0.00	−1.71	−1.71
00293	6.25	6.40	2.40	6.25	6.25	0.00	−2.34	−2.34
00363	11.05	11.20	1.36	11.00	11.00	0.00	−1.79	−1.79
00511	17.70	17.85	0.85	17.75	17.75	0.00	−0.56	−0.56
00941	10.65	11.00	3.29	10.90	10.90	0.00	−0.91	−0.91
01038	14.55	14.55	0.00	14.35	14.35	0.00	−1.37	−1.37

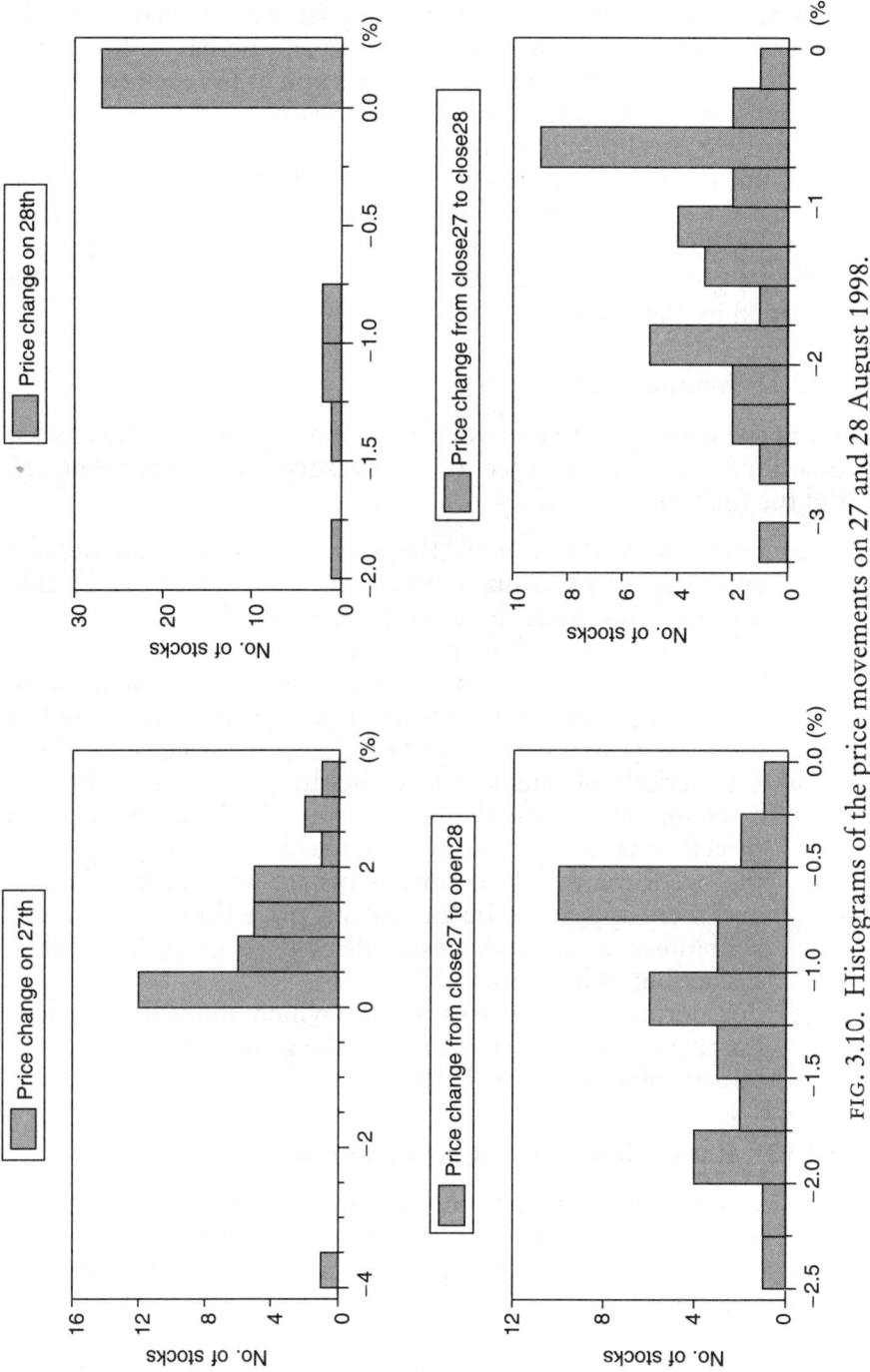

FIG. 3.10. Histograms of the price movements on 27 and 28 August 1998.

anyone could observe from the market. In order to have a better understanding of the entire event, however, one has to know the quantity of purchases made by the government for each stock and on each day. As already mentioned in Chapter 2, the government released the total purchase amount for each stock on 26 October 1998, but no daily details were disclosed.[6] In this section, we give estimates of government purchases using intra-day transaction data based on our own assumptions. Then, we compare our estimates with the government announcement, as well as with information provided by the press.

3.2.3.1 Assumptions

From the common price performance of all the intervened stocks, described in the previous sections, we assume that the government did the following:

(a) For periods when most of the constituent stocks exhibited an up trend, the government was on the buying side of all transactions. This could be a rough assumption because of the existence of other buyers. But we assume that these other buyers who followed in the government's footsteps were mostly small investors; and their participation is filtered as shown later in the discussion on data processing.

(b) For periods of intensive price holding, we assume that the government was on the buying side of all the transactions priced equal to or lower than the held level. By 'price holding' we mean the price movements are within a small range and there appears to be an obvious price floor or ceiling or sometimes a collar. An example will be given later when discussing estimation.

(c) For periods when prices fell, or which showed a random fluctuation with no clear pattern, the government is assumed to have played no part in the market.

3.2.3.2 Rationale Behind the Assumptions

Our assumptions are based not only on the special price patterns observed, but also supported by the institutional details of the order flow and the price formation process in the SEHK described in earlier sections.

---

[6] HKMA news release, http://www.info.gov.hk/hkma, 26 October 1998.

There is a close relationship between investor order submission strategies and the short-term dynamics of asset prices, as well as the transmission of information in security markets. The Hong Kong stock market has the following features that can make it easier to analyse the interaction between the order flow and the evolution of prices: (a) it is a pure order-driven market, which relies solely on the order placement; (b) all the orders are executed based on strict time and price priority; and (c) it is one of the most transparent markets in the world. Detailed information on the order book and transactions are available to all agents and, therefore, their clients. During the intervention, the HKMA assigned several brokers to do the purchases on behalf of the government. They had to submit their orders into the computerized system just as other market participants did. Thus, by tracking the order book changes, we could gain a reasonable understanding of the government behaviour.

Similar to the trading mechanisms of the Paris Bourse,[7] the orders are stored and executed in the sequence in which they are received by the market. The computerized automatching system ensures that the time and price priority rules are enforced. Although only limit orders can be placed, some orders that hit the best price on the opposite side of the limit order book can be grouped as 'market orders'. They are executed immediately, but any excess amount would be converted into a limit order at that price rather than walking up or down the order book.

During the intervention, the government had to use both pushing-up and holding strategies to achieve and maintain the desired index level. When they wanted to lift the prices up, they had to keep inputting 'market orders' to exhaust the supply queue and walk up the limit order book. Thus the order placement had to be aggressive in terms of both price and quantity. Since the presumption is that the speculators, and the arbitrageurs taking advantage of the futures/cash index margin, wanted to push the market lower, the selling pressure must have been heavy and only a large and aggressive buyer could push the price up. Most likely, those buyers were representatives of the Hong Kong government. According to a market observer,[8] the government sometimes used guerrilla tactics—'bombing the market with huge orders and then disappearing'. When they drew back, the selling party would be able to walk

---

[7] For a detailed description of the market structure of the Paris Bourse, please refer to Biais, Hillion and Spatt (1995).

[8] 'Investors unload blue chips', *South China Morning Post*, 22 August 1998.

TABLE 3.5. *Change of the limit order book under a large bid order*

	Limit order book at t_0				Limit order book at t_1	
ASK	162.00	4000		ASK	162.50	
	161.50	6000			162.00	4000
	161.00	2000			161.50	6000
	160.50	2000			161.00	2000
	160.00	4000	← New bid at 160.00 10000 shares		160.50	2000
BID	159.50	2000		BID	160.00	6000
	159.00	6000	Trade Record		159.50	2000
	158.50	200	Price Qty		159.00	6000
	158.50	400	1 160.00 4000		158.50	200
	157.50	800			158.00	400

TABLE 3.6. *An example of walking up the limit order book*

	Limit order book at t_0				Limit order book at t_1	
ASK	162.00	4000		ASK	163.50	
	161.50	6000			163.00	
	161.00	2000	← Bid3=4000 at 161.00		162.50	
	160.50	2000	← Bid2=2000 at 160.50		162.00	4000
	160.00	4000	← Bid1=4000 at 160.00 →		161.50	6000
BID	159.50	2000	Trade Record	BID	161.00	2000
	159.00	6000	Price Qty		160.50	
	158.50	200	1 160.00 4000		160.00	
	158.50	400	2 160.50 2000		159.50	2000
	157.50	800	3 161.00 2000		159.00	6000

down the order book some way and prices should have looked bumpy. Therefore, for those periods when prices were constantly driven up, we count all transactions as government purchases. Actually for these up-periods, most, or all, of the 33 stocks showed similar performances. And for those bumpy periods, we suppose the government representatives stepped back and did not buy.

Two simple examples are given above to illustrate the price formation process: Table 3.5 shows the change of the limit order book when a large bid is posted and Table 3.6 shows how an aggressive bidder can walk up the order book.

For example, when a large bid order (10,000 shares) is submitted at the best ask price (160.00), it is only matched with the orders at that ask price (4,000). The remaining part of the bid order will then remain in the limit order book at the new best bid price of 160.00

A Reconstruction of the Intervention 69

without being matched with less favourable ask prices in the order book.

If the buy side wants to walk up the order book, it has to submit bid orders strategically at each ask price. Table 3.6 gives a simple example without considering any possible dynamic reaction from the sell side. As Table 3.6 shows, to push up the prices, the buyer just has to submit bid orders big enough to absorb the existing selling orders at different ask prices. However, if the sellers are active in their trading, it could be much harder for the buyer to achieve this goal. This is because the sellers can also submit large orders in batches with different but lower prices, and if they can absorb the previous limit bid orders remaining on the books, they would be able to press the price down.

During the price-holding periods, the aim of the government was to keep prices from falling. To do this, bid orders had to be constantly submitted at the same level to set a floor. During such periods, the bid orders would be large and, since they could not be exhausted easily, the bid price shown on the order book should stay unchanged for a long time. If the selling side were speculators, normal investors or arbitrageurs, accepting the best bid was their only real choice. Therefore, when the government was propping up the price, their purchases had to be at a price equal to, or occasionally lower than, the prevailing best bid price. Based on this reasoning, we have formulated our second assumption: no transactions priced higher than the (government-supported) held level is taken into account, since in all likelihood those purchases would be from other liquidity traders who might also wish to acquire some shares for various reasons. Such extraneous 'liquidity' purchases explain the 'pop-ups' during the support periods.

Figure 3.11 plots the best bid price for HSBC on 28 August and its price movement during the same day. It is of course an extreme day but it clearly demonstrates how the government was holding prices.

3.2.3.3 Data Processing

Types of Transactions

In order to estimate the extent of government intervention, we have to take into account all probable purchases by the government-assigned brokers. While it would be valuable to track the performance of every incoming order and the interactive dynamics between the order revisions and the transaction prices, this would

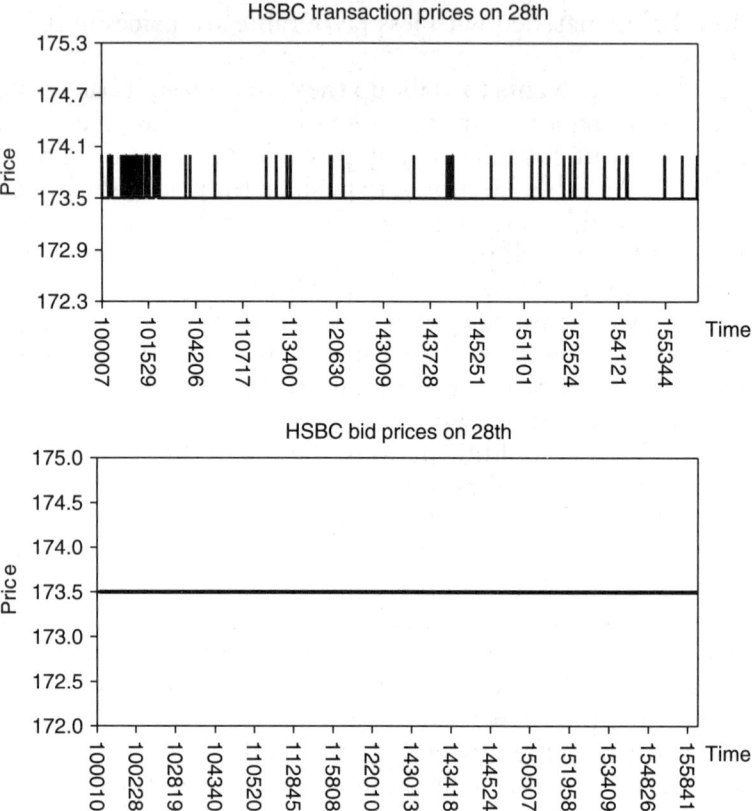

FIG. 3.11. A comparison of the transaction and bid prices on 28 August 1998.

be needlessly time-consuming. Moreover, we only have bid-ask data at 30-second snapshots. When trading activities are intensive, 30-seconds could be long enough to miss quite a lot of information. So, only the trading record, which is a tick-by-tick dataset, was used to do the estimation.

The trading record obtained from the SEHK included not only those transactions automatched by the AMS but also others defined as manual trade, semi-odd trade, special trade, special odd trade, and overseas trade. Table 3.7 defines the different types of transactions. Since we are aware that the government assigned several brokers to trade in large orders, it is unlikely that they adopted any non-automatching trading methods. We have therefore taken into consideration only type 'A' transactions in our estimations, which refer to automatched ones.

TABLE 3.7. *Definitions of different trading methods under AMS/2 of the SEHK (Effective before 7 December 1998)*

Type	Method	Description
A	Automatched trade	A trade which has been generated from two orders being matched by the automatching process.
M	Manual trade	A trade which is reported manually by the seller for a whole number of board lots of a security, which the Exchange has designated as manual, and is executed on the trading floor by telephone negotiation.
O	Semi-odd trade	A trade which has been generated as a result of a trader selecting an odd lot order and confirming that he wishes to trade at the exact price and quantity specified by the order.
S	Special trade	A trade which is reported manually by the seller for a whole multiple of board lots of a security and is executed using other than the Exchange-designated method of trading for that security.
P	Special odd trade	A trade which is reported manually by the seller for a quantity of a security that is not a whole multiple of the board lot for that security and is executed using other than the Exchange-designated method of odd lot trading.
V	Overseas trade	A trade which takes place between a member firm and an individual or organization outside the jurisdiction of Hong Kong. Overseas sales are reported by the member firm, whether it be a buyer or a seller.

Source: User Guide, Trade Record (Equity), SEHK.

Size of the Transactions

Next, we filter the data by the size of the transactions. In their battle with the speculators, the government had to resist selling pressures, in order to push or prop up prices. We assume that the government only became involved in large trades. In all possibility, there were other small buyers in the market. Their buying orders could also have been met alongside government buying, according to either time or price priority. So, we should have reasonable grounds to eliminate those small transactions when we estimate government buying. The definition of 'small' is somewhat arbitrary. For stocks of different prices and different lot sizes, different criteria would be applied to categorize them as large or small. To simplify matters, we chose 10-lots for most of the stocks as a threshold of being counted as part of the intervention; transactions below that were considered small. But for those stocks whose lot size was bigger than 1,000 shares the threshold was fixed at 10,000 shares. This criterion could certainly be biased in some cases, but it is unlikely that any other single criterion can totally avoid biases; and we can assess the effect of this bias later in our results. Table 3.8 gives lot size and spread size of the intervened stocks.

Possibility of Over-estimation

Having accessed the required data and employed the relevant estimation methods, we then went into number crunching. We are still likely to have overestimated government purchases due to the following reasons. First, our method cannot distinguish, and thus filter out, other larger buyers who submit orders at the same prices as the government purchases. These buyers could include large investors, companies doing repurchasing, etc. Second, as mentioned above, 10 lots can be too low a criterion to filter out the small trades for stocks with low prices and small lot size. (For these stocks, even small investors can easily buy 10 lots with a limited investment.)

3.2.3.4 Estimation Process and Results

Figure 3.12 shows some examples of the actual estimation process. For each day, we divided the trading time into different periods, classifying them as pushing-up, holding, or free float. Based on the three assumptions spelt out earlier, we managed to sum up the probable government purchases for each period and then each day. For instance, prices of CLP Holdings (00002) on the morning of 14 August present a clear lifting-then-holding pattern. We identified the levelled price of HK $31.6 as the targeted price before 12:10 hrs, and for this period all the transactions below HK $31.6 were added up, which totalled 2,278,000 shares. The process for 18 August was simpler. HK $32.8 was obviously the held level and the government purchase on that day was calculated as the total amount of transactions below that, which totalled 2,416,000 shares. On 19 August, the price was pushed all the way up from HK $33 to HK $35.2, kept there for about 10 minutes, and then lowered a bit to HK $35.1, where it was held for half an hour. The total purchases for these two stages were 1,461,000 and 2,717,000 respectively. The price was allowed to float freely after that and the government played no part in the market.

We repeated this estimation process for every stock. For some stocks, there were periods when it was difficult to identify the held level, and we had to use our subjective judgement. For example, there may be two parallel price levels as shown in Figure 3.13. In such situations, we first summed up the total shares of transactions at the two prices. If the two sums were widely different, then

TABLE 3.8. Spread and lot size of the intervened stocks

Name	Stock code	Mean price during intervention	Tick size	Lot size	Selection threshold
CHEUNG KONG HDG.	00001	33.27	0.05–0.1	1,000	10,000
CLP HOLDINGS LTD	00002	34.62	0.1	500	5,000
HK.& CHINA GAS	00003	8.85	0.05	1,000	10,000
WHARF HDG.	00004	7.34	0.05	1,000	10,000
HSBC HDG.	00005	169.69	0.5	400	4,000
HONG KONG ELECTRIC	00006	24.43	0.05	500	5,000
CABLE & WIRELESS HKT	00008	15.12	0.05	400	4,000
HANG LUNG DEV.	00010	6.43	0.05	1,000	10,000
HANG SENG BANK	00011	42.57	0.1	100	1,000
HENDERSON LD.DEV.	00012	23.25	0.05	1,000	10,000
HUTCHISON WHAMP.	00013	37.74	0.1	1,000	10,000
HYSAN DEV.	00014	5.16	0.025–0.5	1,000	10,000
SUN HUNG KAI PROPS.	00016	25.24	0.05	1,000	10,000
NEW WORLD DEV.	00017	8.94	0.05	1,000	10,000
SWIRE PACIFIC 'A'	00019	23.36	0.05	500	5,000
WHEELOCK & CO.	00020	4.03	0.025	1,000	10,000
BANK OF EAST ASIA	00023	8.28	0.05	200	2,000
GREAT EAGLE HDG.	00041	6.39	0.05	1,000	10,000
HK.& SHAI. HOTEL	00045	4.08	0.025	500	5,000
HOPEWELL HDG.	00054	0.80	0.01	1,000	10,000
SHANGRI-LA ASIA	00069	4.86	0.025–0.5	2,000	10,000
SINO LAND	00083	2.46	0.01–0.025	2,000	10,000
HENDERSON INV.	00097	4.10	0.025	1,000	10,000
AMOY PROPERTIES	00101	3.76	0.025	500	5,000
FIRST PACIFIC	00142	2.59	0.025	2,000	10,000
CITIC PACIFIC	00267	10.36	0.05	1,000	10,000
GUANGDONG INV.	00270	1.38	0.01	2,000	10,000
CHINA RES.ENTREP.	00291	5.54	0.025–0.05	2,000	10,000
CATHAY PACIFIC	00293	6.19	0.05	1,000	10,000
SHANGHAI INDUSTRIAL HDG.	00363	10.91	0.05	1,000	10,000
TV.BROADCASTS	00511	16.77	0.05	1,000	10,000
CHINA TELECOM	00941	10.83	0.05	2,000	10,000
CHEUNG KONG INFR.	01038	13.63	0.05	1,000	10,000

74 Intervention to Save Hong Kong

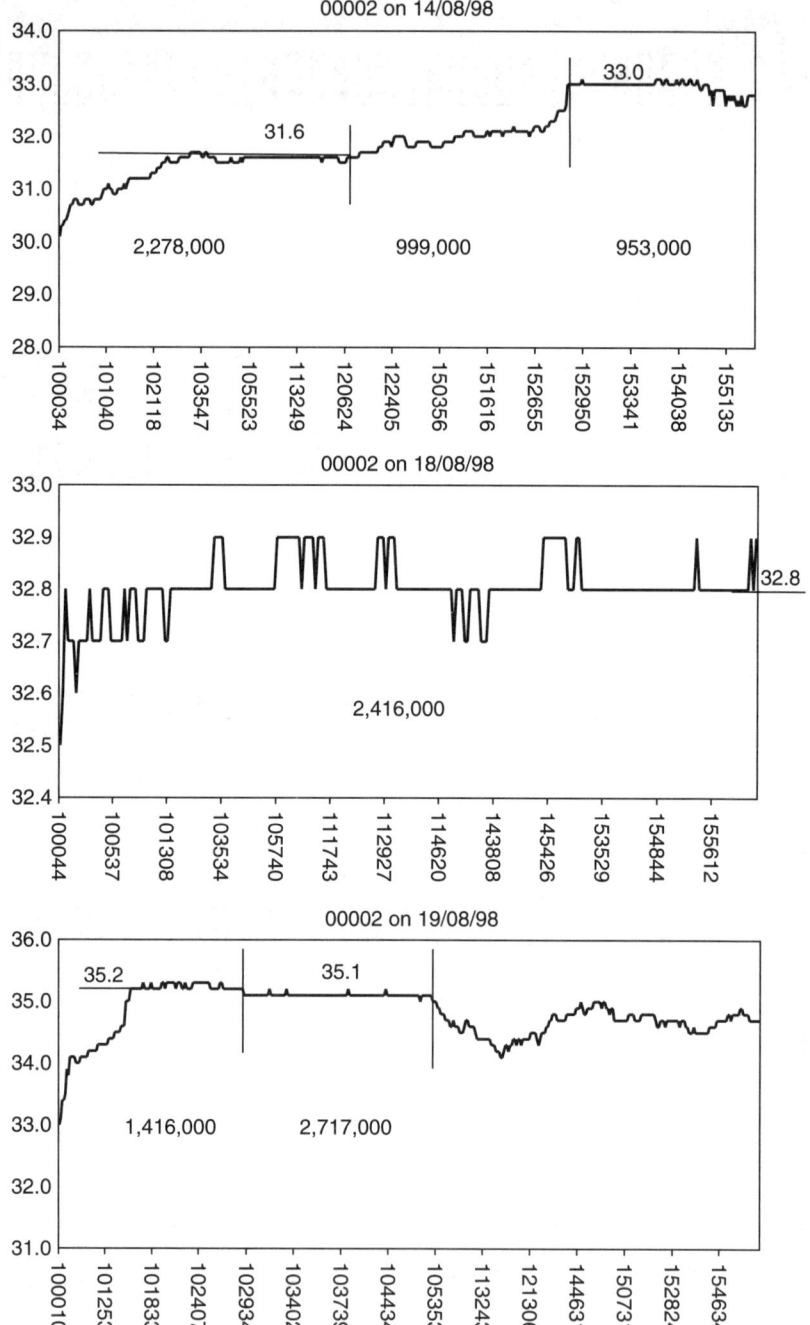

FIG. 3.12. Illustration of the estimation process.

Example I: HSBC (00005) on 18 August 1998

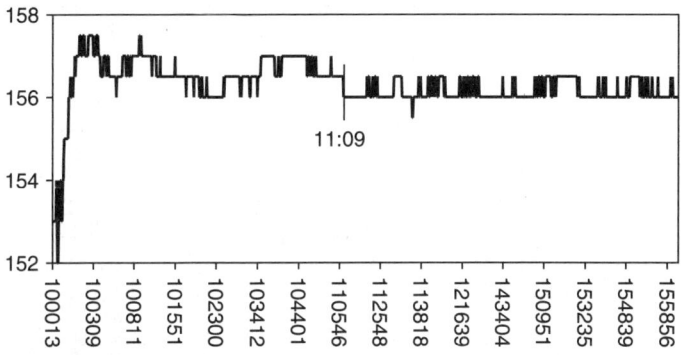

Example II: Swire A (00019) on 25 August 1998

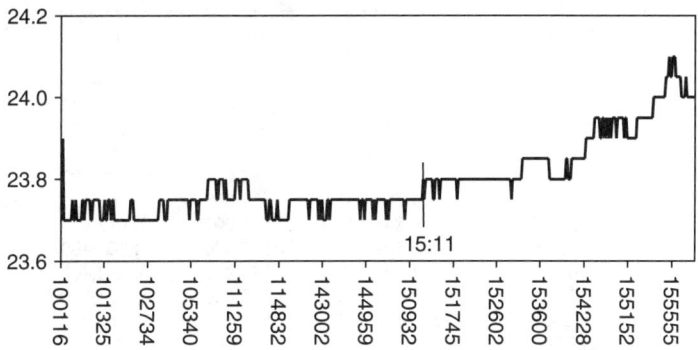

FIG. 3.13. Examples of estimations under parallel prices.

the price with the larger volume was chosen as the held level. In the case of HSBC's trading on 18 August after 11:09 hrs, we assumed the floor of 156 as the government-supported level, while in the case of Swire Pacific (00019) on 25 August, we chose the price of 23.75 before 15:11 hrs. However, if the two sums were close, we chose the 'floor', because we believed the government's goal was only to prevent the market price from going down. Many other 'liquidity' traders could also have entered the market to acquire shares for various reasons. If, according to our estimation method, we chose the higher price as the government held level, all transactions would have to be ascribed to the government buying, which would have been unreasonable.

The detailed estimation result is shown in Table 3.9. Also given in Table 3.9 are the aggregate purchase amounts announced by

76 Intervention to Save Hong Kong

TABLE 3.9. *Estimates of government purchases for each stock*

Date	00001 >= 10000*	00002 >= 5000	00003 >= 10000	00004 >= 10000	00005 >= 4000
14/08	9,886,000	4,230,000	6,701,000	1,491,000	6,911,200
18/08	9,046,000	2,416,000	2,958,000	640,000	3,030,000
19/08	6,360,000	4,178,000	5,710,000	2,807,000	2,827,000
20/08	3,328,000	660,000	3,554,000	470,000	1,974,000
21/08	1,974,000	569,000	2,217,000	1,064,000	1,199,200
24/08	6,382,000	3,769,000	1,069,000	724,000	17,856,400
25/08	4,998,000	6,608,000	11,450,000	5,312,000	4,656,800
26/08	4,048,000	5,780,000	9,777,000	2,466,000	12,982,400
27/08	31,277,000	22,858,500	60,434,000	22,743,000	32,137,200
28/08	161,958,000	86,351,500	190,748,000	83,870,000	130,085,600
Total	239,257,000	137,420,000	294,618,000	121,587,000	213,659,800
Announced	237,628,500	136,022,000	289,040,000	121,679,000	237,001,800
Difference (%)**	0.7	1.0	1.9	−0.1	−9.8

Date	00006 >= 5000	00008 >= 4000	00010 >= 10000	00011 >= 1000	00012 >= 10000
14/08	5,074,500	22,323,600	1,156,000	7,048,700	2,568,000
18/08	3,231,500	19,554,800	925,000	1,921,500	442,000
19/08	1,711,000	10,341,600	622,000	2,690,800	508,000
20/08	523,000	18,219,200	837,000	798,500	458,000
21/08	901,000	9,789,200	652,000	666,100	1,767,000
24/08	2,417,500	58,838,000	2,537,000	10,612,600	6,777,000
25/08	3,749,500	25,502,400	1,591,000	4,007,400	802,000
26/08	6,049,000	41,659,200	948,000	6,142,400	3,449,000
27/08	22,384,500	248,259,200	3,400,000	16,321,700	10,477,000
28/08	81,808,500	546,926,400	20,823,000	65,163,300	55,650,000
Total	127,850,000	1,001,413,600	33,491,000	115,373,000	82,898,000
Announced	124,335,500	972,098,400	33,156,000	109,202,700	85,349,000
Difference(%)	2.8	3.0	1.0	5.7	−2.9

Date	00013 >= 10000	00014 >= 10000	00016 >= 10000	00017 >= 10000	00019 >= 5000	00020 >= 10000
14/08	8,560,000	2,719,000	3,366,000	13,408,000	1,571,500	884,000
18/08	3,837,000	1,388,000	1,016,000	12,031,000	2,208,000	2,073,000
19/08	8,768,000	3,465,000	1,509,000	4,354,000	1,210,500	1,398,000
20/08	1,874,000	1,525,000	3,241,000	4,354,000	238,700	1,828,000
21/08	3,657,000	2,220,000	1,036,000	2,015,000	280,500	957,000
24/08	11,568,000	6,638,000	8,737,000	7,841,000	2,335,000	3,705,000
25/08	3,033,000	6,068,000	4,757,000	6,884,000	5,118,500	4,176,000
26/08	6,352,000	4,618,000	9,601,000	11,118,000	5,356,000	3,661,000
27/08	49,044,000	10,569,000	21,530,000	38,402,000	24,424,000	5,838,000
28/08	200,123,000	25,326,000	128,647,000	152,022,000	74,494,500	39,362,000
Total	296,816,000	64,536,000	183,440,000	252,429,000	117,237,200	63,882,000
Announced	304,550,000	60,524,000	191,660,000	236,470,000	115,433,000	62,391,000
Difference (%)	−2.5	6.6	−4.3	6.7	1.6	2.4

A Reconstruction of the Intervention 77

TABLE 3.9. (continued)

Date	00023 >= 2000	00041 >= 10000	00045 >= 5000	00054 >= 10000	00069 >= 10000	00083 >= 20000
14/08*	1,983,200	293,000	807,500	3,252,000	556,000	3,584,000
18/08	1,434,600	947,000	650,500	6,877,000	542,000	5,092,000
19/08	1,425,400	976,000	675,000	3,104,000	1,228,000	4,482,000
20/08	1,774,000	367,000	630,500	4,262,000	1,688,000	2,622,000
21/08	1,082,000	205,000	624,000	5,079,000	656,000	2,478,000
24/08	1,102,600	840,000	2,093,500	4,998,000	1,510,000	4,120,000
25/08	1,924,800	1,379,000	2,314,500	12,168,000	2,676,000	4,778,000
26/08	3,200,800	908,000	4,655,000	13,949,000	21,524,000	4,790,000
27/08	12,362,800	2,822,000	16,295,500	32,955,000	2,026,000	16,158,000
28/08	63,107,000	16,394,000	29,292,200	140,529,000	30,920,000	76,066,000
Total	89,397,200	25,131,000	58,038,200	227,173,000	63,326,000	124,170,000
Announced	83,017,600	24,652,000	57,494,000	209,323,000	61,674,000	107,238,000
Difference (%)	7.7	1.9	0.9	8.5	2.7	15.8

Date	00097 >= 10000	00101 >= 10000	00142 >= 20000	00267 >= 10000	00270 >= 20000	00291 >= 20000
14/08	1,501,000	1,260,200	5,784,000	8,419,000	8,246,000	5,456,000
18/08	2,396,000	2,208,500	6,590,000	9,611,000	3,606,000	5,280,000
19/08	1,748,000	1,786,500	3,256,000	913,000	5,764,000	5,268,000
20/08	1,843,000	1,452,000	2,894,000	1,188,000	2,922,000	3,382,000
21/08	1,311,000	1,523,000	1,114,000	2,395,000	1,800,000	1,986,000
24/08	1,820,000	2,742,000	16,012,000	3,798,000	5,476,000	6,776,000
25/08	3,909,000	2,756,000	11,716,000	7,846,000	7,382,000	4,564,000
26/08	4,610,000	4,207,000	6,444,000	12,297,000	8,766,000	10,226,000
27/08	16,810,000	9,358,000	53,952,000	21,152,000	15,674,000	20,796,000
28/08	59,753,000	45,959,500	40,890,000	88,309,000	101,572,000	68,980,000
Total	95,701,000	73,252,700	148,652,000	155,928,000	161,208,000	132,714,000
Announced	91,308,000	71,135,000	143,864,000	146,713,000	157,472,000	136,414,000
Difference (%)	4.8	3.0	3.3	6.3	2.4	−2.7

Date	00293 >= 10000	00363 >= 10000	00511 >= 10000	00941 >= 20000	01038 >= 10000
14/08	1,304,000	2,793,000	928,000	23,066,000	3,735,000
18/08	3,875,000	962,000	958,000	25,084,000	2,794,000
19/08	2,075,000	2,682,000	90,000	9,044,000	607,000
20/08	1,511,000	737,000	1,256,000	5,126,000	2,514,000
21/08	376,000	863,000	128,000	4,242,000	1,769,000
24/08	865,000	5,142,000	963,000	40,190,000	1,417,000
25/08	8,254,000	1,311,000	520,000	27,366,000	5,408,000
26/08	5,279,000	2,943,000	1,587,000	14,756,000	1,176,000
27/08	19,029,000	9,623,000	7,518,000	63,784,000	20,910,000
28/08	79,704,000	45,381,000	22,633,000	284,698,000	59,004,000
Total	122,272,000	72,437,000	36,581,000	497,356,000	99,334,000
Announced	119,208,000	71,413,000	35,741,000	478,806,000	96,403,000
Difference (%)	2.6	1.4	2.4	3.9	3.0

*Only trades bigger in size than the selection criteria were included in the estimation.
**The percentage difference between the estimated total and the announced amount of government purchases for each stock.

the government for each stock. The last row indicates the percentage difference between our estimate and the government announcement. As the figures show, we arrived at reasonably good results for most of the stocks. The closest estimation is for Wharf Holdings Ltd. (00004), which is only 0.1 per cent lower than the government announced figure. Multiplied by the daily average prices, we further have an estimation of the intervention value for each stock. The result is given in Table 3.10, with the publicly announced value alongside. The total value we get is HK $118.757 billion, which is very close to the announced HK $118.132 billion.

There are, however, two cases that are far out of line where our estimates are totally off course. One is HSBC (00005) and another is Sino Land (00083). As has been mentioned before, our estimation method tends to overestimate government purchases. In Table 3.9, we see that positive differences are the norm. Only five cases show negative figures. HSBC shows the largest negative difference of −9.8 per cent. Another outlying case—Sino Land—is, on the other hand, far too overestimated. Using the 10-lots filter, the difference is as high as 15.8 per cent. We still needed to find out what happened to these two stocks.

3.2.4 London Market Trading of Hong Kong Shares

3.2.4.1 The London Market and the Data

The underestimation with regard to HSBC brought to the fore the oversight in not considering London market trading. In our analysis, we had only considered the possible situation in Hong Kong, but, as we know, 28 out of the 33 HSI constituent stocks are dually traded on the London Stock Exchange. If the government also intervened in the London market, then we needed to correct our estimations. It was, therefore, necessary to try to find out whether the Hong Kong government had also bought into the London market and, if so, to what extent.

Trading of Hong Kong stocks in London has a fairly long history, but it started to gain more attention only after the introduction of the Hang Seng London Reference Index (HSLRI) on 1 December 1994. Nineteen stocks were chosen to compute the index then; today 28 are included. The entire lot of stocks is from the 33 constituents of the HSI. Table 3.11 lists them. Among these dually-traded stocks, only HSBC is double registered in both the Hong Kong and London markets.

TABLE 3.10. *Summary of intervention values for each stock*

Share Name	Code	Estimated (Hong Kong dollar m)	Announced (Hong Kong dollar m)	Difference (%)
CHEUNG KONG HDG.	00001	8,009	7,968	0.52
CLP HOLDINGS LTD	00002	4,801	4,763	0.79
HK.& CHINA GAS	00003	2,637	2,601	1.37
WHARF HDG.	00004	920	924	−0.38
HSBC HDG.	00005	36,702	40,776	−9.99
HONG KONG ELECTRIC	00006	3,180	3,102	2.51
CABLE & WIRELESS HKT	00008	15,237	14,815	2.85
HANG LUNG DEV.	00010	219	219	−0.22
HANG SENG BANK	00011	5,012	4,778	4.91
HENDERSON LD.DEV.	00012	1,961	2,029	−3.34
HUTCHISON WHAMP.	00013	11,257	11,591	−2.88
HYSAN DEV.	00014	335	316	6.03
SUN HUNG KAI PROPS.	00016	4,728	4,939	−4.27
NEW WORLD DEV.	00017	2,250	2,112	6.55
SWIRE PACIFIC 'A'	00019	2,804	2,770	1.21
WHEELOCK & CO.	00020	262	260	0.95
BANK OF EAST ASIA	00023	751	702	6.93
GREAT EAGLE HDG.	00041	163	162	0.79
HK.& SHAI. HOTEL	00045	240	240	−0.14
HOPEWELL HDG.	00054	185	174	6.48
SHANGRI-LA ASIA	00069	315	310	1.54
SINO LAND	00083	315	277	13.85
HENDERSON INV.	00097	400	386	3.56
AMOY PROPERTIES	00101	281	272	3.14
FIRST PACIFIC	00142	384	373	3.06
CITIC PACIFIC	00267	1,616	1,527	5.81
GUANGDONG INV.	00270	224	220	1.61
CHINA RES.ENTREP.	00291	745	775	−3.85
CATHAY PACIFIC	00293	761	745	2.14
SHANGHAI INDUSTRIAL HDG.	00363	790	785	0.66
TV.BROADCASTS	00511	637	629	1.27
CHINA TELECOM	00941	5,395	5,209	3.56
CHEUNG KONG INFR.	01038	1,405	1,381	1.70
TOTAL		114,953	118,132	−2.69

The London Stock Exchange used to be a typical quote-driven market, where the price formation process is driven by the market-makers' quotes. Investor orders are routed to and executed against a market-maker. A *market-maker* is a broker who is prepared to buy and sell specified securities at all times, thus making a market in them. He takes the opposite side of a trade to the investor, either buying or selling stock from his book. He may then seek to lay off his position elsewhere in the market by dealing with investors

TABLE 3.11. *List of intervened stocks dually traded in London*

ISIN (London code)	Hong Kong code	Name
BMG2098S1008	01038	CHEUNG KONG INFR. (XSQ)
BMG348041077	00142	1ST.PAC.CO. (XSQ)
BMG4069C1486	00041	GREAT EAGLE (XSQ)
BMG8063F1068	00069	SHANGRI-LA ASIA (XSQ)
GB0004004957	00005	HSBC HOLDINGS (XSQ)
HK0001000014	00001	CHEUNG KONG HDG. (XSQ)
HK0002007356	00002	CLP HOLDINGS (XSQ)
HK0003000038	00003	HK.CHINA & GAS (XSQ)
HK0004000045	00004	WHARF HOLDINGS (XSQ)
HK0006000050	00006	HK ELECTRIC (XSQ)
HK0008000066	00008	CABLE & WIRELESS HKT (XSQ)
HK0010000088	00010	HANG LUNG DEV. (XSQ)
HK0011000095	00011	HANG SENG BANK (XSQ)
HK0012000102	00012	HENDERSON LAND (XSQ)
HK0013000119	00013	HUTCHISON WHAMP. (XSQ)
HK0014000126	00014	HYSAN DEV (XSQ)
HK0016000132	00016	SUN H K PROP (XSQ)
HK0017000149	00017	NEW WORLD DEV. (XSQ)
HK0019000162	00019	SWIRE PACIFIC 'A' (XSQ)
HK0020000177	00020	WHEELOCK & CO. (XSQ)
HK0023000190	00023	BANK OF EAST ASIA (XSQ)
HK0083000502	00083	SINO LAND (XSQ)
HK0101000591	00101	AMOY PROPERTIES (XSQ)
HK0267001375	00267	CITIC PACIFIC (XSQ)
HK0291001490	00291	CHINA RES.ENTREP. (XSQ)
HK0293001514	00293	CATHAY PACIFIC (XSQ)
HK0363006039	00363	SHAI.INDUSTRIAL (XSQ)
HK0941007087	00941	CHINA TELECOM (XSQ)

coming the opposite way or he may hold it for some time in the hope of a favourable price movement.

However, on 20 October 1997, the London Stock Exchange introduced a new electronic trading system (SETS). The system enables traders to place, buy, or sell orders for any Financial Times Stock Exchange 100 Share Index (FT-SE 100) stocks in an electronic order book. (These stocks used to be traded under the Stock Exchange Automated Quotations (SEAQ) quote mechanism.) This new system is similar to any other order-driven stock market. Orders are anonymous and are 'good until cancelled', or as otherwise specified by the person who entered the order. These orders are then automatically matched with other opposite orders placed in the market, while under the old system orders were advertised on computer terminals, but actual trades were carried out over the telephone.

A Reconstruction of the Intervention 81

In the London market, domestic and international stocks are traded through different trading systems. The trading of most Hong Kong stocks is conducted through officially endorsed market-makers in the SEAQ International system. SEAQ International is a screen-based price-information system. It is a quote-driven system, which displays real-time prices for overseas listed securities. Market-makers enter prices directly onto the central exchange computer system and these are then distributed across the world through commercial quote vendors including Bridge, Reuters, and Quick, etc. If investors find an attractive dealing price on the information screen, they can contact the appropriate market-maker by telephone to execute the trade. Settlement is determined by both parties at the time of transaction and is carried out in the country of origin of the share.[9] Trading in this market can take place 24 hours a day, although quotations may only be input into the system between the official trading hours from 07:00 to 20:00 London time.

There is one special case though. HSBC is double registered in both the Hong Kong and the London stock exchanges. It is not only one of the biggest listed companies in Hong Kong, but also one of the most actively traded stocks in London. It is classified as a domestic equity on the London Stock Exchange, while all other Hong Kong stocks are classified as overseas equity. Since it is a constituent of FT-SE100, it started to be traded in SETS after October 1997. However, as a Hong Kong stock, it can also be traded through the SEAQ International like other Hong Kong stocks and the transactions are denominated in Hong Kong dollars. Due to these special features of HSBC stocks, we need to separate it from other stocks in our analysis, and give an individual account for it later. (The intra-day trade record is obtained from the Transaction Data Service (TDS) of the London Stock Exchange.[10])

3.2.4.2 Comparing London and Hong Kong Trading of HK Stocks

Trading Volume

The London Traded Hong Kong stocks (referred to as LTHK stocks hereafter) are quoted on SEAQ International. Although they can be traded either in Hong Kong dollars or in some other currencies, such as pound sterlings (GBP) or US dollars, Hong

---

[9] See *IFR Handbook of World Stock & Commodity Exchanges* (1997).
[10] We would like to thank Mr. Stephen Wells for his help in explaining the data.

Kong dollar transactions dominate London trading. To look at the total transaction value of the 27 stocks[11] during August 1998, Hong Kong dollar trades account for 92.5 per cent with a value of GBP 1,518 million, while trades in other currencies account only for 7.5 per cent. This suggests that the investors in these LTHK stocks are most likely from Hong Kong, who may treat the London market as an extension of the Hong Kong market due to the time difference. Therefore, we will only pay attention to the Hong Kong dollar transactions. How big a role, then, did the London market play in these Hong Kong stocks? Table 3.12 compares the volume traded in both Hong Kong and London markets during the 10 days of the intervention.

The volume of London trading was as high as 19.8 per cent (excluding HSBC) in the case of Cheung Kong Holdings (00001), and as low as only 2.7 per cent in the case of Hysan Development (00014). A point to note in interpreting these figures is that Hong Kong's market is an automatching market, whereas SEAQ International is a dealer's market. When there is a trade in Hong Kong, it means a buy order is matched with a sell order, and the result is reflected in one amount. But in London, a transaction means a deal from an investor with a 'middleman', and when this middleman later deals with an opposite investor, it is reflected in another transaction. In this sense, if we compare trading volumes as they are, we actually overestimate the London market, if not double it. Based on this understanding, we conclude that the London market trading is quite small compared to the Hong Kong market.

Besides the comparison between the two markets, we also wanted to know whether there was any change during the intervention periods. As we have seen in the Hong Kong market, the trading volumes increased considerably during the intervention period, especially during the last two days. We now know that it was largely due to government buying. What, then, was the situation in London? We began with plotting the volumes in August 1998 of the three randomly selected stocks to see whether there was any common pattern (Figure 3.14).

In Figure 3.14, the three stocks present no similarity in pattern, except that the volume was generally higher during the second half of the month. In order to check this observation, we calculated the average daily volume for both the pre- and post-intervention periods as well as for the 10-day intervention period. We excluded

[11] The 27 dually traded Hong Kong stocks other than HSBC.

TABLE 3.12. *A comparison of the trading volumes of Hong Kong and London markets (Aggregate turnover in shares from 14 to 28 August)*

Share name	Stock code (HK)	HK volume	LD volume (trades in Hong Kong dollar)	LD/HK (%)	LD volume (trades in GBP)
CHEUNG KONG HDG.	00001	309,254,399	59,283,359	19.2	0
CLP HOLDINGS LTD	00002	178,042,615	27,504,900	15.4	8,500
HK.& CHINA GAS	00003	369,042,106	29,836,650	8.1	0
WHARF HDG.	00004	154,746,104	20,110,800	13.0	0
HSBC HDG.	00005	285,110,811	104,840,222	36.8	156,715,996
HONG KONG ELECTRIC	00006	151,216,926	16,245,865	10.7	0
CABLE & WIRELESS HKT	00008	1,126,766,775	154,684,406	13.7	7,999
HANG LUNG DEV.	00010	47,412,935	5,583,000	11.8	0
HANG SENG BANK	00011	144,029,440	14,425,339	10.0	0
HENDERSON LD.DEV.	00012	119,729,696	12,185,600	10.2	4,000
HUTCHISON WHAMP.	00013	401,033,264	71,018,348	17.7	58,490
HYSAN DEV.	00014	93,145,961	2,514,000	2.7	0
SUN HUNG KAI PROPS.	00016	258,718,141	38,718,200	15.0	0
NEW WORLD DEV.	00017	339,907,300	31,680,676	9.3	0
SWIRE PACIFIC 'A'	00019	138,186,622	12,177,413	8.8	37,229
WHEELOCK & CO.	00020	85,476,754	8,827,652	10.3	6,000
BANK OF EAST ASIA	00023	102,451,965	6,939,600	6.8	0
GREAT EAGLE HDG.	00041	35,450,609	3,854,622	10.9	0
HK.& SHAI. HOTEL	00045	64,918,185	N.A.	N.A.	0
HOPEWELL HDG.	00054	281,740,513	N.A.	N.A.	0
SHANGRI-LA ASIA	00069	79,417,536	8,462,708	10.7	0
SINO LAND	00083	179,903,596	13,070,156	7.3	0
HENDERSON INV.	00097	116,761,566	N.A.	N.A.	0
AMOY PROPERTIES	00101	108,424,676	14,834,000	13.7	48,000
FIRST PACIFIC	00142	199,265,854	29,967,292	15.0	0
CITIC PACIFIC	00267	224,389,314	17,253,276	7.7	22,000
GUANGDONG INV.	00270	233,812,499	N.A.	N.A.	0
CHINA RES.ENTREP.	00291	256,166,211	21,286,254	8.3	7,000
CATHAY PACIFIC	00293	156,763,397	21,030,600	13.4	28,999
SHANGHAI INDUSTRIAL HDG.	00363	131,961,872	4,950,000	3.8	0
TV.BROADCASTS	00511	43,355,914	N.A.	N.A.	0
CHINA TELECOM	00941	742,917,217	115,244,580	15.5	0
CHEUNG KONG INFR.	01038	130,225,960	7,507,500	5.8	0

Example I: CLP Holdings (00002)

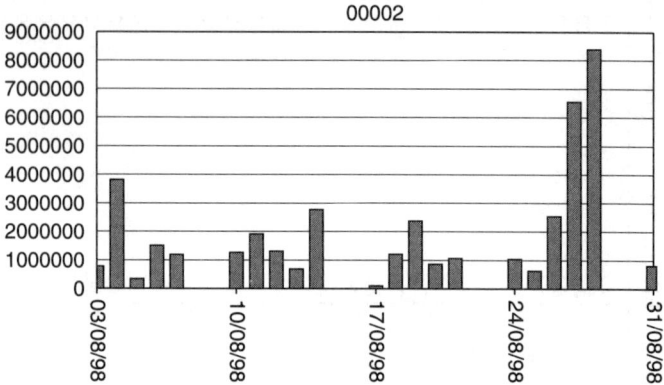

Example II: Henderson Land Development (00012)

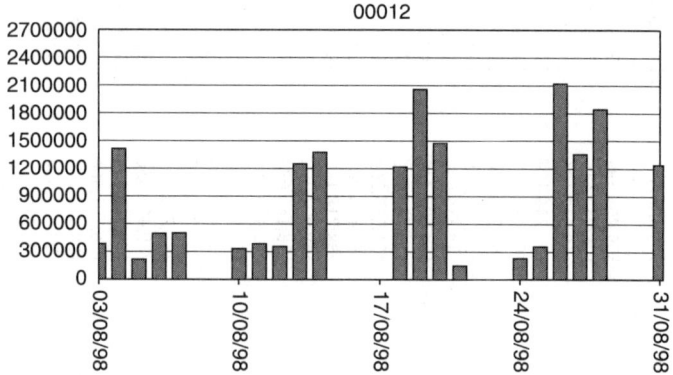

Example III: Chinese Resources Enterprise (00291)

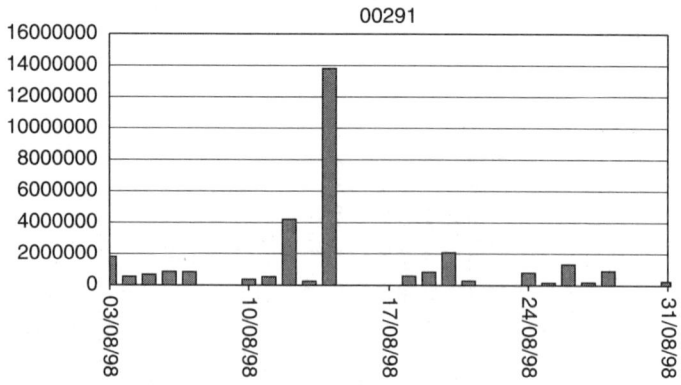

FIG. 3.14. London (Hong Kong dollar) trading volume of Hong Kong stocks during August 1998.

17 August in the computation because the Hong Kong market was closed on that day. (The trading volume is usually small on the London market when the Hong Kong market is closed.) The result is shown in Table 3.13. For most of the stocks, the average shares traded daily from 14 to 28 August was much higher than the other two periods. This signifies that the trading volumes of Hong Kong stocks on the London market also saw a general increase during the intervention period, although the increases were not similarly concentrated on the last two or three days. Was this because of the government buying? So next we examined the price details of London trading during the intervention.

TABLE 3.13. *Average daily trading volumes of Hong Kong stocks on the London market*

Share name	Stock code	3–13 August	14–28 August (Exclude 17th)	1–11 September
CHEUNG KONG HDG.	00001	2,242,138	5,903,206	2,736,479
CLP HOLDINGS LTD	00002	1,421,856	2,740,490	645,247
HK.& CHINA GAS	00003	2,735,284	2,983,665	1,787,337
WHARF HDG.	00004	844,490	2,010,000	1,427,456
HSBC HDG.	00005	6,632,491	10,446,585	3,877,911
HONG KONG ELECTRIC	00006	1,021,548	1,624,587	643,958
CABLE & WIRELESS HKT	00008	4,500,852	15,448,441	5,661,242
HANG LUNG DEV.	00010	252,444	558,300	256,516
HANG SENG BANK	00011	509,133	1,342,534	528,064
HENDERSON LD.DEV.	00012	592,889	1,218,560	676,289
HUTCHISON WHAMP.	00013	2,443,561	7,089,335	2,694,548
HYSAN DEV.	00014	347,222	251,400	238,889
SUN HUNG KAI PROPS.	00016	2,203,948	3,861,600	1,771,744
NEW WORLD DEV.	00017	2,649,796	3,168,068	566,147
SWIRE PACIFIC 'A'	00019	1,229,315	1,217,481	712,789
WHEELOCK & CO.	00020	587,889	882,765	238,707
BANK OF EAST ASIA	00023	450,022	693,960	932,951
GREAT EAGLE HDG.	00041	98,333	385,462	56,879
SHANGRI-LA ASIA	00069	298,333	846,271	154,500
SINO LAND	00083	3,084,667	1,307,016	1,142,892
AMOY PROPERTIES	00101	1,208,033	1,483,400	2,443,417
FIRST PACIFIC	00142	1,067,889	2,996,729	932,653
CITIC PACIFIC	00267	1,605,694	1,725,328	498,357
CHINA RES.ENTREP.	00291	1,120,600	2,128,625	1,570,122
CATHAY PACIFIC	00293	1,648,611	2,103,060	1,514,411
SHANGHAI INDUSTRIAL HDG.	00363	557,000	483,000	634,450
CHINA TELECOM	00941	8,838,667	11,454,458	6,413,344
CHEUNG KONG INFR.	01038	444,000	3,110,896	290,625

Price Examination

As we did with the Hong Kong data, we plotted the London intra-day price path of Hong Kong dollar transactions for all the LTHK stocks during August 1998. Figure 3.15 gives two examples. It is clear that London trading is much sparser and there seems to be no special pattern, such as the price-holding pattern in the SEHK,

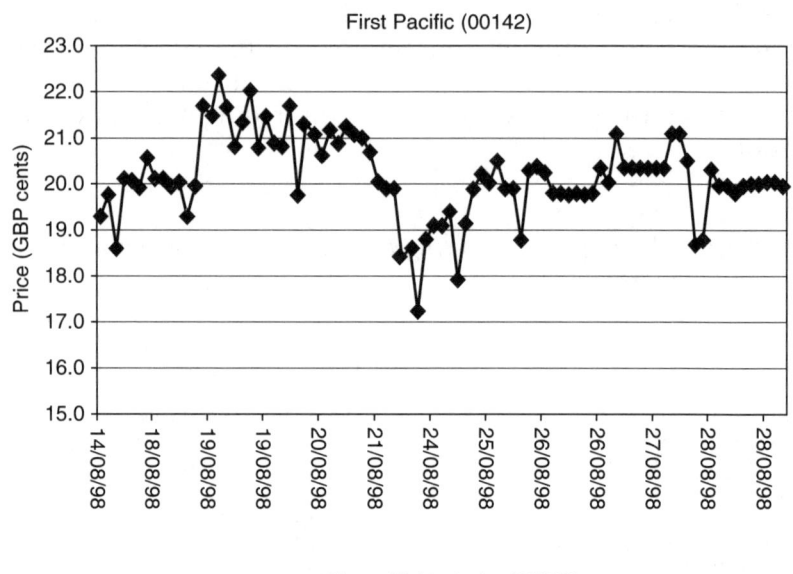

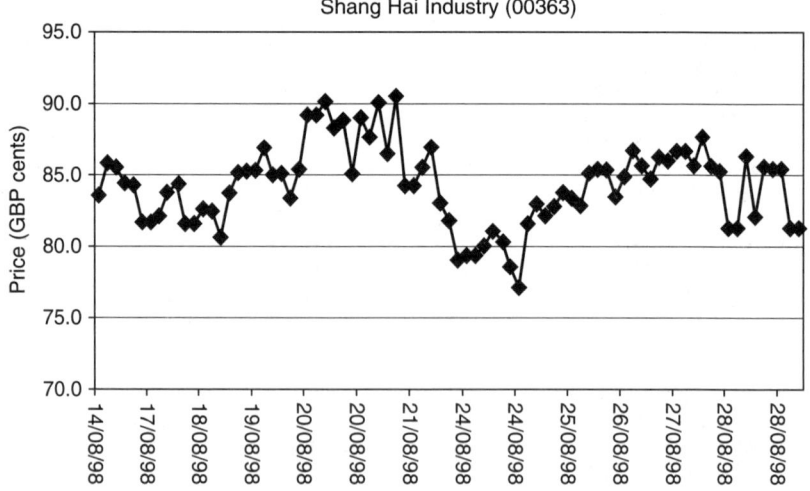

FIG. 3.15. Intra-day price performance of Hong Kong stocks on the London market during the intervention period.

during most of the intervention days. In the case of First Pacific (00142), there are two periods on 26 and 27 August that suggest that prices might have been held. However, since there are too few transactions and the pattern does not show in every stock, we would rather not attribute those transactions to Hong Kong government buying. Based on our analysis, we can conclude that there was hardly any intervention in the London market.

The reason why the Hong Kong government did not intervene in the London market could be the following. The government left it to the arbitrageurs to take care of the London market. How well did the arbitrageurs do the job? We compared mean prices (MP) of the London and Hong Kong markets. Mean prices of the London market are calculated only for transactions done in Hong Kong dollars. Mean prices of the Hong Kong market are calculated only using the prices of automatched transactions. Since London market prices are quoted in sterling while Hong Kong market prices are quoted in Hong Kong dollars, we transformed the Hong Kong market price into sterling-denominated using the Datastream daily exchange rate. Two examples are given in Figure 3.16. It can be seen that, although there were hardly any price-holding activities in London, prices closely followed the Hong Kong market. Prices in London were, on an average, a bit lower than the Hong Kong prices, but this small discrepancy was not unique to the intervention period. We actually compared the price differences for all the LTHK shares between the pre-intervention period and the intervention period. The result is given in Table 3.14. Clearly, the small negative discrepancy is the norm for both periods and it could be due to different transaction costs in the two markets.

Summary

Compared with the Hong Kong market, the trading volume was much lower in London, and there was hardly any peculiar price pattern during the intervention period. We concluded that the government did not buy in the London market because they considered the market size quite small, and were confident that inter-market arbitrageurs could take care of the market. If the London market fell too much behind the Hong Kong market, the arbitrageurs could buy in London and sell the next day in Hong Kong as long as they believed the market intervention would continue. They actually did a good job. We can observe that the prices of the two markets were kept quite close to each other during the intervention period. So, we can reasonably say that London trading did not pose any problems for our estimation results for all the LTHK stocks except for HSBC. The apparent price holdings for some stocks during the last two or three days can be dismissed on *de minimis* grounds, since the amounts were insignificant. Our next step was to examine the London trading of HSBC.

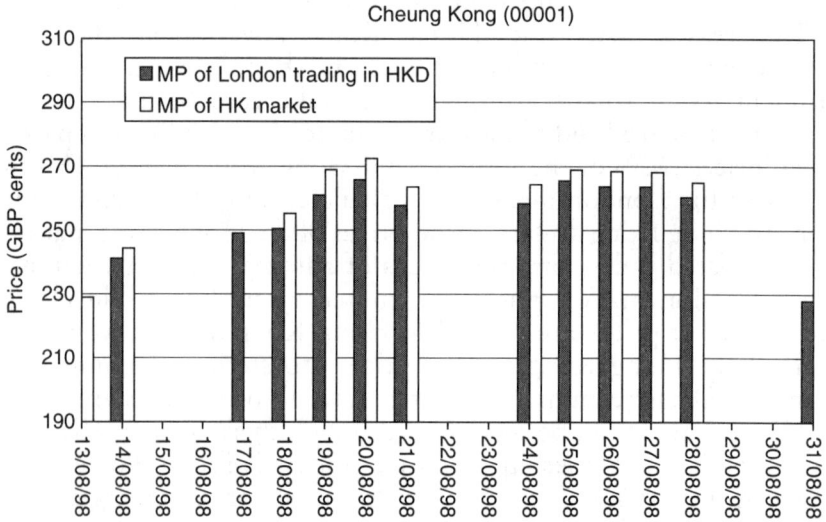

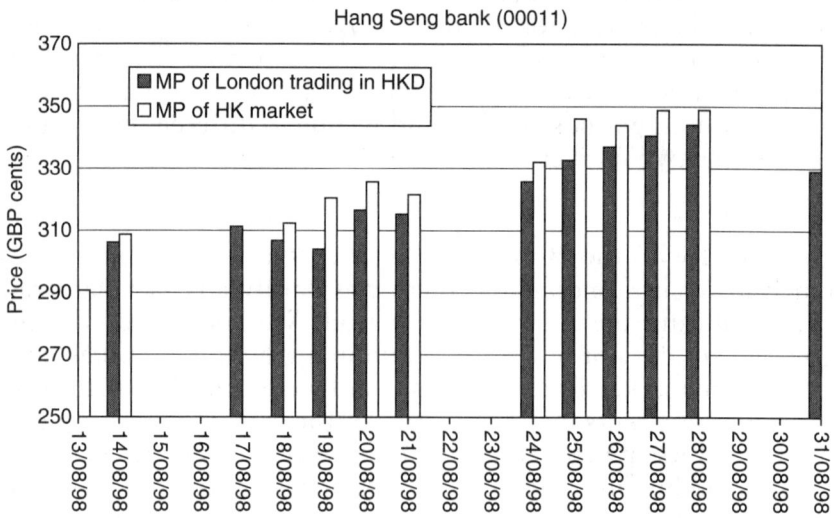

FIG. 3.16. Price comparison between the Hong Kong and London markets.

TABLE 3.14. *Average daily price difference between the Hong Kong and London markets*

Share name	Stock code	Average price difference during 3–13 August	Average price difference during 14–28 August
CHEUNG KONG HDG.	00001	−1.68	−1.63
CLP HOLDINGS LTD	00002	−1.66	−1.77
HK.& CHINA GAS	00003	−1.61	−1.33
WHARF HDG.	00004	−1.60	−1.57
HSBC HDG.	00005	−1.69	−2.22
HONG KONG ELECTRIC	00006	−1.39	−1.53
CABLE & WIRELESS HKT	00008	−1.37	−1.85
HANG LUNG DEV.	00010	−1.32	−1.46
HANG SENG BANK	00011	−1.57	−1.82
HENDERSON LD.DEV.	00012	−1.57	−1.66
HUTCHISON WHAMP.	00013	−1.65	−1.94
HYSAN DEV.	00014	−1.31	−0.69
SUN HUNG KAI PROPS.	00016	−1.43	−1.64
NEW WORLD DEV.	00017	−1.61	−1.20
SWIRE PACIFIC 'A'	00019	−0.85	−0.82
WHEELOCK & CO.	00020	−1.46	−1.40
BANK OF EAST ASIA	00023	−1.27	−1.54
GREAT EAGLE HDG.	00041	−1.59	−1.36
SHANGRI-LA ASIA	00069	−1.64	−1.89
SINO LAND	00083	−1.94	−1.56
AMOY PROPERTIES	00101	−1.42	−1.84
FIRST PACIFIC	00142	−1.39	−1.56
CITIC PACIFIC	00267	−1.87	−1.31
CHINA RES.ENTREP.	00291	−1.63	−2.41
CATHAY PACIFIC	00293	−1.75	−1.31
SHANGHAI INDUSTRIAL HDG.	00363	−1.93	1.60
CHINA TELECOM	00941	−1.25	−1.63
CHEUNG KONG INFR.	01038	−1.20	−1.27
Average		−1.52	−1.45

*Price differences were calculated for each day and then averaged over each sub-period.

3.2.4.3 The Case of HSBC

Headquartered in London, HSBC Holdings is one of the largest banking and financial service organizations in the world. In the London Stock Exchange, it is classified as a domestic equity, but it can be traded in both SETS (transactions done in GBP) and SEAQ International (transactions done in Hong Kong dollars). From Table 3.12 we see that HSBC was very actively traded in London both in Hong Kong dollars and in GBP. In terms of total shares, London Hong Kong dollar trading is equal to 36.8 per cent of the Hong Kong market and London GBP trading is equal to 55.0 per cent.

In comparison with other LTHK stocks, the Hong Kong dollar transaction of HSBC counts for a sizeable portion of the value of total trading of LTHK stocks. From 14 to 28 August, the Hong Kong dollar transaction value of HSBC accounted for 54.5 per cent of the total LTHK stocks' transaction value. It was our suspicion that the government did intervene in HSBC trading due to its relative importance. To check this possibility, we first compared the daily prices of three kinds of trading during August 1998. The three kinds of trading refer to the Hong Kong market trading, London trading in Hong Kong dollars, and London trading in GBP respectively. These actually can be treated as three different markets, with different participants trading the same share. The result is presented in Figure 3.17.

Recall that London trading occurs after Hong Kong trading in time. The Hong Kong market was closed on 17 August, and there was no London trading in GBP on 31 August since it was a local holiday. From the daily mean price comparison, it is easy to observe some abnormalities. The three types of prices follow each other closely on most trading days. However, on the last two intervention days, there was a diversion. The prices of London GBP trading dropped considerably, while the other two prices remained much higher. The price in the Hong Kong market was higher because the government took great effort to hold up the price on the last two

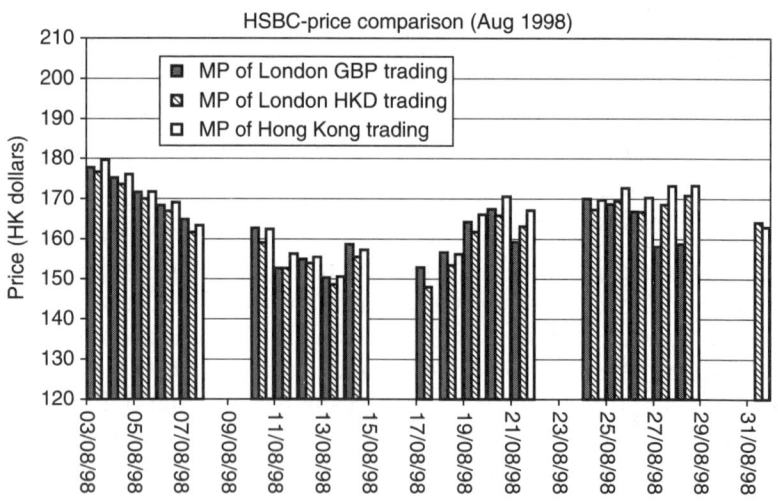

FIG. 3.17. Comparison of daily average price of HSBC in August 1998.

days. But why did a price differential open up in the London market between the Hong Kong and United Kingdom registered lines? Although the transactions were carried out in different trading systems, the shares were the same, weren't they? What explains the difference?

As mentioned earlier in section 3.2.4.1, London trading of Hong Kong stocks gained prominence only after the HSLRI came into operation. The London market opens after the Hong Kong market closes. Although the trading of Hong Kong stocks on SEAQ International can take place 24 hours a day, the HSLRI has a daily close level, cutting off at 23:30 hrs Hong Kong time or 16:30 London time. The Hong Kong market is aware of this close price of HSLRI before the next day's opening. Therefore, although the London market is relatively small in terms of market turnover, it could have some indicative or psychological influence on the Hong Kong market. Second, the Index is compiled using the following formula:

HSLRI=(*Current Aggregate Market Capitalization of HSLRI stocks*)/ (*Today's Hong Kong closing Aggregate Market Capitalization of HSLRI stocks*) × (*Today's Hong Kong Closing HSI*)

Thus the HSLRI is actually a measurement of the relative performance of London prices to Hong Kong prices. However, the compilation of the HSLRI uses only the price on the SEAQ International and, therefore, only the Hong Kong dollar trading prices of HSBC are reflected in the HSLRI.

Calculating from transaction data of London trading, we saw that the London market, in aggregate, was a heavy seller of the Hong Kong registered line and a buyer of the United Kingdom registered line on 27 and 28 August. The United Kingdom registered line recorded net buys of 47.3 million shares and the Hong Kong registered line net sales of 29.1 million shares. Over the period from 3 to 26 August, the market had been a modest seller of both lines of stock, with 4.2 million in the United Kingdom registered line and 4.5 million in the Hong Kong registered line.[12] Our guess is that there was heavy buying from outside the market of the Hong Kong registered line, perhaps by the HKMA. In order to win the battle, the government wanted to sustain the spot HSI level on the futures contract expiration day (28 August). The government definitely did not want the HSLRI to be too much lower, because it could place

---

[12] The calculation was originally provided by Mr. Stephen Wells.

more psychological pressure on the next day's trading in the Hong Kong market. Further, since the volume of trading of HSBC stocks in the London market is quite large, the government, in order not to give speculators an easy way-out by covering their short positions in the London international market, could have purposefully pushed the price higher to raise the cost for the speculators.

London dealers supplied this purchase from the HKMA, but did not have the required inventory, i.e. they sold short. They covered themselves by buying United Kingdom registered stock but possibly borrowed Hong Kong registered stock to meet settlement obligations in Hong Kong. The Hong Kong registered line is settled in Hong Kong using Hong Kong dollars, and the settlement should be within T+2,[13] while the settlement for the United Kingdom line is carried out in London using GBP with a much longer settlement period.[14] The reason that there seemed to be no arbitrage activities to bring the two lines together could be that the arbitrage was only available to people who could borrow stock; other investors were presumably happy to sell the United Kingdom registered line at £12, seeing this as a good price.

Intra-day transactions of the London market on 27 and 28 August are plotted in Figures 3.18 and 3.19. On 27 August, the price deviation started from about 9:30 hrs. After that, the Hong Kong dollar trading prices were held higher than £13.00 all the way till the end of 28 August, while during the same time, the GBP trading prices fell below £12.50. Based on these plots, we can assume that the Hong Kong government propped up the Hong Kong dollar trading prices of HSBC on these two days; it is therefore necessary to add these two days of government buying in the London market to the estimation result.

To calculate the estimation amount, we add up all Hong Kong dollar transactions above £13.00 from 9:30 hrs on 27 August till the end of 28 August. This gives us the possible intervention quantity of 37 million shares in the London market. Adding this number to our original estimation pushes up government purchases of HSBC to

---

[13] According to the London Stock Exchange Rule 3.24, 'Unless otherwise agreed at the time of dealing, a transaction effected by a member firm in an international equity market security shall be settled in accordance with the rules of the exchange on which the transaction was executed and the clearing system used.' Hong Kong stock market uses T+2 settlement rule.

[14] Usually it is T+5 for normal investors, but a member firm can agree on a due date up to 25 days for settlement of an on-Exchange transaction in a domestic equity market security. (Rule 10.2-a of the London Stock Exchange)

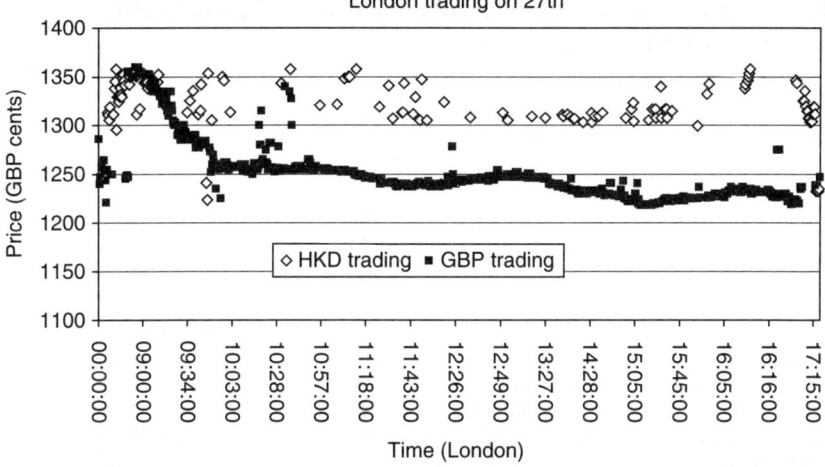

FIG. 3.18. Intra-day trading of HSBC in London on 27 August 1998.

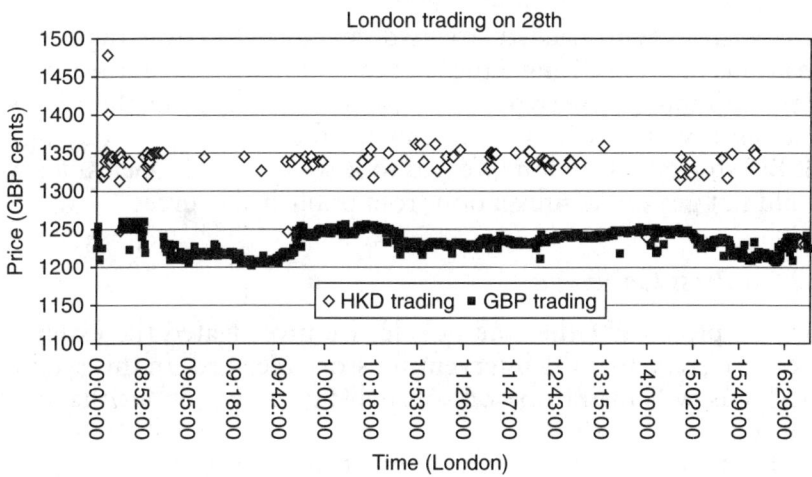

FIG. 3.19. Intra-day trading of HSBC in London on 28 August 1998.

249,719,430 shares, which is 5.4 per cent higher than the announced amount (Table 3.15). This result is more consistent with other stocks.

At this stage, however, we need to point out two possible challenges to our above estimation: (1) Why did the government need to hold up the London price even on 28 August *after* the intervention in the Hong Kong market had ceased? (2) Could the deviation of Hong Kong dollar trading prices from GBP trading prices be due to

TABLE 3.15. *Estimation of the government purchase of HSBC shares in both Hong Kong and London*

Date	(+LD)	HSBC (00005) >= 4000(HK)	LD + HK
14/08		6,911,200	
18/08		3,030,000	
19/08		2,827,000	
20/08		1,974,000	
21/08		1,199,200	
24/08		17,856,400	
25/08		4,656,800	
26/08		12,982,400	
27/08	9,890,797	32,137,200	
28/08	26,168,833	130,085,600	
Total	36,059,630	213,659,800	249,719,430
Announced		237,001,800	237,001,800
Difference (%)		−9.8	5.4

other parties who needed stocks desperately to cover their short positions in Hong Kong either in the spot market or in the futures market? Taking these two questions into consideration, there is also a possibility that we have overestimated the government's buying of HSBC stocks in London. We had to leave the result open since we could not get any confirmation from published sources.

3.2.5 Press Coverage

Having pieced together the puzzle, we investigated the extent of press coverage that the intervention story received. In this section, the focus will mainly be on journalistic reports about the stock market.

The first day of the government intervention received the following press coverage: 'The government yesterday launched its first-ever defence of the local stock and futures markets with a concerted intervention, which drove the HSI 8.5 per cent higher .... Market analysts estimated that the buying of 33 constituent stocks could have cost the government up to HK $3 billion.' It was also reported that: 'The government was forced into the action after unnamed investment banks, acting on behalf of international hedge funds, undertook heavy speculative selling of Hong Kong dollars in the past few days. The speculators' aim was to drive up local interest rates, which would result in sharp falls in stock and futures markets.' (*South China Morning Post*, 15 August 1998)

Then for the following week from 18 to 21 August, there were hardly any estimates regarding the intervention amount in the newspapers. Only the weekend edition of the *South China Morning Post* (23 August 1998) carried a summary, which estimated that the government might have spent HK $6 billion to 8 billion since it began buying into the market on 14 August. Starting from 24 August, the first day of the second phase, as the intervention became heavier and more problematic, government action drew greater attention from the press. There were estimates of the HKMA's purchases almost every day: 'Most brokers estimate the government (to) have spent between $10 billion and $15 billion intervening in the share market in the past six trading sessions, and at least one believes the figure could be as high as $22 billion.' For 24 August alone, 'Estimates suggested government spending accounted for at least half of yesterday's (24 August) $9.8 billion in turnover, probably the largest one-day intervention since the Exchange Fund began buying Hong Kong equities on 14 August.' One sales director, who put the entire intervention bill at $22 billion, said that the government's move on 24 August accounted for $6 billion (*South China Morning Post*, 25 August 1998).

For 25 August, the market's estimate of government spending was $4 billion and the intervention was concentrated mostly in the last hour of trading, with the buying focusing on a new mix of blue-chip stocks, including Cathay Pacific Airways, Wharf (Holdings) and Cheung Kong Infrastructure (*South China Morning Post*, 26 August 1998). The newspapers carried no estimation for 26 August. Purchases on 27 August were estimated to be at least $18 billion (*South China Morning Post*, 28 August 1998) and on 28 August the estimate was $70 billion (*South China Morning Post*, 30 August 1998). The entire two-week intervention was estimated to have cost the government US $15 billion.

As can be seen, the extent of government intervention was tracked by the market quite closely. 'In arriving at their estimates, brokers said that they assumed large buy orders supported by a single broker were part of the intervention effort.'[15] This method is clearly different from the one adopted by us and, most importantly, the broker information that they used is only displayed on the screens of their terminals but not recorded in our dataset of intra-day transactions. In Table 3.16 we summarize the various estimates

---

[15] 'Market step-in bill may top $22b', *South China Morning Post*, 25 August 1998.

TABLE 3.16. *Intervention estimation from the news*

Date	Our estimation (HK $ bn)	Estimation from news (HK $ bn)		
14/08	3.59	3		
18/08	2.22			
19/08	2.59		6~8	10~15
20/08	1.70			
21/08	1.40			
24/08	7.11	6		
25/08	3.52	4		
26/08	5.30			
27/08	19.38	18		
28/08	72.11	70		
Total	118.80	116.25*		
Announced	118.13			

*The estimated US $15 billion were converted at the rate of US $1 = HK $7.75.

gathered from the newspapers and compare them with our estimates.

Another finding from our news search related to Sino Land (00083). Besides HSBC, Sino Land was the other outlier in our previous intervention estimation. Compared to the announced figure, our estimated result was 15.8 per cent higher. It indicates that other large buyers may have been included in our estimation. On 21 August, it was reported (*South China Morning Post*), that Sino Land was the only constituent stock to buy back shares during the intervention. Their estimated buying on the first day of the intervention was about 2 million. Although no further information on Sino Land was available, this could explain the exceedingly large overestimation made with regard to this stock.

CHAPTER 4

An Assessment of the Effects of the Intervention

4.1 Introduction

In Chapter 3, we reviewed the process of the Hong Kong government's intervention in the stock market. We not only examined the price behaviour of every intervened stock, but also estimated the quantity that the government had purchased based on our assumptions about the government's likely actions. The robustness of our research was revealed by the fact that our estimates were very close to the government's announced results. In this chapter, we will assess the Hong Kong government's actions at different phases of the intervention. We will also evaluate their achievement in relation to both Hong Kong non-intervened stocks and stocks from the London market.

Table 4.1 summarizes the daily trading information culled from the estimates in Chapter 3. In terms of the distribution of government expenditures, the second week was clearly much more heavily intervened than the first week, with the final two days accounting for slightly over 75 per cent of the total intervention value. By comparing the aggregate intervention value with the total market turnover for the 33 constituent stocks, we can also calculate that, during the 10 days of the intervention, the government's purchases amounted to as much as 79 per cent of the whole market turnover in these stocks.

The government's achievements in terms of affecting the percentage price movement of the intervened stocks also varied. The most successful day was, not surprisingly, 14 August, the first day of intervention when the intervention was unexpected. With HK $3.5 billion, accounting for nearly half of the market turnover, the

TABLE 4.1. *Aggregate intervention value by each day*

Date	Intervention value	Market turnover	% of market turnover	% change of HSI	Accumulated change of HSI	% of total purchase
14/08	3,488,280,074	7,010,921,386	49.75	8.47	8.47	2.94
18/08	2,216,186,305	4,269,552,219	51.91	−0.19	8.27	1.87
19/08	2,586,632,733	5,616,070,941	46.06	5.71	14.45	2.18
20/08	1,695,250,345	5,046,278,634	33.59	1.57	16.25	1.43
21/08	1,396,368,298	3,603,214,712	38.75	−2.78	13.02	1.18
24/08	7,112,117,217	8,770,229,740	81.09	4.22	17.79	5.99
25/08	3,523,141,545	8,903,436,389	39.57	0.57	18.46	2.97
26/08	5,299,714,098	8,333,679,579	63.59	−0.71	17.63	4.46
27/08	19,377,639,193	21,601,513,298	89.71	1.13	18.96	16.31
28/08	72,106,096,421	76,909,082,975	93.75	−1.18	17.56	60.69
Total	118,801,426,228	150,063,979,872	79.17	17.56		100.00
Announced	118,132,000,000					

government achieved an 8.5 per cent increase in the HSI. Then, on 19 August, the government seemed to have given the market another big push. A 5.7 per cent daily increase was achieved with about HK $2.6 billion, and the accumulated percentage increase of the HSI reached 14.5 per cent over its close on 13 August of 6,660. From 20 to 26 August, the index was mostly maintained at a level over 7,500, and the accumulated percentage change was around 17 per cent. On Friday, 21 August, there was a drop in the index, and only a small amount was purchased. However, the push on 24 August, which cost the government HK $7.1billion, helped the index recover. Subsequently, the government seemed to be content with maintaining that level without trying to push the index much higher.

The major confrontation with the speculators took place on the last two days, with an abrupt increase in both government buying and market turnover. It appeared that the government had tried to push the index up on 27 August, but clearly the selling pressure was too heavy on 28 August. They could not continue holding the level, but had to allow the market to decrease slightly to release pressure. On these last two days, the Hong Kong government became almost the sole buyer in the market, with their purchases accounting for around 90 per cent of the market turnover of the 33 stocks (89.7 per cent on 27 August and 93.6 per cent on the 28th respectively). The selling pressure came from arbitrageurs and speculators, as well as other normal investors. Market observers believed that the government would stop buying after the August contract expired, and the

An Assessment of the Effects of the Intervention

market would then fall sharply. A report in one of the local dailies typifies the general concern: 'A confidential report by investment bank Goldman Sachs is recommending Fund Managers to sell 10 major blue-chip Hong Kong stocks. The report warns that without continued HKMA support, the HSI could plunge to below 6,000 points in one day.'[1] The prognostications of such reports was one reason why the government ended up spending more and purchasing more shares than they had expected to.

We will assess the three sub-stages of the intervention separately: 14–19 August—the first successful push; 20–26 August—the steady slog phase; and 27–28 August—the serious confrontation phase with the speculators.

4.1.1 First Success

From 14 to 19 August, the government was engaged in pushing, holding, and then driving the market up again. After these three days, the HSI rose by nearly 1,000 points to 7,622. During this phase, the government spent HK $8.3 billion, which amounted to only about 7 per cent of the total invested money. But this 7 per cent investment accounted for over 80 per cent of the increase of the index for the whole intervention period. We therefore group these three days as the first success of the intervention.

This success was achieved mainly because the government's action had been unexpected. This was particularly the case on 14 August. '"It felt like our clients were caught in an ambush," said one sales director.'[2] 'It caught speculators by surprise, pushed the HSI safely over the 7,000 mark at the start of a long weekend...'[3]

Although the government announced later that they had bought a small amount on the futures market on 13 August to test the market,[4] that amount was too small to be noticed by the market. No mention of this action was found in the newspapers on the following two days. The element of surprise in the intervention gave the government an edge, enabling them to successfully reverse

---

[1] 'Goldman recommends selling 10 blue chips', *South China Morning Post*, 31 August 1998.
[2] 'Intervention brightens trading day', *South China Morning Post*, 15 August 1998.
[3] 'Skirmish won: but now for the war', *South China Morning Post*, 16 August 1998.
[4] 'Government statement on HKMA test operation', http://www.hknews.com.hk, 31 March 1999.

the downward trend in the market before 14 August. As revealed in Chapter 3, the government gave the stock market a boost during both the morning and the afternoon trading sessions, and the market closed with a 564 increase in the index.

On 18 August, Tuesday (Monday having been a public holiday in Hong Kong), the market saw the government buying for the second day. This buying was somewhat expected because, on 17 August, Moscow unexpectedly announced that it would allow the rouble to depreciate as much as a third by the end of the year and would restructure all treasury bills to avert a payment crisis.[5] As a consequence of this announcement, all the surrounding Asian markets experienced a significant drop, because Russia's problems clearly compounded the level of anxiety in Asia. With HK $2.2 billion spent on 18 August, the government shored up the market from sliding alongside neighbouring Asian markets. The market closed only 0.19 per cent lower than its close on 14 August.

On 19 August, the government's buying again surprised the market. 'Yesterday's (19 August) intervention surprised the market, as pressure on the Hong Kong dollars declined and interbank rates eased as the yen rose.'[6] The market did not expect the government to continue their action of buying stocks and pushing up prices even higher.

To evaluate the government's achievement for each stock during the first phase, we list both the price change and the percentage of the outstanding shares that the government bought in each stock (Table 4.2). During this phase, there was almost a 15 per cent price increase on average, and the increase was achieved by buying only 0.50 per cent of the outstanding shares. In the case of Hopewell Holdings (00069), where 0.13 per cent of the outstanding shares were bought, and the price increased by 38.24 per cent, the achievement[7] was noteworthy; while in the case of New World Development (00142), where the price changed only by 2.91 per cent with 0.71 per cent of government buying, it was a marginal achievement.

In terms of the relative increase in valuation per HK$ worth of shares bought, Hopewell Holdings (00069) finds a place at the top

---

[5] 'Regional stocks fall in aftermath of devalued rouble', *South China Morning Post*, 19 August 1998.

[6] 'HKMA chief warns of long-term battle as buying continues despite limited dollar pressure', *South China Morning Post*, 20 August 1998.

[7] The 'achievement' is defined here as percentage price change per percentage point of outstanding shares bought by the government.

TABLE 4.2. *First success (14–19 August)*

Stock code	% change in price			% of outstanding shares bought			'Achievement'
	End price (13/08)	End price (19/08)	% chg (1)	Outstanding	Bought	% chg (2)	%(1)/%(2)
00001	28.85	33.6	16.46	2,297,556,240	25,292,000	1.10	14.96
00002	30.1	34.7	15.28	2,448,916,500	10,824,000	0.44	34.58
00003	8.05	8.95	11.18	4,320,213,174	15,369,000	0.36	31.43
00004	6.2	7.15	15.32	2,295,086,583	4,938,000	0.22	71.22
00005	151.0	167.5	10.93	1,812,187,182	18,572,000	1.02	10.66
00006	21.45	23.95	11.66	2,020,334,691	10,017,000	0.50	23.51
00008	12.55	14.7	17.13	11,949,377,176	52,220,000	0.44	39.20
00010	5.45	6.0	10.09	1,328,730,245	2,703,000	0.20	49.61
00011	36.8	40.2	9.24	1,911,842,736	11,661,000	0.61	15.15
00012	20.3	22.65	11.58	1,722,140,000	3,518,000	0.20	56.67
00013	31.7	38.0	19.87	3,875,593,490	21,165,000	0.55	36.39
00014	4.725	5.05	6.88	1,026,942,204	7,572,000	0.74	9.33
00016	21.6	25.2	16.67	2,391,389,866	5,891,000	0.25	67.66
00017	7.95	9.4	18.24	1,984,931,571	29,793,000	1.50	12.15
00019	20.0	22.55	12.75	940,111,885	4,990,000	0.53	24.02
00020	3.33	3.83	15.04	2,026,932,899	4,355,000	0.21	69.99
00023	7.25	8.05	11.03	1,374,732,387	4,843,200	0.35	31.32
00041	5.35	5.95	11.21	546,366,811	2,216,000	0.41	27.65
00045	3.15	3.95	25.40	1,156,704,599	2,133,000	0.18	137.72
00054	0.64	0.76	18.75	4,379,910,606	13,233,000	0.30	62.06
00069	3.4	4.7	38.24	1,794,254,988	2,326,000	0.13	294.94
00083	2.03	2.35	16.05	3,112,622,259	13,158,000	0.42	37.97
00097	3.45	3.98	15.22	2,817,327,395	5,645,000	0.20	75.95
00101	3.13	3.68	17.60	2,858,786,257	5,255,200	0.18	95.74
00142	2.58	2.65	2.91	2,373,627,935	17,444,000	0.73	3.96
00267	9.35	11.05	18.18	2,127,367,160	18,943,000	0.89	20.42
00270	1.17	1.32	12.82	2,488,314,570	17,616,000	0.71	18.11
00291	4.58	5.3	15.85	1,553,000,000	14,920,000	0.96	16.49
00293	5.15	6.1	18.45	3,384,199,848	7,254,000	0.21	86.06
00363	10.35	10.95	5.80	841,320,000	6,437,000	0.77	7.58
00511	14.55	15.4	5.84	417,645,500	1,976,000	0.47	12.35
00941	9.3	11.1	19.35	11,780,788,000	54,676,000	0.46	41.70
01038	11.15	13.15	17.94	2,254,209,945	7,136,000	0.32	56.66
Average			14.82			0.50	29.64

102 *Intervention to Save Hong Kong*

of the list. On a purchase worth only HK $9.2 million, the market value of the stock increased by HK $2,333 million. The 'leverage'[8] reached 253 times (Table 4.3). However, the largest purchase in value terms and the biggest change in market value were seen in relation to the HSBC stocks. The government invested HK $2,910 million in HSBC, which accounted for more than 35 per cent of the total government money used during this phase. The total

TABLE 4.3. *Actual market value (MV) changes (14–19 August)*

Stock code	Actual Change in MV (HK$ mn)			Value of purchases (HK$mn)	'Leverage' (1)/(2)
	MV 13/08	MV 19/08	Chg (1)		
00001	66,284.50	77,197.89	10,913.39	799.34	13.65
00002	73,712.39	84,977.40	11,265.02	351.12	32.08
00003	34,777.72	38,665.91	3,888.19	128.90	30.17
00004	14,229.54	16,409.87	2,180.33	32.40	67.30
00005	273,640.26	303,541.35	29,901.09	2,909.69	10.28
00006	43,336.18	48,387.02	5,050.84	225.14	22.43
00008	149,964.68	175,655.84	25,691.16	714.81	35.94
00010	7,241.58	7,972.38	730.80	16.11	45.37
00011	70,355.81	76,856.08	6,500.27	455.70	14.26
00012	34,959.44	39,006.47	4,047.03	77.07	52.51
00013	122,856.31	147,272.55	24,416.24	741.94	32.91
00014	4,852.30	5,186.06	333.76	36.95	9.03
00016	51,654.02	60,263.02	8,609.00	138.85	62.00
00017	15,780.21	18,658.36	2,878.15	259.92	11.07
00019	18,802.24	21,199.52	2,397.29	107.80	22.24
00020	6,739.55	7,753.02	1,013.47	15.19	66.71
00023	9,966.81	11,066.60	1,099.79	36.71	29.96
00041	2,923.06	3,250.88	327.82	13.01	25.19
00045	3,643.62	4,568.98	925.36	7.47	123.92
00054	2,803.14	3,328.73	525.59	9.22	56.97
00069	6,100.47	8,433.00	2,332.53	9.20	253.47
00083	6,303.06	7,314.66	1,011.60	29.21	34.63
00097	9,719.78	11,198.88	1,479.10	20.44	72.38
00101	8,933.71	10,506.04	1,572.33	18.23	86.25
00142	6,112.09	6,290.11	178.02	45.22	3.94
00267	19,890.88	23,507.41	3,616.52	200.09	18.07
00270	2,911.33	3,284.58	373.25	21.41	17.43
00291	7,104.98	8,230.90	1,125.93	69.86	16.12
00293	17,428.63	20,643.62	3,214.99	41.09	78.25
00363	8,707.66	9,212.45	504.79	68.55	7.36
00511	6,076.74	6,431.74	355.00	30.06	11.81
00941	109,561.33	130,766.75	21,205.42	576.15	36.81
01038	25,134.44	29,642.86	4,508.42	84.22	53.53
Total			184,172.47	8,291.10	22.21

[8] 'Leverage': change in market value as a percentage of the value of government purchases.

value of government purchases during this first phase was HK $8,291 million, moving the market value of the 33 stocks up by HK $184,172 million. The average leverage is, therefore, more than 22 times. It has been difficult to access comparable 'leverage' data for other cases of market intervention in other markets, in other countries and at other times. However, it is obvious that the scale of 'leverage' in this instance is surprisingly large.

4.1.2 Steady Slog

After the first successful phase of intervention, the government changed its strategy. The market index was seen as being held rather than being pushed up. 'Brokers said it was difficult to find the patterns in government tactics.'[9]

On 20 and 21 August, the intervention amounts were very small. Our estimates are only 1.7 billion and 1.4 billion respectively. The market closed for the week at 7,531, with an increase of 1.6 per cent on 20 August and a drop of 2.8 per cent on 21 August.

On 24 August, the market opened somewhat lower at 7,443 points, but was then pushed steadily back up to 7,844 points by the time it closed, returning to the level that had been achieved on 20 August. The index level was then maintained thereabouts on 25 and 26 August, but this holding process was not as easy as in the first week. HK $3.5 billion and HK $5.3 billion were spent on each day, which was higher than any daily purchase during the first week. The market index was thus kept stable on these two days. But on 26 August, the market began to show signs of strong selling pressure. The index experienced a sudden drop of almost 300 points within a few minutes of trading opening in the afternoon. It could be that either the government was testing the market, or just had not been prepared for a sudden surge in sales. But clearly the market could not sustain itself, and the government then pushed it back to the desired level. The market closed with a slight drop of 0.71 per cent.

During this steady slog phase, the performance of the stocks was quite diverse. Six out of 33 experiencing two-digit percentage increases while four stocks had negative price changes. Obviously the government did not simply put their money into every stock but played tactically in the market. Although they did a good job in keeping the market and the speculators guessing, their activities

---

[9] 'Investors unload blue chips', *South China Morning Post*, 22 August 1998.

were not as unexpected as in the first phase. The market had expected, especially starting from the second week, that the government would stay in the market at least till the expiration day of the futures contracts on Friday, 28 August. The newspapers reported: 'By boosting the HSI, the government hopes to force speculators to take big losses when the August index futures expires on the 28th.'[10] 'The government has indicated that the intervention will not end when the August futures contract expires on Friday. It has vowed to stay in the market as long as necessary to drive out speculators profiting from a double-play in the currency and stock market.'[11]

With this expectation in the market, it was not as easy any more for the government to support the level of prices. Over these five days, the government spent more than HK $19 billion in the market, but managed to lift the HSI up by only another 2.77 per cent.

A closer examination of each stock (Table 4.4) reveals that, although the 'achievements' varied from stock to stock, they were, in general, much lower than the achievements in the first phase (compare with Table 4.2). The top performer was Cheung Kong Infrastructure (01038) with a purchase of only 0.54 per cent of its outstanding shares, its price was raised by 10.65 per cent. The simple average of the rates of price increase to percentage of stock bought for all stocks is only 6.69 during this phase, while the average for the first phase is 48.28. In terms of the value (Table 4.5), the story is similar. The 'leverage' effect was greatly reduced in comparison with the first three days of intervention. The average figure dropped sharply from 22.21 to 2.11.

4.1.3 Serious Confrontation

The most serious problems for the authorities arose in the last two days before the expiration of the August futures contract. On 27 August, most of the 33 blue chips ended up either level or a bit higher. The index rose slightly to 7,923 at the close, but it cost the government HK $19.38 billion to achieve this marginal increase. Our guess is that the government wanted to push the index

---

[10] 'HKMA chief warns of long-term battle as buying continues despite limited dollar pressure', *South China Morning Post*, 20 August 1998.

[11] 'Market step-in bill may top $22b', *South China Morning Post*, 25 August 1998.

TABLE 4.4. *Steady slog (20–26 August)*

Stock code	% change in price			% of outstanding shares bought			'Achievement' %(1) /%(2)
	End price (19/08)	End price (26/08)	% chg (1)	Outstanding	Bought	% chg (2)	
00001	33.6	34.0	1.19	2,297,556,240	20,730,000	0.90	1.32
00002	34.7	35.1	1.15	2,448,916,500	17,386,000	0.71	1.62
00003	8.95	9.1	1.68	4,320,213,174	28,067,000	0.65	2.58
00004	7.15	7.6	6.29	2,295,086,583	10,036,000	0.44	14.39
00005	167.5	171.5	2.39	1,812,187,182	49,768,800	2.75	0.87
00006	23.95	25.1	4.80	2,020,334,691	13,640,000	0.68	7.11
00008	14.7	15.5	5.44	11,949,377,176	154,008,000	1.29	4.22
00010	6.0	6.65	10.83	1,328,730,245	6,565,000	0.49	21.93
00011	40.2	44.0	9.45	1,911,842,736	22,227,000	1.16	8.13
00012	22.65	23.75	4.86	1,722,140,000	13,253,000	0.77	6.31
00013	38.0	38.2	0.53	3,875,593,490	26,484,000	0.68	0.77
00014	5.05	5.35	5.94	1,026,942,204	21,069,000	2.05	2.90
00016	25.2	26.2	3.97	2,391,389,866	27,372,000	1.14	3.47
00017	9.4	9.05	-3.72	1,984,931,571	32,212,000	1.62	-2.29
00019	22.55	24.25	7.54	940,111,885	13,328,700	1.42	5.32
00020	3.83	4.2	9.80	2,026,932,899	14,327,000	0.71	13.87
00023	8.05	8.45	4.97	1,374,732,387	9,084,200	0.66	7.52
00041	5.95	6.55	10.08	546,366,811	3,699,000	0.68	14.89
00045	3.95	4.2	6.33	1,156,704,599	10,317,500	0.89	7.10
00054	0.76	0.83	9.21	4,379,910,606	40,456,000	0.92	9.97
00069	4.7	4.9	4.26	1,794,254,988	28,054,000	1.56	2.72
00083	2.35	2.63	11.70	3,112,622,259	18,788,000	0.60	19.39
00097	3.98	4.25	6.92	2,817,327,395	13,493,000	0.48	14.45
00101	3.68	3.85	4.76	2,858,786,257	12,680,000	0.44	10.74
00142	2.65	2.63	-0.94	2,373,627,935	38,478,000	1.62	-0.58
00267	11.05	10.35	-6.33	2,127,367,160	27,524,000	1.29	-4.90
00270	1.32	1.43	8.33	2,488,314,570	26,346,000	1.06	7.87
00291	5.3	5.85	10.38	1,553,000,000	27,659,000	1.78	5.83
00293	6.1	6.25	2.46	3,384,199,848	16,285,000	0.48	5.11
00363	10.95	11.05	0.91	841,320,000	10,996,000	1.31	0.70
00511	15.4	17.7	14.94	417,645,500	4,454,000	1.07	14.00
00941	11.1	10.6	-4.50	11,780,788,000	87,777,000	0.75	-6.05
01038	13.15	14.55	10.65	2,254,209,945	12,284,000	0.54	19.54
Average			5.04			1.02	4.94

Intervention to Save Hong Kong

TABLE 4.5. *Actual market value changes (20–26 August)*

Stock code	Actual change in MV (HK$ mn)			Value of purchases (HK$ mn)	'Leverage' (1)/(2)
	MV (19/08)	MV (26/08)	Chg (1)		
00001	77,197.89	78,116.91	919.02	700.45	1.31
00002	84,977.40	85,956.97	979.57	605.43	1.62
00003	38,665.91	39,313.94	648.03	248.12	2.61
00004	16,409.87	17,442.66	1,032.79	72.50	14.25
00005	303,541.35	310,790.10	7,248.75	8,473.22	0.86
00006	48,387.02	50,710.40	2,323.38	334.33	6.95
00008	175,655.84	185,215.35	9,559.50	2,374.01	4.03
00010	7,972.38	8,836.06	863.67	41.43	20.84
00011	76,856.08	84,121.08	7,265.00	948.65	7.66
00012	39,006.47	40,900.83	1,894.35	304.18	6.23
00013	147,272.55	148,047.67	775.12	1,014.67	0.76
00014	5,186.06	5,494.14	308.08	108.86	2.83
00016	60,263.02	62,654.41	2,391.39	703.08	3.40
00017	18,658.36	17,963.63	−694.73	286.91	−2.42
00019	21,199.52	22,797.71	1,598.19	315.22	5.07
00020	7,753.02	8,513.12	760.10	56.58	13.43
00023	11,066.60	11,616.49	549.89	73.49	7.48
00041	3,250.88	3,578.70	327.82	23.41	14.00
00045	4,568.98	4,858.16	289.18	41.69	6.94
00054	3,328.73	3,635.33	306.59	32.34	9.48
00069	8,433.00	8,791.85	358.85	147.35	2.44
00083	7,314.66	8,170.63	855.97	45.83	18.68
00097	11,198.88	11,973.64	774.77	54.69	14.17
00101	10,506.04	11,006.33	500.29	46.41	10.78
00142	6,290.11	6,230.77	−59.34	98.06	−0.61
00267	23,507.41	22,018.25	−1,489.16	276.51	−5.39
00270	3,284.58	3,558.29	273.71	36.57	7.48
00291	8,230.90	9,085.05	854.15	156.19	5.47
00293	20,643.62	21,151.25	507.63	101.91	4.98
00363	9,212.45	9,296.59	84.13	116.00	0.73
00511	6,431.74	7,392.33	960.58	72.12	13.32
00941	130,766.75	124,876.35	−5,890.39	946.42	−6.22
01038	29,642.86	32,798.75	3,155.89	169.96	18.57
Total			40,232.80	19,026.59	2.11

over 8,000 but was unable to do so. Then on 28 August, the last trading day of the August futures contracts, the Hong Kong market saw a most remarkable day of trading. As on the previous day, the HKMA maintained outstanding bids for all HSI stocks. Selling orders were unexpectedly huge. To quote Joseph Yam's speech on 30 August 1998: 'It (the cost of the defence) is larger than expected because some of the investors took advantage of our very clear strategy...to unload some of their stocks. That's

An Assessment of the Effects of the Intervention 107

something we have to live with. We ended up with more than we anticipated.'[12]

From Table 4.6, we see that the HKMA, on average, bought about 5 per cent of every Hang Seng constituent stock on 28 August. Such purchases even reached more than 10 per cent in the case of Swire Pacific 'A' (00019). (Note that, for HSBC, we have not added in the possible London buying that we estimated in the previous chapter since the action has not been confirmed by the government.) Using the same definition as in the previous two phases, the government 'achievement' was, on average, negative. The average price drop over these two days was −0.36 per cent and the market value of all 33 stocks fell by HK $2.73 billion (Table 4.7). The 'leverage' effect was negative in most of the cases. This was because the HKMA, which was coordinating the government's buying, allowed the market to fall slightly, especially during the afternoon trading. They released some pressure by doing so, as the goal of posting an inflated close level for the August futures contract was still seemingly being achieved, although they had not reached the index level of 8,000 (which we believe was their underlying target, though we have no firm evidence to support our assumption). This last day's battle cost the Hong Kong government HK $72 billion, which accounts for more than 60 per cent of the total intervention value, as shown in Table 4.1.

The scale of intervention on this final day was gigantic, both in its own right and even more so when you consider that Hong Kong is a small economy. The authorities ended up buying nearly 5 per cent of the total capitalization of the index on one day. By comparison, 5 per cent of the capitalization of the Dow Jones Industrial Average was US $122.4 billion, of the Financial Times 100 was US $93.6 billion (£58.4 billion), (end 1998 data).[13]

---

[12] 'Lies by speculators pressure peg', *South China Morning Post*, 31 August 1998.

[13] The total purchased amount on 28th August was HK $72.1 billion and the total capitalization of HSI stocks was HK $1611.3 billion. Total capitalization was US $2448.7 billion of Dow Jones Industrial Average and GBP1167.3 billion of FT-SE 100.

TABLE 4.6. *Serious confrontation (27–28 August)*

	% change in price			% of outstanding shares bought			'Achievement'
Stock code	End price (26/08)	End price (28/08)	% chg (1)	Outstanding	Bought	% chg (2)	%(1) /%(2)
00001	34.0	33.2	−2.35	2,297,556,240	193,235,000	8.41	−0.28
00002	35.1	35.2	0.28	2,448,916,500	109,210,000	4.46	0.06
00003	9.1	9.0	−1.10	4,320,213,174	251,182,000	5.81	−0.19
00004	7.6	7.55	−0.66	2,295,086,583	106,613,000	4.65	−0.14
00005	171.5	173.5	1.17	2,659,952,862	168,044,000	6.32	0.18
00006	25.1	25.15	0.20	2,020,334,691	104,193,000	5.16	0.04
00008	15.5	15.1	−2.58	11,949,377,176	795,185,600	6.65	−0.39
00010	6.65	6.7	0.75	1,328,730,245	24,223,000	1.82	0.41
00011	44.0	44.3	0.68	1,911,842,736	81,485,000	4.26	0.16
00012	23.75	23.9	0.63	1,722,140,000	66,127,000	3.84	0.16
00013	38.2	37.8	−1.05	3,875,593,490	249,167,000	6.43	−0.16
00014	5.35	5.25	−1.87	1,026,942,204	35,895,000	3.50	−0.53
00016	26.2	25.7	−1.91	2,391,389,866	150,177,000	6.28	−0.30
00017	9.05	8.85	−2.21	1,984,931,571	190,424,000	9.59	−0.23
00019	24.25	24.0	−1.03	940,111,885	98,918,500	10.52	−0.10
00020	4.2	4.23	0.60	2,026,932,899	45,200,000	2.23	0.27
00023	8.45	8.5	0.59	1,374,732,387	75,469,800	5.49	0.11
00041	6.55	6.6	0.76	546,366,811	19,216,000	3.52	0.22
00045	4.2	4.2	0.00	1,156,704,599	45,587,700	3.94	0.00
00054	0.83	0.83	0.00	4,379,910,606	173,484,000	3.96	0.00
00069	4.9	4.8	−2.04	1,794,254,988	32,946,000	1.84	−1.11
00083	2.63	2.63	0.00	3,112,622,259	92,224,000	2.96	0.00
00097	4.25	4.25	0.00	2,817,327,395	76,563,000	2.72	0.00
00101	3.85	3.93	1.95	2,858,786,257	59,317,500	2.07	0.94
00142	2.63	2.58	−1.90	2,373,627,935	95,592,000	4.03	−0.47
00267	10.35	10.4	0.48	2,127,367,160	109,461,000	5.15	0.09
00270	1.43	1.42	−0.70	2,488,314,570	117,246,000	4.71	−0.15
00291	5.85	5.75	−1.71	1,553,000,000	104,846,000	6.75	−0.25
00293	6.25	6.25	0.00	3,384,199,848	98,733,000	2.92	0.00
00363	11.05	11.0	−0.45	841,320,000	55,004,000	6.54	−0.07
00511	17.7	17.75	0.28	417,645,500	30,151,000	7.22	0.04
00941	10.6	10.9	2.83	11,780,788,000	349,718,000	2.97	0.95
01038	14.55	14.35	−1.37	2,254,209,945	79,914,000	3.55	−0.39
Average			−0.36			4.86	−0.07

TABLE 4.7. *Actual market value changes (27–28 August)*

Stock code	Actual change in MV			Value of purchases (2) (m)	'Leverage' (1)/(2)
	MV26 (m)	MV 28 (m)	(1)Chg (m)		
00001	78,116.91	76,278.87	−1,838.04	6,509.89	−0.28
00002	85,956.97	86,201.86	244.89	3,845.08	0.06
00003	39,313.94	38,881.92	−432.02	2,260.18	−0.19
00004	17,442.66	17,327.90	−114.75	815.50	−0.14
00005	456,181.92	461,501.82	5,319.91	29,123.58	0.18
00006	50,710.40	50,811.42	101.02	2,620.74	0.04
00008	185,215.35	180,435.60	−4,779.75	12,148.66	−0.39
00010	8,836.06	8,902.49	66.44	162.32	0.41
00011	84,121.08	84,694.63	573.55	3,608.24	0.16
00012	40,900.83	41,159.15	258.32	1,580.38	0.16
00013	148,047.67	146,497.43	−1,550.24	9,501.08	−0.16
00014	5,494.14	5,391.45	−102.69	189.58	−0.54
00016	62,654.41	61,458.72	−1,195.69	3,886.18	−0.31
00017	17,963.63	17,566.64	−396.99	1,703.80	−0.23
00019	22,797.71	22,562.69	−235.03	2,381.71	−0.10
00020	8,513.12	8,563.79	50.67	191.03	0.27
00023	11,616.49	11,685.23	68.74	641.10	0.11
00041	3,578.70	3,606.02	27.32	126.81	0.22
00045	4,858.16	4,858.16	0.00	191.83	0.00
00054	3,635.33	3,635.33	0.00	144.18	0.00
00069	8,791.85	8,612.42	−179.43	158.61	−1.13
00083	8,170.63	8,170.63	0.00	239.96	0.00
00097	11,973.64	11,973.64	0.00	325.64	0.00
00101	11,006.33	11,220.74	214.41	232.69	0.92
00142	6,230.77	6,112.09	−118.68	248.86	−0.48
00267	22,018.25	22,124.62	106.37	1,140.05	0.09
00270	3,558.29	3,533.41	−24.88	166.69	−0.15
00291	9,085.05	8,929.75	−155.30	605.64	−0.26
00293	21,151.25	21,151.25	0.00	618.60	0.00
00363	9,296.59	9,254.52	−42.07	606.40	−0.07
00511	7,392.33	7,413.21	20.88	535.39	0.04
00941	124,876.35	128,410.59	3,534.24	3,822.17	0.92
01038	32,798.75	32,347.91	−450.84	1,151.16	−0.39
Total			−1,029.66	91,483.74	−0.01

Even taken by itself, the intervention of HK $72 billion, equal to US $9.3 billion or £5.6 billion at the prevailing exchange rates,[14] dwarfs any other daily intervention. Perhaps the other large daily intervention occurred when the UK monetary authorities vainly attempted to hold their dollar-peg in October 1964 and their Exchange Rate Mechanism (ERM) peg in September 1992.

[14] The exchange rates on 28 August 1998 were HK $12.86: £1 and HK $7.74:US $1, respectively.

110 *Intervention to Save Hong Kong*

It is probable that the Hong Kong authorities had failed to anticipate the flood of sales that would be unleashed on 28 August. The decision on that day whether to fight and use up untold billions of taxpayers' money, or to fold before the onslaught, must have been a hard one to make.

4.1.4 Summary

In this section, we have assessed the government's efforts and achievements during the three different intervention phases. In the initial phase, the government took the market by surprise with its unprecedented actions and the market was raised by nearly 15 per cent from its bottom level of 6,660 on 13 August. It cost the government only HK $8.3 billion to achieve this recovery. Then, as the market became accustomed to the intervention and as the expiration day of the August futures contract approached, the market's selling pressure started to build up. Market turnover increased, and more investors took advantage of the higher price level that government purchases had brought about. During this phase of steady slog, the HSI increased slightly by 2.77 per cent; yet the government had to spend more than HK $19 billion to effect this change.

The last two intervention days posed major problems. The selling orders were enormous and the government had to build a wall of bid orders to prevent the HSI from falling. The HKMA appeared to be the sole buyer in the market. According to our estimates, the government purchased an amount accounting for 89.71 per cent and 93.75 per cent of the market turnover on 27 and 28 August respectively. So, although the government was successful in sustaining the index level and thus securing a loss for speculators in the futures market, they eventually paid a fortune to make it happen. (The information is summarized in Table 4.8.)

TABLE 4.8. *Summary of the three phases*

Phase	Average price change (%)	Index change (%)	Average % of outstanding shares bought	Total change in MV	Total value of purchase
First success	14.82	14.45	0.50	184,172.47	8,291.10
Steady slog	5.04	2.77	1.02	40,232.80	19,026.59
Serious confrontation	−0.36	−0.06	4.86	−1,029.66	91,483.74

An Assessment of the Effects of the Intervention   111

Let us look at some of the problems posed by such government intervention. The government intervened with an obvious purpose to hit speculators in order to drive them away. It amounted to telling the market that they would support the index till the expiration of the August futures contract. In all likelihood, without the government's buying, the market would have fallen back sharply. Rational investors would choose to sell high to the government and later buy lower from the market. In Chapter 5, we will argue that the government added to its problems by contributing to the price depression of the September futures contract. The authorities may have been lulled into a false confidence by their relatively easy experience during the opening days of the intervention. Perhaps they should have anticipated that the real battle, both in the spot and in the futures market, would come right at the end, when the August futures contract expired. Even so, it is hard to see how anyone could have possibly forecast the likely size and scale of the market battle on the final two days. How far could, and should, the authorities have appreciated the risks involved? We will never know, unless and until the authorities choose to reveal the inside story of the entire episode. This time around, the government has won; but whether the strategy was right or not, is another issue. If there should ever be another occasion in the future for the government to intervene, the possible risks involved would have to be considered beforehand.

4.2   Performance Comparison with Non-intervened HK Stocks

4.2.1   Choice of Comparison Pairs

To fully assess the government's intervention, it would be useful to compare the performance of the intervened stocks with the non-intervened ones. Since the 33 stocks that the government bought are the top stocks in the Hong Kong equity market, it is hard to construct a control group. So we have to make do with a few comparable pairs. We began with grouping the 33 stocks into sectors. Then, for each sector, we identified the next largest stocks in terms of market capitalization. If these stocks were comparable in size with at least one of the intervened stocks within the same sector, then that pair was chosen. Using this method, we obtained the following five pairs (Table 4.9):

TABLE 4.9. *Comparable non-intervened Hong Kong stocks*

Sector	Companies	Stock code	Market capitalization (HK $ mn)
Property development	Hang Lung*	00010	12,823
	Kerry Prop	00683	12,578
	Great Eagle*	00041	7,486
	Tsim Sha Tsui	00247	7,080
Finance	Bank of East Asia*	00023	27,084
	Dao Heng Bank	00223	26,599
Utility	Cheung Kong Infr*	01038	37,536
	Johnson Electric	00179	32,148
Hotel	HK & S Hotels*	00045	7,866
	CDL Hotels Intl	00557	6,529

*Intervened stocks

We compared price movements of these pairs both in the short term and in the long term. The performance of the HSI was also included as a benchmark.

4.2.2 Comparison

For a short-term high-frequency comparison, we first grouped the tick-by-tick transaction prices into minute-by-minute data and calculated the mean price for each minute. Then we used the opening prices on 14 August 1998 as the base prices and computed the minute-by-minute relative prices from 13 to 31 August. Two pairs are shown in Figure 4.1 as examples.

Both examples, as well as the other three pairs, presented a similar picture. Initially, the market had access to limited information, and some non-intervened stocks followed the HSI trend, with the stock value rising. However, once the market became aware of the scale of the government intervention, the non-intervened stocks immediately delinked themselves from the market trend. Their prices either stayed at the same level or even dropped, while the index and the intervened stocks showed greater price escalation. Technically, this could have been because market attention had wholly shifted to the intervened constituent stocks. On the last two days, however, the index was sustained, with an abrupt increase in market turnover, while at the same time there was a sharp drop in the prices of non-intervened stocks. Market selling pressure, therefore, was not restricted to the index constituent stocks alone, but also spread to the other stocks. This could have been an indication

Example I: Hang Lung Development (00010) vs. Kerry Property (00683)

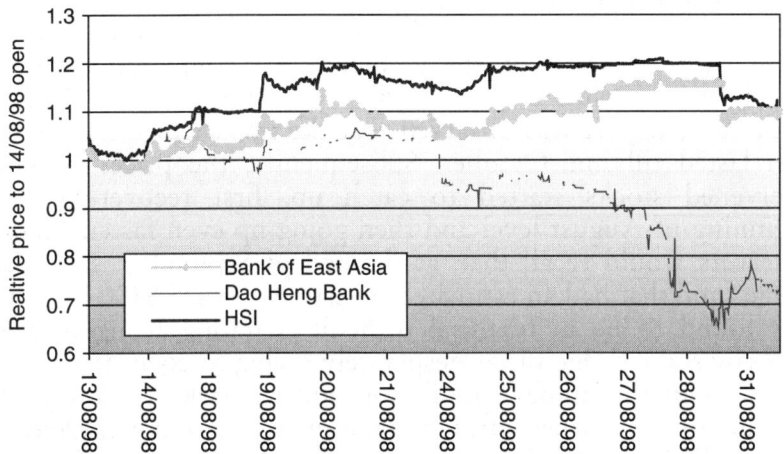

Example II: Bank of East Asia (00023) vs. Dao Heng Bank (00223)

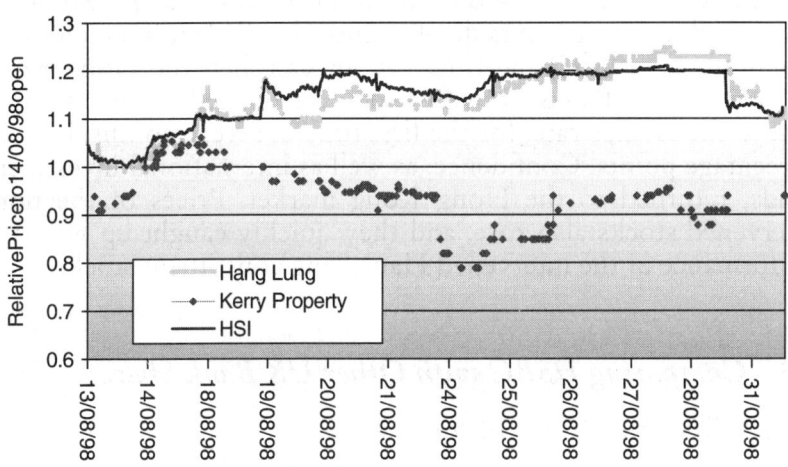

FIG. 4.1. Performances of intervened and non-intervened Hong Kong stocks (13–31 August 1998).

of a market consensus: the government-supported level was unsustainable, prompting players to exit from the market. The performance of the non-intervened stocks gives us a rough idea as to the extent to which the intervened stocks might have fallen without the government's effort. On 31 August, the first day after the government had withdrawn from the market, the prices of

114 *Intervention to Save Hong Kong*

the intervened stocks dropped immediately. The prices of the non-intervened stocks, on the contrary, rose slightly.

In order to examine the full impact of the intervention, we extended the period of study. Figure 4.2 compares the daily closing prices, using 3 August (the first trading day in August) as the base day. It was observed that the impact of the intervention lasted till mid-October. Subsequently, the prices of non-intervened stocks started to catch up, first recovering their beginning-of-August level and then going up even faster. Market observers would recall that, at the end of September, LTCM, a hedge fund that had an estimated investment of US $100 billion,[15] was found to be in financial difficulties. Hong Kong markets also saw some hedge funds desperately trying to cover their short positions in the money, bond, and equity markets. Slowly, the pressure on the market started to fade away. Beginning in October, surrounding economic conditions improved. The Japanese yen appreciated, instead of continuing its downward trend. The Federal Reserve System of the US cut the interest rate three times in a row, including once outside of a scheduled Federal Open Market Committee (FOMC) meeting. On 16 October, the Hong Kong Association of Banks (HKAB) also announced its decision to reduce the savings rate, for the first time in seven months, by 0.25 percentage points. Confidence, as well as international investment funds, returned to the Hong Kong market. Prices of the non-intervened stocks also rose, and they quickly caught up with the performance of the intervened Hang Seng constituent stocks.

4.3   Comparing HSBC with Other UK Bank Shares

4.3.1   Choice of Comparator

Besides comparing intervened with local non-intervened stocks, we would also like to evaluate the relative performance of these intervened stocks with stocks from other markets. However, it is not easy to find many comparable pairs. In the UK market, the dually traded Hong Kong stocks (except for HSBC) are traded in a separate system from the domestic stocks, and therefore cannot be paired. There are also some Hong Kong stocks that are listed in the US market through the American Deposit Receipt (ADR)

[15] 'Hedge funds—the high rollers of the markets', Reuters 24 September 1998.

An Assessment of the Effects of the Intervention

Example I: Hang Lung Development (00010) vs. Kerry Property (00683)

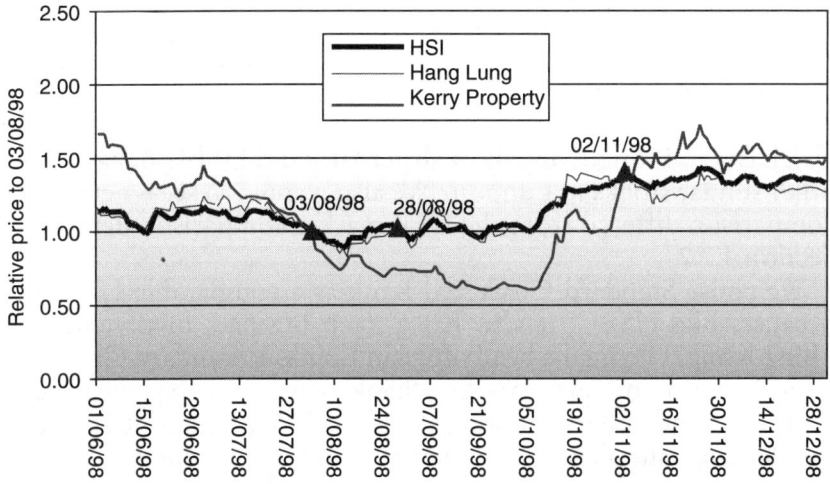

Example II: Bank of East Asia (00023) vs. Dao Heng Bank (00223)

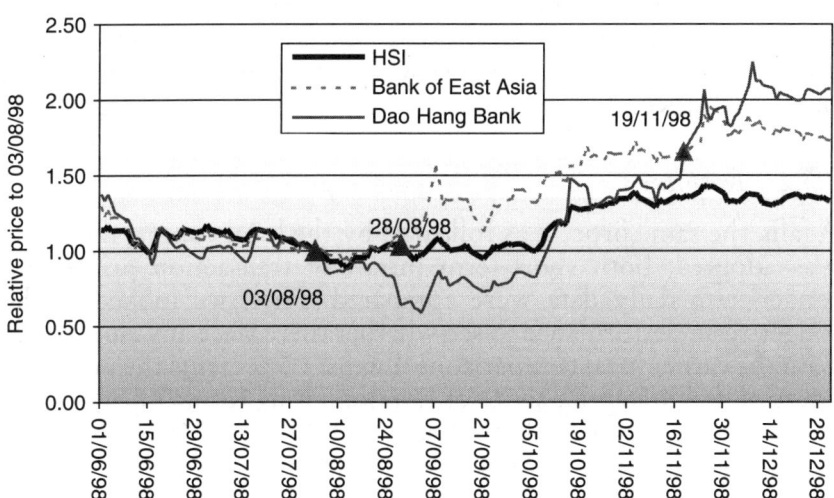

FIG. 4.2. Long-term comparison of intervened and non-intervened Hong Kong stocks.

116 *Intervention to Save Hong Kong*

program.[16] But they usually have thin trading and it is difficult to form comparable pairs. Luckily, HSBC is a double registered company which is big and famous in both the Hong Kong and London markets. It thus provided an opportunity to examine the effect of the government intervention by comparing local stock performances with performances in an outside market. Given government purchases in Hong Kong, how differently did HSBC behave from other similar stocks in London? We also wanted to see whether this comparison differed from the local market comparison detailed in Section 4.2.2.

We chose Standard Chartered Bank as a comparable UK stock because, like HSBC, it also has a deep business involvement in Hong Kong. Having its head office in London, Standard Chartered is, in fact, an emerging markets bank, with a strong presence in both Asia and other emerging areas. In Hong Kong, it is one of the leading suppliers of personal banking products. Another common point with HSBC is that both of them are notes-issuing banks of Hong Kong.[17] Although HSBC Holdings is almost twice as big as Standard Chartered in terms of market capitalization (end 1998 data),[18] Standard Chartered Bank can be taken as a comparable share to HSBC. In addition, we also chose another bank share—Barclays—to make a similar comparison, just to avoid any possible bias which may occur by considering only one individual stock.

4.3.2 Results

Again, the same process as followed by the local comparable pairs was adopted; both short-term intra-day transaction prices and longer-term daily data were compared. First, we looked at the longer-term performance to see whether there were any similarities with the earlier local comparisons. Figure 4.3 presents the performances of the three price series of London Hong Kong dollar trading of HSBC, London GBP trading of HSBC, and one UK bank. Again, the price on 3 August was chosen as the base level and relative prices were computed for all the other trading days.

---

[16] American Deposit Receipt, a program for dual-listing foreign companies on the US stock market.
[17] Hong Kong has three notes-issuing banks currently. Bank of China is the third one, besides HSBC and Standard Chartered.
[18] Market capitalization of HSBC Holdings and Standard Chartered was GBP 16.1 billion and GBP 8.1 billion respectively at the end of 1998.

An Assessment of the Effects of the Intervention 117

We observe a very familiar picture of relative price movements. In both examples, the three price series moved with each other quite closely before the intervention. Even after the intervention began, there was very little variation until the second week. We know from our earlier estimation (see Chapter 3) that the government put more effort into sustaining the HSI level during the second week. The prices on the London market also started to diverge at the same time. On 24 August, the day that the government gave the Hong Kong market a long push after 12 noon, the London Hong Kong dollar trading of HSBC also started to emerge as distinct. However, the difference became marked only on 27 and 28 August, especially in the case of Standard Chartered Bank. Table 4.10 gives the exact figures.

In the UK, 31 August was a holiday, so the prices recorded were the same as on 28 August. Subsequently, the prices of all three stocks declined, while the relative price differentials remained relatively stable for quite a long time. But the trajectories of the two comparators were different, with Standard Chartered Bank catching up with HSBC much faster than Barclays. From Figure 4.3, we see that Standard Chartered caught up immediately after the market started to turn around in early October, yet in the case of Barclays the gap remained until late February 1999.

The performance of Standard Chartered was quite similar to those of the local non-intervened stocks. This can be seen more clearly when a detailed intra-day price comparison is done. Figure 4.4 charts the hourly data from 13 to 31 August.

Both the Hong Kong dollar and GBP prices of HSBC fell sharply on 21 August 1998, bringing it back in line with Standard Chartered Bank. Considering that there was a 4 per cent drop in HSBC's price in Hong Kong on the same day, this movement was understandable. Ordinary investors worried that the price might not be sustained under selling pressure in Hong Kong, and felt that it might be sensible not to hold the shares over the weekend of 22/23 August. The arbitrageurs, on the other hand, would not buy HSBC at a high price because they were afraid that they would not be able to unload the shares profitably without the government supporting the price. There were probably many doubts whether the intervention would continue after the weekend, and, if it did, at what price level.

Entering the second week, when the market perceived the continuing intervention, the gap between the performance of HSBC and Standard Chartered Bank reappeared. The gap was relatively

Example I: HSBC and Standard Chartered Bank

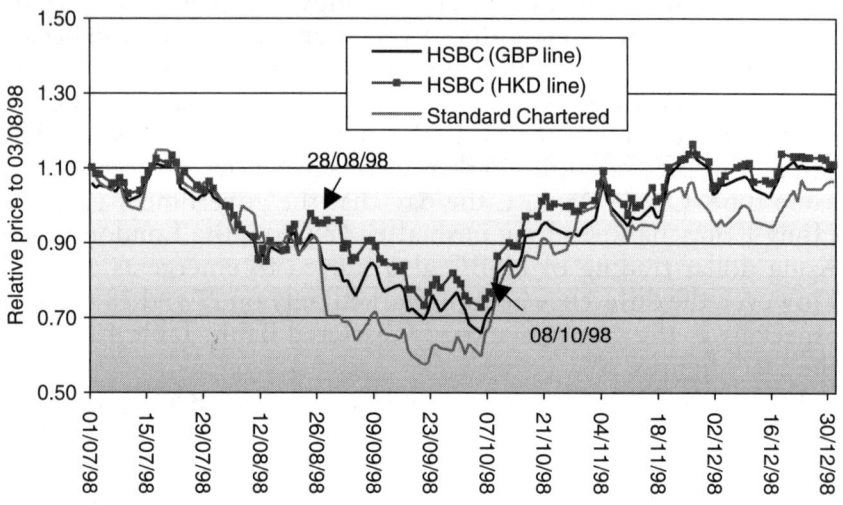

Example II: HSBC and Barclays Bank

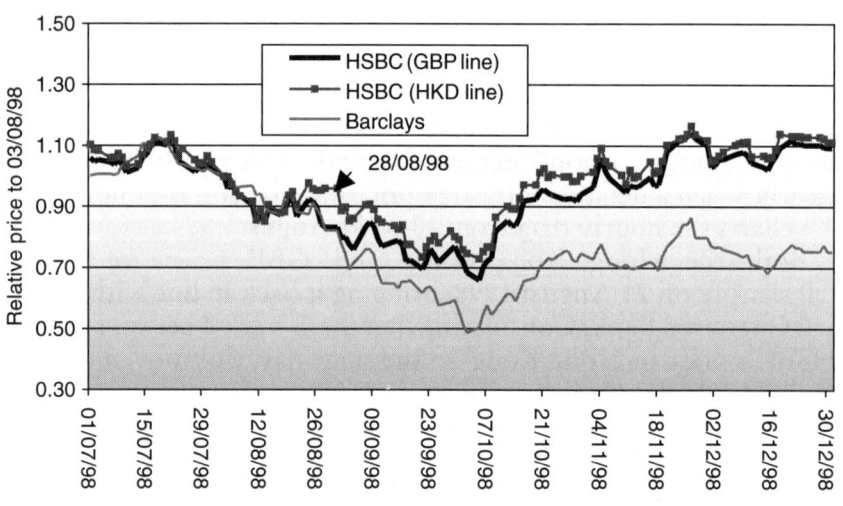

FIG. 4.3. Daily comparison of HSBC with other UK bank shares.

stable until the end of trading on 26 August. Then all three price-series diverged. The Standard Chartered Bank stock fell abruptly on 27 and 28 August, and the GBP trading of HSBC also declined on 27 August, but stabilized on the 28th. The fall in both the Standard Chartered and the GBP trading price of HSBC, relative to the Hong

An Assessment of the Effects of the Intervention 119

TABLE 4.10. *A comparison of HSBC with other UK banks**

	HSBC			
Date	HK $ trading	GBP trading	Standard Chartered	Barclays
14/08/98	0.91	0.89	0.89	0.88
17/08/98	0.88	0.87	0.90	0.88
18/08/98	0.88	0.89	0.92	0.93
19/08/98	0.94	0.92	0.92	0.95
20/08/98	0.95	0.93	0.90	0.92
21/08/98	0.90	0.87	0.87	0.88
24/08/98	0.98	0.92	0.91	0.87
25/08/98	0.96	0.92	0.92	0.91
26/08/98	0.95	0.90	0.90	0.89
27/08/98	0.95	0.84	0.78	0.87
28/08/98	0.96	0.83	0.70	0.82

*Prices are converted to relative levels to the average trading price on 3 August 1998.

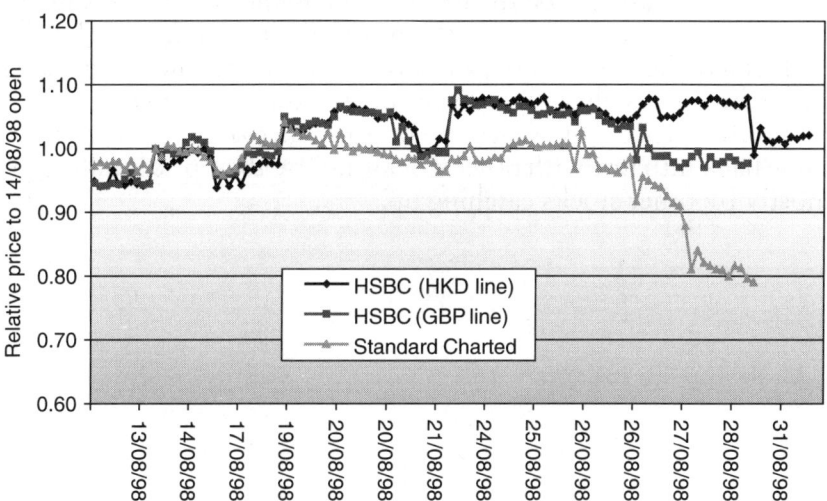

*Prices are converted to relative levels to the average trading price on 3 August 1998.
FIG. 4.4. Hourly comparison of HSBC with Standard Chartered Bank.

Kong dollar trading price of HSBC on 27 August revealed the special features of the Hong Kong dollar trading of HSBC. We have earlier hypothesized that this was possible because the Hong Kong government was on the buying side of these transactions, at least on 27 August if not on the 28th. But we still cannot satisfactorily and fully explain why arbitrage could not bridge the gap between the GBP trading prices and the Hong Kong dollar trading prices. Although a difference between the two prices of HSBC emerged on these two days, there did seem to be some arbitrage activities to hold the GBP prices of HSBC from dropping the way other UK bank shares did.

4.3.3 Summary

In the last two sections, we compared the performance of the intervened stocks with comparable stocks chosen from both the Hong Kong and London markets. The comparison has revealed the extent to which, and the period when, the prices of the different groups of stocks diverged. It is now known that, when the market could predict the government's actions, the latter had to put in more effort to achieve their target. The performance difference between the intervened and non-intervened stocks can be taken as an indication of the extent to which the government had to bolster the prices of the HSI stocks. In fact, it offers us another possible metric for the government's efforts: the more the intervened stocks outperformed the non-intervened stocks, the more the government had to buy. Also, the longer-term comparison gives us some indication of the process by which the performance of intervened stocks came back into line with other stocks–not by their prices falling but mostly by other stocks catching up.

CHAPTER 5

Confrontation on the Futures Market

5.1 *Introduction and Review of News Coverage*

In the previous chapters, we reviewed the confrontation between the Hong Kong government and the speculators in the stock market. We not only covered the local equity market, but also studied the London market—another important market for trading Hong Kong's blue chips. The government took the unprecedented action of intervening in the market because they felt the need to protect local financial markets from being destroyed by the speculators' 'double play' strategy. An important part of this strategy was shorting the futures market. Therefore, for a more complete understanding of the entire episode, an overview of this market is in order. This section will briefly describe the HSI futures trading scenario, and then review the news coverage of the event.

5.1.1 *HSI Futures and the Futures Market*

Index futures trading is considered to be more efficient than stock trading, not only because it involves standardized and homogeneous contracts, but also because of its leverage effect. Buyers and sellers of index futures can obtain exposure to the overall movement of the spot market with only a fraction of the capital—the margin deposit, which is the amount of money paid to the clearinghouse when a position is created to cover short-term fluctuations in the value of the contract. As distinct from other commodity futures contracts, index futures are settled in cash according to the closing value of the index.

The HSI futures contract was introduced in May 1986 to meet the growing interest in the Hong Kong stock market and rising demand for related hedging tools. The availability of HSI futures has brought maturity and sophistication to the Hong Kong financial market. Trading volume increased substantially after its introduction until the 1987 stock market crash. Thereafter, it revived in 1992 when the stock market began to rise, and became one of the most liquid contracts in the world in terms of trading volume by 1998.[1]

One important characteristic of the Hong Kong futures market is the active participation of both retail and institutional investors. According to the Member Transaction Survey conducted by the Hong Kong Futures Exchange (HKFE)[2] for the year 1998–99, local retail investors' transactions constituted 48.7 per cent of the total HSI futures trades in 1998–99. Meanwhile, the proportion of institutional investors' transactions in HSI futures rose to 45.4 per cent in 1998–99 from 39.2 per cent in 1993–94, of which the share of overseas institutional investors increased to 26.3 per cent from 22.3 per cent, while local institutional participation rose from 16.9 per cent to 19.1 per cent. Investors use the HSI and other futures products mainly for the following three purposes: (i) arbitrage, (ii) hedging, or (iii) one-way trading as either investment or speculation. However, according to the survey, two major changes were observed for HSI trading in 1998–99. The proportion of one-way transactions rose to 71.7 per cent, while arbitrage transactions dropped to 8.5 per cent.

Among the many products of the HKFE, the HSI futures contract is definitely the flagship, accounting for over 70 per cent of the Exchange's total turnover. There are four contract-months available at any time for this contract, namely the spot month, the next calendar month, and the next two months from the quarterly cycle: March, June, September, and December. Usually trading is focused on the spot-month contract for the first three weeks of each month and then trading falls away quickly and the market's attention switches to the next calendar-month contract. Figure 5.1 shows a typical example of how the trading volume changes during one month.

The spot-month contract expires on the business day immediately preceding the last business day of each month. The final settlement day is the first trading day after the expiration day. The HSI futures contract is settled using an Asian-style procedure, which means that the settlement price is the average of the

---

[1] The International Federation of Stock Exchanges, http://www.fibv.com.
[2] Special reports from the website of HKFE, http://www.hkex.com.hk.

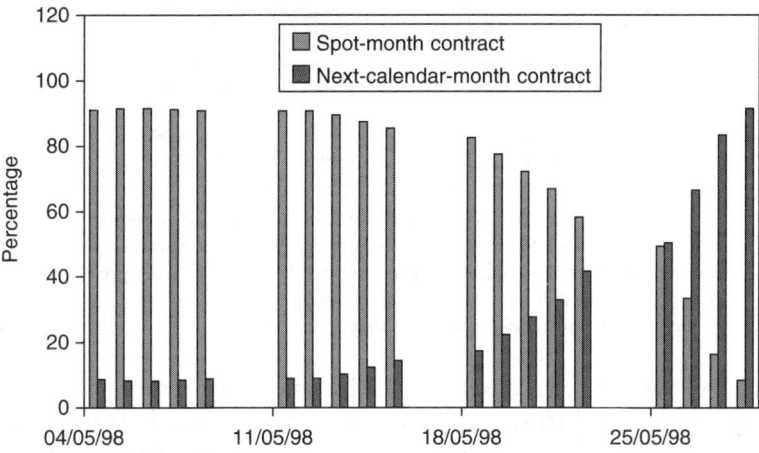

FIG. 5.1. Percentage of futures trading volume.

quotations on the HSI taken at every 5-minute interval during the last trading day of the contract. Before 5 June 2000, HSI futures contracts trading was conducted via an open outcry system on the trading floor, but was then shifted to an electronic order matching system.[3] Just as in the equity market, trading is split into morning and afternoon sections. However, the exact trading time may vary from time to time (Table 5.1).

During the speculative attack and government intervention in 1998, the futures market was definitely one of the most important battlefields. The government thought that the speculators had accumulated a large short position in the HSI futures contracts in order to profit from the rising interest rate that could have been induced by their huge selling of Hong Kong dollars. We shall now look at the news coverage of the futures market behaviour and the Hong Kong government's participation in the futures market around the intervention period.

5.1.2 Relevant Information from News Releases

The official stock market intervention started on 14 August 1998. However, it was disclosed later that some trial buying on the futures market had been carried out on 13 August. In response to media enquiries, a government spokesman made a statement on 30 March 1999 that, 'In order to prepare for the August market operation, the

[3] The Hong Kong Futures Automated Trading System (HKATS).

TABLE 5.1. *Trading time of the HKFE*

Period	Morning Section	Afternoon Section
Before 20 November 1998	10:00–12:30	14:30–16:00
Since 20 November 1998*	09:45–12:30	14:30–16:15†

*From 5 June 2000, a pre-market opening mechanism was introduced in the HSI futures market to determine an opening price for the HSI futures contracts. This facilitates the price discovery process of the market in response to overnight information.[4]
†On the last trading day, the closing time is 16:00.

HKMA, with the agreement of the Financial Secretary, transacted a small number of futures contracts twenty minutes before the close of trading on 13 August 1998. As a result of these test transactions, 491 August HSI futures contracts were purchased by the HKMA. This accounted for only 1.98 per cent of the total turnover of August HSI futures contracts traded at the HKFE on that day (24,794 contracts).'[5]

The spokesman said that the HKMA needed to conduct these trial transactions to 'reassure the Financial Secretary that all the resources and the logistical arrangements required were in place for the launch of the operation planned for the following day.' However, 'the government did not consider it necessary to report on these preparatory details.'

When the mass intervention started, market attention was largely focused on the stock market. Although the HKMA also bought into the futures market, very little market information on their purchases was made public. This could be partly attributed to the fact that compared with the huge investments in the stock market, the government money deployed in the futures market was rather small, due to the leverage effect of the futures market. Further, no matter how the futures prices fluctuate before maturity, the futures market has to converge to the cash market level at the maturity day.

The speculators kept selling, thereby pressing down on the futures price in the hope that it would have a leading effect on the spot market. The Hong Kong government, in order to obstruct

[4] For more information, refer to the website of HKFE, http://www.hkex.com.hk.
[5] 'Government statement on HKMA test operation', http://www.hknews.com.hk, 31 March 1999.

this plan and keep public confidence, put more effort into supporting the cash market. Nevertheless, developments in the futures market remain one of the most interesting parts of the story. Later in the literature review, we will also see that many research reports on the earlier 1987 market crash focused on, or at least mentioned, the role that the index futures played, as well as the interrelationship between the futures market and the spot market.

At the beginning of the second week of the intervention, some brokers estimated that the government had bought at least 10,000 August and September contracts (*South China Morning Post*, 25 August 1998). Then the picture started to get more complicated when the government was noticed to have been selling September positions while buying the August ones during that week. Presumably, the government's purpose was to make it more expensive for those who wanted to roll over their positions. 'Traders said yesterday's cost of rolling a short contract forward was about 1.33 per cent of the value of the position.'[6] Some other brokers estimated that 'the government has hedged up to 20 per cent of its equity investment through the sale of September futures'.[7]

As mentioned in Chapter 2, whereas the government announced their stock market purchases in late October 1998, their trading in the futures market was not disclosed until early December 1998. The Secretary for Financial Services, Rafael Hui, made the following statement to the Legislative Council on 2 December 1998:[8]

The government's trading in the futures market in August is part of the open market operations to frustrate double market play by manipulators. The objective of the operations is to protect the stability and integrity of the monetary and financial systems of Hong Kong.

(a) At present, the government does not hold any HSI futures and options contracts.

(b) The government purchased 36,935 August HSI futures contracts, 1,100 August HSI options contracts and 10,176 September HSI futures contracts but none of both October HSI futures and options contracts.

(c) The net profit generated from the transactions in HSI futures and options contracts as mentioned in part (b) above was about $350 million.

---

[6] 'Peg speculators chase futures', *South China Morning Post*, 26 August 1998.
[7] 'Massive buying sets stage for August futures showdown', *South China Morning Post*, 28 August 1998.
[8] 'Govt's trading in the futures market', http://www.hknews.com.hk, 2 December 1998.

Although the statement provides us with an overall idea of how much the government had bought and how much they had made, it is not clear when the government entered and exited the market. Also, it does not mention whether the government's position of 10,176 September contracts was short or long. We suppose that it was a short position since the government was subsequently seen to be selling the September contracts low during the last week of August 1998.

5.2 Hong Kong's Futures Market During the Intervention

As mentioned in the news review, the HSI futures contracts also behaved abnormally during the Hong Kong financial market turmoil in August/September 1998. Those abnormalities are described in more detail below.

5.2.1 Volume

The government claimed that the speculators had been accumulating a short index-futures position in order to make huge gains from the sharply increased interest rate induced from their currency selling. Before the intervention, the government estimated that positions held by those speculators totalled about 80,000 contracts. Is there any way of confirming this estimate? When did the speculators probably start to accumulate this position? Let us first take a look at both the trading volumes and the open interests in the Hong Kong futures market.[9]

5.2.1.1 Summary of all Futures Contracts

For every trading day, there are four contract months available, but most of the open positions and trading volume are concentrated in the spot month and the next calendar month. We will first look at the gross open interest of all four contract months and then go into more detail about the different contracts.

Figure 5.2 shows the daily gross open interest for a span of two years from 2 January 1998 to 31 December 1999. The yearly average was 70,450 contracts for 1998 and 49,365 contracts for 1999. Clearly the months from May to September 1998 were far

---

[9] The daily information of HSI futures contracts has been acquired from the website of HKFE, http://www.hkex.com.hk.

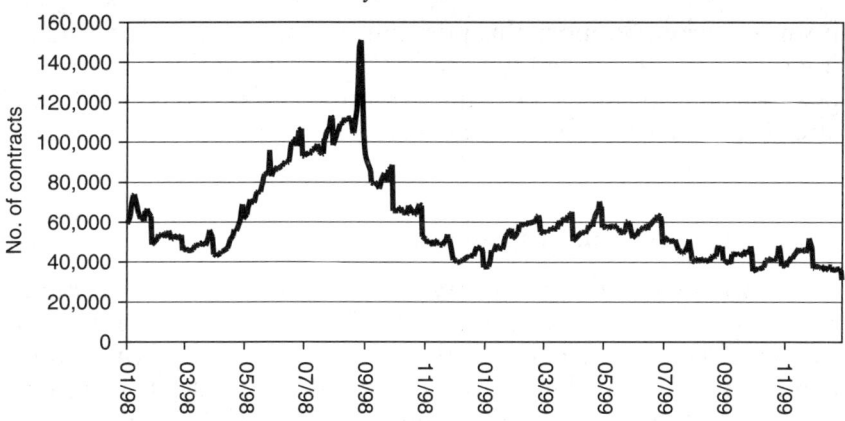

FIG. 5.2. Daily gross open interests (January 1998–December 1999).

TABLE 5.2. *Average amount of gross open interests by month (1998–99)*

Month (1998)	Contracts	Month (1999)	Contracts
January	65,614	January	47,328
February	52,920	February	58,242
March	48,661	March	58,590
April	51,494	April	58,981
May	75,398	May	57,432
June	92,957	June	57,735
July	99,002	July	48,490
August	115,469	August	42,565
September	84,637	September	43,197
October	65,869	October	40,401
November	50,291	November	43,892
December	42,887	December	37,182
Average for the year	70,540	Average for the year	49,365

more active than the other months. Table 5.2 gives the daily average gross open interest for the different months. From May 1998, the average open interest started to pick up, reaching 115,469 contracts in August. September saw a big drop from the August record, but only in October did the daily open interest return to a level close to that of the pre-intervention period. Comparing the speculators' 80,000 contracts that the Hong Kong government had estimated with the information given above, it does appear that the speculators had taken a massive position in Hong Kong's futures market. Suppose this position was only reached in August, it would have accounted for nearly 70 per cent of the daily market position on average. For the months before May 1998 and after October 1998, the average daily gross open interest is usually below 60,000.

5.2.1.2 Information by Contract

When we look at the by-contract information captured in Figure 5.3, the picture becomes even clearer. Normally, the open interest in a contract is at its peak around the beginning of its maturity month, and the amount quickly drops during the latter half of the month. Figure 5.3, however, reveals several abnormalities. First, the peak positions of the June, July, August and September contracts are much higher than the ones for other contracts. The June, July and August ones can be attributed to the speculators' accumulation, but the September contracts' position was partly due to the Hong Kong government selling. Second, we can see that the terminal positions of the August and September contracts, especially the August one, were much higher than the other contracts, i.e. there were many more contracts of these two months left to expire on the maturity day. For the August contracts, the figure was as high as 42,905. Third, the open position in the September contracts showed a much sharper decline after reaching its peak at the end of August

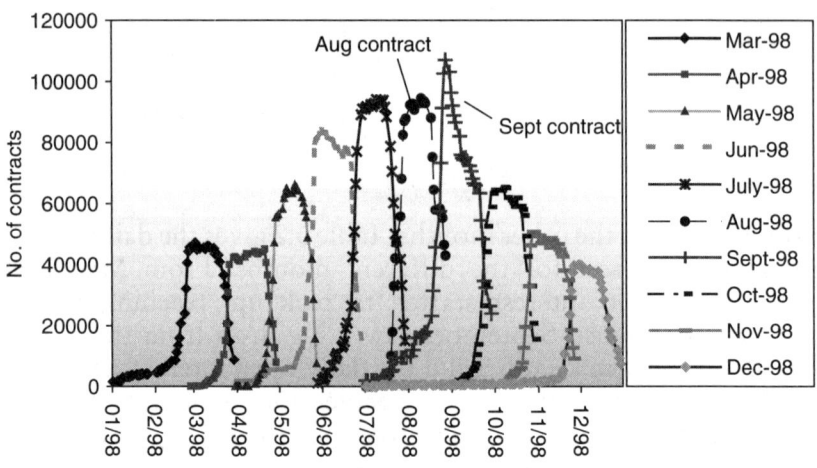

FIG. 5.3. Daily trading volumes of contracts with different maturities.

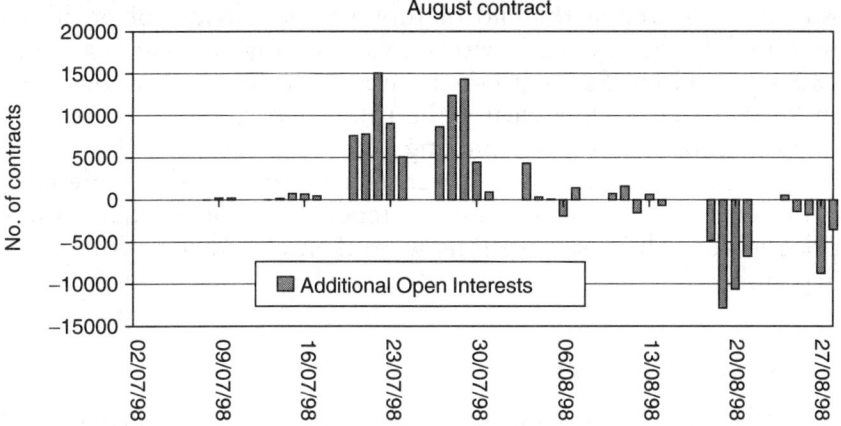

FIG. 5.4. Additional open interests for August futures contract.

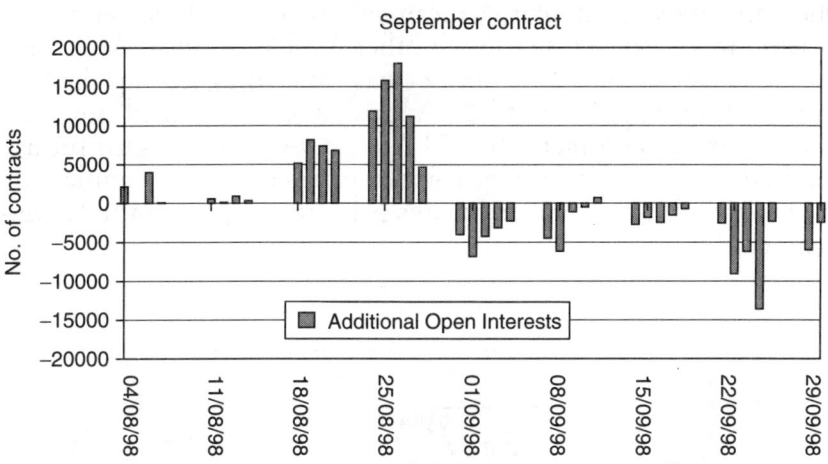

FIG. 5.5. Additional open interests for September futures contract.

1998. These two months can be examined more closely. Figures 5.4 and 5.5 present the daily additional open interest for the August and September contracts.

For each futures contract traded, the buyer (or the seller) can either be establishing a new position or offsetting an existing position; so the information reflected in the additional open interests is usually very mixed. However, for the August and September contracts, the speculators were presumably the main players (on the short side) and the change in open interests may well offer us some insight into their activities. For the August contracts, accumulation was concentrated at the end of July and the closure of positions was mainly in the last two weeks of August, starting from 18 August. Combined with the figure for the September contracts, those two weeks were clearly the rollover period, with positions in September contracts picking up very quickly. However, recall that the Hong Kong government also sold the September contracts short at this point, intending to push the futures price lower. All these positions were then closed out throughout September.

5.2.2 Price Behaviour

In addition to the enormous open interest positions around the intervention, we also note the deviations between the spot index and the different futures contracts. Figure 5.6 charts the daily movement of the mean prices of the three series: the prices moved very close to each other until 24 August. After that, it looks as if the spot index was first dragged up by the August futures prices until 28 August, and then pulled down by the September contracts after 28 August when the August futures expired. Nevertheless, the spot-index prices remained significantly higher than the September futures price throughout until 21 September.

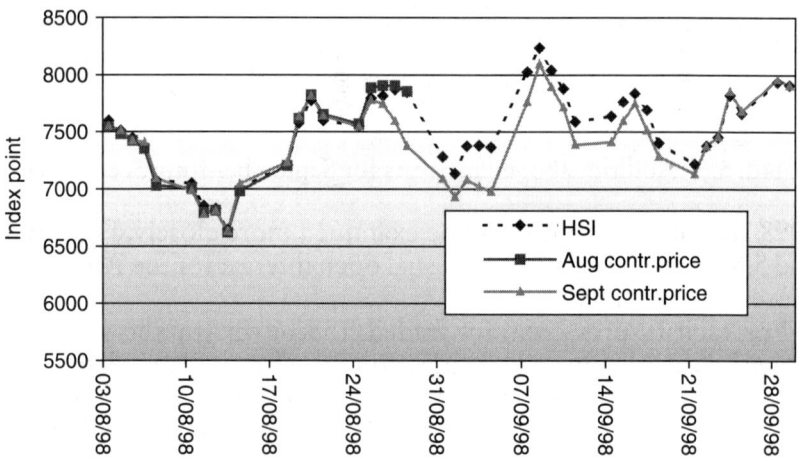

FIG. 5.6. Daily average of HSI spot index and August and September futures.

5.2.3 The basis

The basis is defined as the current price of a futures contract minus the spot price of the underlying asset: *basis* = $F - S$, and the theoretical no-arbitrage price of the index futures should be

$$F_t = S_t[1 + (r - d)(T - t)] \tag{5.1}$$

i.e., where S_t is the spot index level, r the riskless rate of interest, d the dividend yield of the equity index and $(T - t)$ the time to maturity in number of years. Thus the basis of the index futures should be equal to

$$\text{Basis}_t = F_t - S_t = S_t(r - d)(T - t) \tag{5.2}$$

Since the riskless rate of interest (r) is usually higher than the dividend yield of the equity index (d), the basis should normally be positive before maturity and zero at maturity (when $t = T$). To compare the basis at different index levels, we also define the *standardized basis* (*SB*) as the percentage of the spot index for later use.

$$SB_t = 100 \, (F_t - S_t)/S_t \tag{5.3}$$

In the 1987 crash, the basis was much larger than usual, and on 19 October 1987 it became negative. During the span of the intervention, the basis also behaved abnormally. Figure 5.7 shows the basis for the spot month futures contracts during August–October 1998.

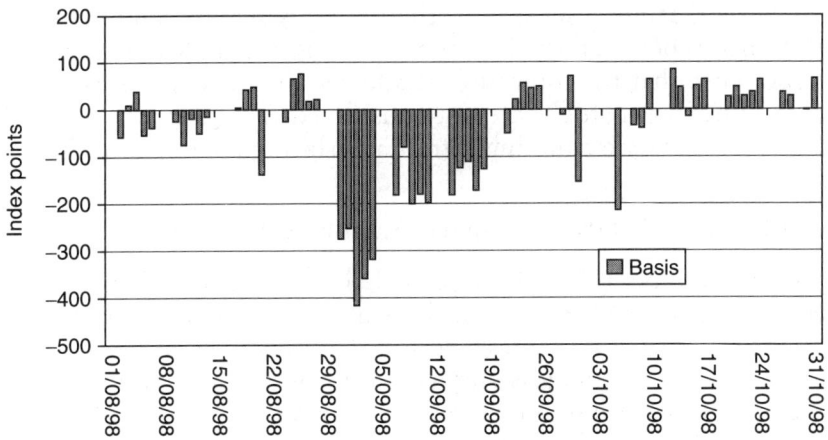

FIG. 5.7. The basis of spot-month HSI futures (August–October 1998).

The last trading days (28 August, 29 September, and 29 October) are not included in the figure because of the 'Asian' settlement style of HSI (settlement prices of HSI futures are the average of values of HSI at every 5-minute interval). Before the intervention, the basis was negative more often than positive, but the bases were not very large. The largest negative bases were concentrated in the three weeks starting from 31 August 1998. In the most serious instance, the basis went lower than −400 points. This irregular behaviour was corrected only in the last week of September, and thereafter the positive basis dominated throughout October 1998.

According to Fung and Lam (2000), the index basis could be used to identify occasions of overreaction in the index-futures market. When investors buy index futures after observing a negative basis, the returns should be higher than buying after a day that closes with a positive basis, i.e. the more negative the basis, the higher the returns of buying index futures. The relationship between the returns of index futures and the magnitude of the basis at the previous market close was tested (see Appendix I). We found that the normal negative relationship elucidated by Fung and Lam (2000) did not exist in the chosen pre-intervention period from May to July 1998, signifying that either the signalling effect of the basis was distorted or the trading activities on the futures market were abnormal. However, the relationship was restored after the period of government intervention.

5.2.4 Mispricings of HSI Futures

The basis that we discussed in the previous section simplifies the relationship between the futures prices and the underlying indices in the sense that the interest cost and the dividend yield from the index constituent stocks are not considered. That gap will be filled in this section by examining intra-day arbitrage opportunities.

5.2.4.1 Daily Arbitrage Opportunities by Contracts

Fung and Draper (2000) have provided a fairly detailed analysis of index futures arbitrage relationships during the financial crisis and the government intervention period. Compared with their study, the analysis here puts less emphasis on precise calculation of mispricings, and is going to be more descriptive. Also, we will review contract-specific price/mispricing behaviour. Our purpose is to pick out the time period(s) and the contracts that experienced particularly abnormal behaviour around the time of the government intervention. Therefore, the span is relatively short, covering a half-year of daily data from June 1998 to January 1999. We will continue to adopt a graphical approach.

Figure 5.8 shows the daily mispricings of the August, September and October futures in 1998. The mispricings are the gaps between the market prices of the futures contracts and their theoretical prices. The theoretical prices are calculated from equation 5.1, with the Hong Kong interbank one-month rate being the risk-free interest rate (r) and the actual month-end weighted average dividend yields being the dividend rate of the HSI (d). For the spot index and the index-futures price, we simply adopted the day-end levels.[10] Again, the last trading days were eliminated from the data series due to the 'Asian' settlement practice.[11] What we can see from

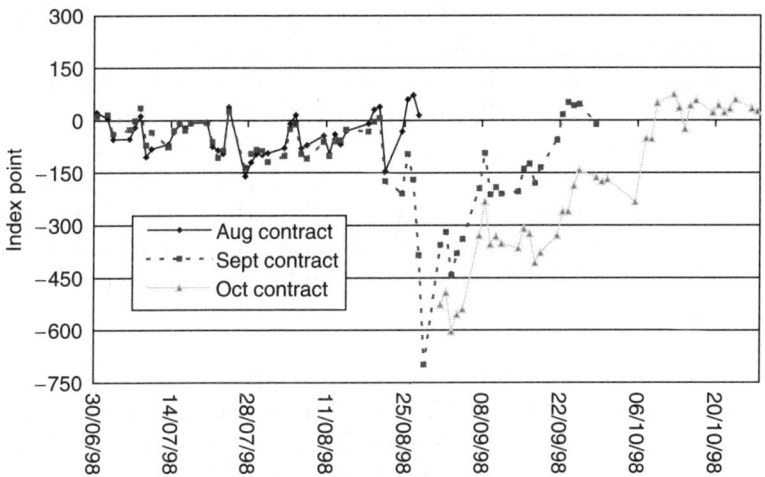

FIG. 5.8. The mispricings of August/September/October 1998 futures contracts.

[10] Note that the futures market and the spot market of Hong Kong closed at the same time (16:00) before 20 November 1998, but the futures market close was subsequently extended to 16:15.

[11] In Appendix II, we provide graphs showing the price performances of the selected futures contracts on their expiration days. We also checked the correlation coefficients between different futures bases and the index returns on the next trading day. The results suggest that the day-end bases of the spot month futures on their expiration days no longer carry any predictive power for the next day's index return, but instead, the bases of the second month futures do. However, this signalling effect of the second month futures was apparently distorted on 28 August 1998.

134 *Intervention to Save Hong Kong*

Figure 5.8 is that the abnormal mispricings started from the end of August 1998. The government was presumed to have been selling the September contracts at the time, with an aim to increase the rollover cost of the speculators. However, the underpricings of the futures contracts lasted long after that—the September contract went back to its normal range of pricing only near its expiration, while the pricing gap of the October contract closed in early October.

5.2.4.2 Mispricings of Futures Contracts and Short-selling Activities

So far we have not taken transaction costs of arbitrage activities into consideration, but even after allowing for those cost items, the abnormal mispricings still exist.

According to Fung and Draper (2000) (Table 5.3), during the intervention and in the following month, the transaction costs of index futures arbitrage was less than 70 index points for member firms and less than 110 for non-members. The mispricings of August, September and October 1998 contracts (see Figure 5.8) reveal that, even after the discount for the highest cost of 110 points, negative arbitrage gaps existed on all trading days between 31 August and 30 September for the October contract, and on most trading days until close to its expiration for the September contract (Table 5.4).

So, even after taking into account the transaction costs for members and non-members, negative arbitrage gaps existed on all occasions during September for the October contracts' trading, and on most of the days for the September contracts from end-August till one week before its expiration. Why did these large arbitrage gaps continue for such a long time? As we know, usually arbitrage activities tie the spot and futures markets together and are regarded as a normal feature of well-functioning markets. Although many previous studies have found that some arbitrage opportunities exist in various markets, including the US, UK, and Japan, those opportunities have usually been short-lived; and arbitrage gaps of the size which occurred in Hong Kong during August and September 1998 have seldom been seen before. What would explain this unusual phenomenon?

When the futures prices are relatively lower than their theoretical price, arbitrageurs should buy the underpriced assets, i.e. futures contracts in the stock index, and sell the overpriced asset, i.e. spot

TABLE 5.3. *Transaction costs for index-futures arbitrages in Hong Kong*

Groups		14/08/1998~04/09/1998	07/09/1998~30/09/1998	05/10/1998~30/10/1998
Members*	Halfway percentage cost[†]	0.84	0.84	0.84
	Average HSI	7543.00	7729.00	9195.00
	Average cost[‡]	63.36	64.92	77.24
Non-members	Halfway percentage cost	1.41	1.39	1.41
	Average HSI	7543.00	7729.00	9195.00
	Average cost	106.36	107.43	129.65

*In addition to the trading and settlement fees that member firms of the SEHK and the HKFE have to pay, non-members have to pay commissions to their brokers (or the member firms).
[†]Information on the halfway percentage cost was extracted from Fung and Draper (2000), which refers to the one-side percentage arbitrage cost.
[‡]Besides those fees and commissions, the bid-ask spread of trading the spot index portfolio has also been included in the transaction cost.

TABLE 5.4. *Arbitrage gap after deduction of different transaction costs*

Date	September contract		October contract	
	Member	Non-member	Member	Non-member
14/08/1998	0*	0		
18/08/1998	0	0		
19/08/1998	0	0		
20/08/1998	0	0		
21/08/1998	−111	−68		
24/08/1998	−147	−104		
25/08/1998	0	0		
26/08/1998	−107	−64		
27/08/1998	−323	−280		
28/08/1998	−637	−594		
31/08/1998	−294	−251	−463	−420
01/09/1998	−257	−214	−429	−386
02/09/1998	−380	−337	−541	−498
03/09/1998	−317	−274	−492	−449
04/09/1998	−276	−233	−477	−434
07/09/1998	−131	−89	−264	−222
08/09/1998	−28	0	−168	−126
09/09/1998	−147	−105	−290	−248
10/09/1998	−127	−85	−267	−225
11/09/1998	−146	−104	−288	−246
14/09/1998	−140	−98	−300	−258
15/09/1998	−73	−31	−245	−203
16/09/1998	−59	−17	−260	−218
17/09/1998	−115	−73	−343	−301
18/09/1998	−70	−28	−314	−272
21/09/1998	0	0	−265	−223
22/09/1998	0	0	−196	−154
23/09/1998	0	0	−195	−153
24/09/1998	0	0	−123	−81
25/09/1998	0	0	−77	−35
28/09/1998	0	0	−98	−56
29/09/1998	0	0	−109	−67
30/09/1998			−103	−61
Total trading days	32	32	23	23
Arbitrage days	20	19	23	23

*0 means the mispricing is within the transaction cost bound.

shares in the index. But such observed opportunities may be left unexplored due to the high risk involved. When calculating the theoretical price of the futures contracts, we have actually made several assumptions, such as no marking to the market, constant riskless interest rate, certain dividends, no transaction cost, no restrictions on short-selling and simultaneous trading, etc. Many previous studies have, therefore, focused on the non-practicality of arbitrage activities when there are violations of some of these assumptions. The difficulty with trading too many constituent stocks at the same time and restrictions on short-selling in the spot market are also mentioned in many studies.[12]

Short-selling is often used in arbitrage activities when the futures market is underpriced. It involves sales of stocks that the seller does not own. In some markets, this activity is subject to certain restrictions or even forbidden. In the US, a share can only be sold short if its last price movement was upwards (uptick rule). In the UK, on the other hand, any trader can short-sell shares and there is no uptick rule; however, share-borrowing facilities are only available to UK market-makers and certain members of the London International Financial Futures Exchange (LIFFE). In Japan, restrictions on short-selling were tightened in the early months of 2002. In Germany, the banks are prevented from lending shares to their customers for use in a short sale; it is also banned in Singapore and Norway. In Hong Kong, short-selling was a criminal offence until 3 January 1994. Later, 17 HSI constituent stocks were allowed to be sold short on an uptick. The uptick rule was lifted and short-selling was opened up for all 33 stocks of the index since 25 March 1996. However, Fung and Draper (2000) suggest that many more difficulties and risks were involved in short-selling activities during the intervention and the period which followed, and that it led to the abnormally large arbitrage gaps.

First, a lack of stock-lenders in the market could limit the supply of stocks and thus increase the difficulty of short-selling. Lenders of Hong Kong stocks are mostly overseas institutions, lending through their custodian banks. A lending fee is charged to borrowers with a varying rate, which could be very high when the market is tight. Moreover, liquidity was seriously reduced after the massive purchases made by the government. Arbitrageurs who needed to short-sell the stocks had to face both a high lending rate and a considerable uncertainty of finding a lender when they were faced with a call notice. Since buying in the open market could be equally expensive, this lack of lending facilities could seriously handicap investors from shorting stocks. Clearly, these factors made short-selling much more difficult.

Second, after the intervention, several restrictive measures on short-selling in Hong Kong were immediately put into effect. The measures included a special margin rate of 150 per cent on

[12] See, for example, Sofianos (1993), Puttonen (1993), and Pope and Yadav (1994).

large open positions announced on 29 August 1998, the uptick rule reintroduced on 7 September 1998[13], and the strict implementation of the $T+2$ delivery requirement from 27 September.[14] Besides, 2 September 1998 also saw a suspension of short-selling on three big HSI stocks: HSBC Holdings Plc (00005), Hong Kong Telecommunications Ltd (00008), and China Telecom (Hong Kong) Ltd (00941). This decision was made because the Hong Kong Securities Clearing Company reported settlement failures in these three stocks for some transactions conducted on 27 and 28 August. These three stocks represent a large proportion of the HSI, with HSBC accounting for 28.29 per cent, China Telecom 8.45 per cent and Hong Kong Telecom 11.09 per cent of the index's weighting. The short-sales volume slumped immediately to 1.508 million shares on that day from 6.898 million on the previous day. Table 5.5 gives the short-sales turnovers in August and September 1998.

By using a regression of mispricings of spot month futures prices on the short sale/total underpricings ratios, as well as futures return volatility and time to maturity of futures contract, Fung and Draper (2000) concluded that the coefficient for the short sales/total underpricings ratio was significantly negative (P-value = 0.0570). Here we would offer a simpler correlation analysis. Since the short-sale constraints started after the intervention, we separate the data into two periods: pre-intervention as from 3 to 28 August and post-intervention as from 29 August to 29 September 1998.

Since it would have been more difficult for arbitrageurs to bridge the spot-index gaps when short-selling was restrained, we expected a positive correlation between mispricings of futures contracts and short sale turnovers after the intervention. The above result confirmed our understanding that the short selling constraints can offer an explanation for the existence of arbitrage gaps in both spot-month futures and the second-month futures. But we would conjecture that the huge mispricings on 27 and 28 August 1998 are in large part because of the government's intervention to drive down the September futures contract. By doing this as well as by propping up the spot-market prices, the government was

---

[13] Measures to tighten up securities and futures markets, http://www.hknews.com.hk , 7 September 1998.

[14] Although the $T+2$ rule was always specified for delivery, overdue settlement was usually allowed during $T+3$ to $T+5$. This practice, however, was restrained from 24 September 1998 onwards.

TABLE 5.5. *Number of short-sold shares (August–September 1998)*

Date	No. of shares	Date	No. of shares
03/08/98	36,132,200	01/09/98	6,898,000
04/08/98	3,339,800	02/09/98	1,508,000
05/08/98	8,354,300	03/09/98	3,682,300
06/08/98	18,085,600	04/09/98	1,614,500
07/08/98	18,073,900	07/09/98	4,847,200
10/08/98	5,913,200	08/09/98	8,489,700
11/08/98	18,047,800	09/09/98	3,714,400
12/08/98	5,491,000	10/09/98	8,998,200
13/08/98	13,252,300	11/09/98	9,595,100
14/08/98	13,243,300	14/09/98	10,368,000
18/08/98	4,995,600	15/09/98	7,631,400
19/08/98	5,979,200	16/09/98	6,826,300
20/08/98	4,870,000	17/09/98	7,282,600
21/08/98	2,903,600	18/09/98	11,676,600
24/08/98	29,651,400	21/09/98	5,729,500
25/08/98	11,342,100	22/09/98	7,529,000
26/08/98	45,757,600	23/09/98	7,012,100
27/08/98	104,265,200	24/09/98	14,972,000
28/08/98	401,654,382	25/09/98	12,147,200
31/08/98	9,873,300	28/09/98	8,732,600
		29/09/98	16,242,500
Average	38,061,289	Average	7,462,735

Source: Stock Exchange of Hong Kong monthly bulletin.

attempting to cut the linkage between the two markets. They might have thought that it would be difficult for arbitrageurs to undertake arbitrage deals because share-lending facilities were running out in Hong Kong. Whether the Hong Kong authorities realized it or not, the arbitrageurs still had access to overseas lending sources. For example, in an extraordinary disclosure to the London Stock Exchange, HSBC Holdings revealed that HSBC Investment Bank held about 29.1 million of the group's sterling-denominated shares between 4 and 7 September 1998. The report stated that more than 82 per cent of the total quantity of shares was related to customer-driven stock lending and borrowing. Some analysts suspected that,[15] following the HKMA's acquisitions, HSBC Investment Bank—the securities arm of HSBC Holdings—had been warehousing the stock and was borrowing some of it to service its short-selling clients. The short-selling turnover was huge on 28 August,

---

[15] 'HSBC stock made available for shorts by own offshoot', *South China Morning Post*, 10 September 1998.

TABLE 5.6. *Correlation between the volume of short-sell turnover and mispricings of the spot/second-month futures*

Correlations	Short-sell shares 30/6/98–13/8/98	31/8/98–29/10/98
Mispricings* of spot month futures	−0.4974	0.5523
P-value	0.0038	0.0002
Mispricings* of second-month futures	−0.4526	0.5440
P-value	0.1193	0.0003
Corrleations	Total value of short sell 30/6/98–13/8/98	31/8/98–29/10/98
Mispricings* of spot month futures	−0.3601	0.2164
P-value	0.0429	0.1800
Mispricings* of second-month futures	−0.3725	0.2321
P-value	0.0358	0.1495

*Mispricing without deduction for transaction cost: Mispricing >0 if futures contract is overpriced, and <0 if underpriced.

with 401.65 million shares being sold short. By the end of the day, although they successfully maintained the massive gap between the spot index and the September futures, the Hong Kong authorities ended up with a vastly larger number of shares than they had planned or, we think, expected to buy. Had they failed to anticipate the deluge of shares on 28 August that the massive arbitrage gap, in practice, brought about? And did this deluge so withdraw liquidity from the market that, combined with the added restrictions, the arbitrage gap then continued for weeks afterwards?

CHAPTER 6

Financing the Intervention

6.1 What was the Source of the Funds Used?

At various points in this book, it may have sounded as if the government used taxpayers' money for the intervention. In the literal sense that the funds employed by the HKMA came directly from inflows of tax receipts, this is not the case. The one sense in which the authorities were, however, using *taxpayers' money* was that any loss/profit from the intervention would (ultimately) accrue to the taxpayers.

It would have been entirely impossible to levy taxes with such speed and to such a large extent to fund the intervention purchases. Instead, as described below, the funds were obtained by financial rearrangements, selling existing Exchange Fund assets and issuing additional HKMA debt.

As will be reported subsequently in Chapter 7, in this instance the taxpayers benefited considerably, with a dramatic improvement in the authorities fiscal position. The previously projected deficit of HK $36.5 billion for the fiscal year (1999–2000) turned out to be only HK $1.6 billion, being almost entirely offset by the capital gain from the intervention. According to Donald Tsang, Financial Secretary of HKSAR at that time, 'The increase in the HSI from 10,049 at the end of 1998 to 16,962 at the end of 1999 has boosted the value of the portfolio of Hong Kong stocks acquired by the Exchange Fund in 1998.... As a result, the investment earnings on our fiscal reserves have soared to HK $44 billion, almost double our original estimate of HK $22.2 billion'.[1]

---

[1] 'Hong Kong finances in better shape than expected', *China Daily*, 9 March 2000.

Nevertheless, those in authority who take decisions on intervention do not, in general, share in the pecuniary outcome of their decisions. It is sometimes held that such freedom to gamble with other peoples' money may unduly bias officials towards excessive intervention. But this view ignores the non-pecuniary incentives. Those responsible for the intervention, notably Donald Tsang, the Financial Secretary, and Joseph Yam, the head of the HKMA, were putting their careers on the line by taking this step. If the exercise came to be perceived as a failure, there was a strong likelihood that they would be forced to resign. The upside for personal success was, we believe, much less than the downside for failure for the officials involved.

This asymmetry in non-pecuniary incentives, we would argue, is a significant factor in restraining official intervention much more widely. Even where central banks perceive their currencies as fundamentally misaligned, they are generally reluctant to take steps to intervene (i.e. sterilised intervention). This is so even when such interventions are perceived as having an expected positive net value to taxpayers, because of the fear of what possible failure might do to the institution's (and to the individual's) reputation and credibility.

In the British television programme *Yes, Minister* the official's most serious act of warning to his minister is to suggest that some proposed line of action would be a 'brave policy'. There is no doubt that intervention was a 'brave policy'!

One reason it could be termed thus is that such intervention is both high profile and transparent. This book, put together entirely from the public records, is itself witness to the transparency with which government bodies work. Compare and contrast this with the opacity on the side of the counter-party speculators. We know nothing about them from the public records, not even their identities, let alone their positions and profits/losses. All the information we have is inferential, and largely derived from our assessment of the official side. If the speculators had 'won' to the extent that the authorities actually did in this case, Tsang and Yam would probably have lost their jobs and endangered their careers. We have no idea whether this setback made the slightest difference to the 'losing' speculators, to their careers, or even who they were.

It is surely right that governments should adhere to higher standards of accountability and transparency, since they are wagering moneys initially raised by non-voluntary, state-power imposed taxation. On the other hand, those who transfer savings voluntarily to commercial financial intermediaries can observe and, to an extent, choose the governance controls on managerial risk-taking. Even so, the discrepancy between the relative transparency of, and subsequent incentives on, the official side and those applying to the speculators has raised some concerns and questioning, at least in Asia, though less so elsewhere.

The above discussion has been somewhat of a digression. In the first instance, a central bank, or a monetary authority, like the HKMA, does not need to obtain any outside funding to buy a financial asset. It simply pays for its purchase by writing a cheque upon itself. This is a standard open market operation (injecting liquidity into the system). From one viewpoint, the HKMA's intervention in the equity market can be seen as a massive positive open–market operation, albeit in a financial market that is not normally used as a vehicle for such an exercise. Nevertheless, the direct effect of such an intervention, after settlement, is to leave the seller of the stock with a claim on the central bank. The payee will then deposit the cheque with his commercial bank, of which a proportion, (selecting a number which can only be a rough approximation), say *two-fifths*, will go towards reducing an existing overdraft or loan, while the remaining *three-fifths* goes towards raising deposits. Abstracting from the special currency board arrangements in Hong Kong, and starting from an illustrative position as shown:

Let us now assume that the government buys 10 equities from the private sector. The direct result is:

TABLE 6.1. *Illustration of monetary effect of equity market purchase. (a–d)*

(a)

Items	Private sector investors		Commercial banks	
	Assets	Liabilities	Assets	Liabilities
Deposits	100			100
Bank loans		70	70	
Cash	20		10	
Central Bank debt	20		10	
Equity	1000			15
Other assets	?		25	
Total	?	70	115	115

(b)

	Central Bank (Exchange Fund)	
Items	Assets	Liabilities
Cash		30
Debt		30
Owed to government (accumulated surplus)		200
Foreign Exchange	230	
Domestic Assets	30	
Total	260	260

(c)

	Private sector investors		Commercial banks	
Items	Assets	Liabilities	Assets	Liabilities
Deposits	106 (+6)			106
Bank loans		66(−4)	66 (−4)	
Equities	990 (−10)			
Cash	unchanged		20 (+10)	
Total			+6	+6

(d)

	Central Bank	
	Assets	Liabilities
Cash		40 (+10)
Domestic assets	40 (+10)	

The direct result of such positive open market operations is, of course, an injection of enormous liquidity into the system. But such liquification of the banking system would be totally inappropriate when the currency is under attack, in part because excessive cash reserves would drive interest rates rapidly down to zero, hardly a desired response in such cases. Moreover, and just as important, such massive expansion of the monetary base under such circumstances would be completely at odds with both the spirit and the letter of a currency board system.

So the cash injection from the intervention had to be sterilised by a sale of existing HKMA assets, or by the sale of additional HKMA/ government liabilities. As shown in the illustrative tables above, the largest part of the HKMA's assets was its foreign exchange holdings. As of June 1998, the HKMA held some US $96.5 billion as foreign currency reserve assets (Table 6.2). By comparison, as shown in the Exchange Fund balance sheet for end-June 1998 (Table 6.3), the monetary base[2] amounted to HK $90.5 billion, while the Exchange Fund Bills and Notes, which were in effect to be added to the monetary base by the currency board reforms of September 1998,[3] amounted to another HK $88 billion, or about HK $180 billion in all, or US $23 billion. So the HKMA had some US $70 billion of 'free' reserves, over and above the amount strictly needed as backing for the monetary base under the currency board system.

Central banks tend to keep their reserves primarily in the form of liquid, short-dated foreign government debt, mostly in US debt, treasury bills, and short bonds. Given the 'link', the HKMA held its foreign currency assets largely in such US government securities.[4] The market for such assets was very liquid, and they could be mobilized immediately at very little transaction cost without moving the market against the seller.

The second leg of the speculators' 'double play' was to attack the Hong Kong dollar directly by sales of futures and forwards in the foreign exchange market. So, for the authorities, the natural counter to the double play was to support the foreign exchange market too. While the speculators were selling futures (and forwards) in both the equity and the foreign exchange markets, the authorities were countering by buying the spot market in both cases. The statistics for HKMA foreign currency reserve assets show a decline from US $96 billion at end-July to US $87.6 billion at end-August, a fall of

---

[2] The monetary base in Hong Kong includes Certificates of Indebtedness, coins in circulation, and the aggregate balance of the banking system.

[3] To further strengthen the currency board arrangements and make them less susceptible to manipulation by speculators to produce extreme conditions in the interbank market and interest rates, the HKMA announced, on 5 September 1998, a package of seven technical measures. Freer access to end-day liquidity through the use of Exchange Fund paper, which is fully backed by foreign currency reserves, is allowed. New Exchange Fund paper is to be issued only when there is an inflow of funds. This will ensure that all new Exchange Fund paper will be fully backed by foreign currency reserves.

[4] The Exchange Fund is managed as two distinct portfolios. The first is a backing portfolio to ensure that the monetary base is fully backed by highly liquid, short-term US dollar-denominated interest-bearing securities. The second is an investment portfolio to preserve the long-term purchasing power of these assets.

146 *Intervention to Save Hong Kong*

TABLE 6.2. *HKMA foreign currency reserve assets as at 30 June 1998*

At the end of		(US$ mn)
Foreign currency reserve assets	Exchange Fund[5]	77,858
	Land Fund	18,645
	Total	96,503
Unsettled forward transactions	Exchange Fund	24
	Land Fund	(17)
	Total	7
Foreign currency reserve assets (including forward transactions)	Exchange Fund	77,882
	Land Fund	18,628
	Total	96,510

Source: http://www.info.gov.hk/hkma.

TABLE 6.3. *Exchange Fund balance sheet as at 30 June 1998*

ASSETS	(HK$ mn)
Cash and short-term funds	98,615
Fixed deposits	50,565
Certificates of deposit	43,522
Investments	446,774
Mortgage loans	4,141
Fixed assets	287
Other assets	15,633
Total assets	659,537
LIABILITIES	
Certificates of Indebtedness	84,675
Coins in circulation	5,648
Balance of the banking system	497
Exchange Fund Bills and Notes	87,758
Placements by other government funds	246,775
Placements by other institutions	24,887
Other liabilities	7,272
Total liabilities	457,492
NET ASSETS	202,045
Representing	
Accumulated surplus	201,949
Minority interests	96
Total	202,045

Source: http://www.info.gov.hk/hkma.

[5] From October 1997, the foreign currency assets have been adjusted to exclude the loans extended to Thailand under the financing package organized by the International Monetary Fund (IMF).

$8.4 billion. It takes two working days to settle foreign exchange transactions and 29–30 August 1998 was the weekend. Table 6.3 shows that unsettled forward transactions on 31 August amounted to the relatively huge amount of US $4.45 billion, probably representing spot deals made on 28 August but not yet completed.

Even though US $8.4 billion is a massive amount, it only represents half the total amount spent on the intervention. In addition, as we will record later, HKMA's outstanding Exchange Fund Bills and Notes rose by about HK $9.5 billion (US $1.2 billion) between end-June and end-December 1998 which can reasonably be ascribed to the need to finance the equity purchases. But this means that we have only identified the source of US $9.6 billion to offset the total cost of purchasing equities worth US $15 billion.

Until and unless the HKMA reveals the precise financing details, we are not in a position to identify the source of finances for the remaining amount. In our view, it is very likely that the HKMA would have offset the effect of the initial, immediate expenditure of equity purchases by domestic money market operations, repos, and outright sales of bills and notes. This is more probable since they would not have been able to gauge the likely expenditure on each day until the end of business on that day. Thereafter, on the next day or so, the HKMA would have been able to decide what proportion of the finance should come from external or internal assets. Since about two-thirds of the equity purchases were done on the final two days, and almost half on the final day, 28 August, we believe that much of the external financing of the August equity purchases was probably pushed into September, the details of which will have been obscured by other events, including a possible flow-back of reserves to the HKMA in the course of the month. Moreover, statistics on foreign currency reserves can always be manipulated, for example by swaps, and until recent years was so manipulated by many central banks. There is no evidence whatsoever to suggest that the HKMA engaged in such practices on this occasion. However, the fact that Table 6.4 only reveals a fall in foreign exchange reserves of US $8.4 billion to end-August, with marginal increases thereafter till end-December, is consistent with the view, which we hold, that the greater majority of the financing of the intervention was funded by the sale of foreign exchange assets.

Indeed, we can look at the whole episode from a slightly different angle—as an example (with some idiosyncratic elements) of sterilised intervention in the foreign exchange market. Under such

TABLE 6.4. *Month-end foreign currency reserves (June–October 1998) (Includes both Exchange Fund and Land Fund)*

Date	Excluding unsettled foreign exchange contracts (US$ bn)	Unsettled foreign exchange contracts (US$ bn)	Including unsettled foreign exchange contracts (US$ bn)
June	96.503	0.007	96.510
July	96.541	(0.530)	96.007
August	92.069	(4.450)*	87.624
September	88.394	(0.160)	88.231
October	88.669	(0.140)	88.534

*This arises from 'spot' transactions (settlement in two days) done at the end of August for settlement at the beginning of September.
Source: http://www.info.gov.hk/hkma.

sterilised intervention, the central bank sells (buys) foreign exchange securities, which withdraws (injects) domestic cash from the market. Then, to sterilise the effect of such cash flows on the money market and banking system, the central bank has to buy (sell) other domestic assets. Normally, with sterilised intervention, such assets would be domestic government debt. In this unusual case, they were private sector equities, but the effect on the monetary base, money market, and monetary aggregates would, to a first approximation, be the same.[6]

Tables 6.1a–6.1d illustrate the effect of an equity purchase of 10 by a central bank. We now show in Table 6.5(a)–6.5(b) what happens when this starting point is financed by a sale of 10 foreign exchange assets. As can be seen from these Tables, sterilised intervention, as effected by the HKMA, will simply turn foreign exchange assets into domestic assets (Hang Seng equities) offset by a contrary shift in the portfolio of Hong Kong private investors, leaving unchanged the monetary base, the money market (and the level of interest rates), and the monetary aggregates, to a first approximation. As noted in footnote 6, there can be some second-order effects depending on the various identities of the counterparties to this exercise, and how they, in turn, finance their own

[6] Insofar as the respective counterparties in the equity market, for example Hong Kong resident non-bank investors, non-Hong Kong non-bank investors, Hong Kong banks, etc., might be expected to be somewhat different from those in the government debt market, there could be some second-order differential effects. We would, however, hesitate even to give a sign to such effects, let alone any quantification.

TABLE 6.5. *Illustration of money market sterilisation of equity market purchase. (a–b)*

(a)

	Private sector investors		Commercial banks	
Items	Asset	Liability	Asset	Liability
Deposits	106 − 6 = 100			106 − 6 = 100
Bank loans		66 + 4 = 70	70	
Equities	990			
Foreign exchange assets	10			
Cash	20		20 − 10 = 10	

(b)

	Central Bank	
Items	Asset	Liability
Cash		30
Domestic assets	30 + 10 = 40	
Foreign exchange assets	230 − 10 = 220	
Total		260

transaction, but these, we suggest, are likely to be both second-order and unpredictable in advance.

Thus the expectation should be that this massive (sterilised) intervention would have no effect on the monetary base, or the monetary aggregates on the balance sheets of the commercial banks. (Table 6.6 lists the related data for the months from June to October 1998.)

There is no indication of any significant jump in any of these series in August or September. The Hong Kong monetary system was largely insulated from the disturbances in the other financial markets.

Although it is our belief that considerably more of the US $15 billion market intervention was funded from foreign exchange assets than the US $8.4 billion shown at end-August, nevertheless some, probably smaller, proportion could have come from the sale of domestic assets by the HKMA. The Exchange Fund balance sheet shows a large jump between June 1998 and December 1998 in Bills and Notes—from some HK $88 billion in June 1998 to HK $98 billion in December 1998.

The HKMA wanted to make the Hong Kong bond market larger and more liquid, as part of their general campaign to

Intervention to Save Hong Kong

TABLE 6.6. *Money supply of Hong Kong (June–October 1998)*

Money supply		June	July	August	September	October
M1	HK $	170,182	170,439	167,163	168,944	173,238
	FC*	18,030	19,659	19,073	19,792	21,549
	Total	188,212	190,099	186,236	188,737	194,787
M2	HK $	1,681,941	1,747,638	1,758,351	1,771,012	1,801,464
	FC	1,135,043	1,169,993	1,202,651	1,222,227	1,257,642
	Total	2,816,983	2,917,631	2,961,002	2,993,238	3,059,106
M3	HK $	1,696,290	1,761,541	1,773,388	1,783,759	1,813,702
	FC	1,181,753	1,218,207	1,252,296	1,269,022	1,306,918
	Total	2,878,043	2,979,747	3,025,683	3,052,781	3,120,619

*FC: foreign currencies.

Source: http://www.info.gov.hk/hkma.

TABLE 6.7. *Liabilities of the Exchange Fund*

Liabilities	December 1997	June 1998*	December 1998[†]
Certificates of Indebtedness	87,015	84,675	86,465
Coins in circulation	5,399	5,648	5,778
Balance of the banking system	296	497	2,527
Exchange Fund Bills and Notes	89,338	87,758	98,334
Placements by other government funds	237,629	246,775	424,562
Placements by other institutions	21,062	24,887	21,401
Other liabilities	5,740	7,272	39,902
Total liabilities	446,479	457,492	678,969

*Unaudited figures.

[†]As from November 1998, the assets of the Land Fund were merged into the Exchange Fund.
Source: HKMA Monthly Statistical Bulletin.

foster a well-functioning, liquid bond market, in which private companies—both mainland and Hong Kong—could raise bonds (as an alternative and diversification from equities and bank loans).[7] They may have seen the need to raise funds to sterilise the equity purchases as a useful opportunity to extend and enlarge the available outstanding portfolio of their Exchange Fund Bills and Notes.

In addition, and finally, any (perhaps seasonal) inflow of net tax receipts could have gone directly into equity purchases. Only to

---

[7] See, for example, the speech by Andrew Sheng at the First Annual Pan-Asia Bonds Summit, 'Future Directions for Hong Kong's Debt Market', 29–30 November 1994, or the keynote address by Joseph Yam at the Asian Debt Conference, 'Development of the Debt Market', 14 July 1997.

this, almost certainly fairly minimal, degree could the intervention be said to have directly used *taxpayers' money*. Also there might have been some other, again probably fairly minimal, rearrangement of HKMA and the Exchange Fund domestic assets to fund the equity purchases, for example, running down existing deposit balances already held with Hong Kong commercial banks, but, if used at all, these were probably both de minimis and temporary.

6.2 How did the Speculators' Attack and the Government Intervention Affect the Foreign Exchange Market?

During the period from 1 July to 30 October 1998, which saw the major speculative attack on the Hong Kong dollar, and on the Hang Seng market, the spot level of the Hong Kong dollar was held within very narrow bands, between 7.7500 (on the weak side) on 7 August and 7.7440 (on the strong side) on 25 August. Figure 6.1 records the end-daily data for the Hong Kong dollar against the US dollar from 1 July till 30 October 1998.

Why did the spot rate remain so stable, despite the speculative attack? As will be discussed shortly below, the speculators were selling forwards (futures). This opened up a sizeable discount, i.e. the forward rate stood above the spot rate on the weaker side, indicating a possible risk of a devaluation. To the extent that there was a forward discount on the Hong Kong dollar, *given* unchanged interest rates, there would be a virtually riskless profit to be made by arbitrageurs, via covered interest arbitrage.[8] They could sell the

---

[8] Covered interest arbitrage is a process designed to take advantage of interest rate differentials between two currencies that exceed the foreign exchange premium or discount implied by forward prices. There are many textbook accounts of this. We give the following example. In the case of Hong Kong dollar/US dollar, the interest rate parity condition can be restated as:

$$(1 + r_{hk}) = (1 + r_{us})(F_t/S_0) = (1 + r_{us})[1 + (F_t - S_0)/S_0]$$

r_{hk} and r_{us} are, respectively, the interest rate of Hong Kong and the United States over the period of t months.

F_t is the t-month forward exchange rate and S_0 the spot exchange rate.
$[(F_t - S_0)/S_0]$ is the forward premium or discount.

Suppose that the 3-month interest rates (per annum) for the two countries are 8 per cent and 6 per cent, then r_{hk} and r_{us} are 2 per cent and 1.5 per cent, respectively. If the spot exchange rate is 7.7500 and F_t is 7.8000, then it follows that $(1 + r_{hk})/(1 + r_{us}) < (F_t/S_0)$.

An arbitrageur can then benefit from a strategy of selling Hong Kong dollar spot, and buying forward. A numerical example is given in footnote 9.

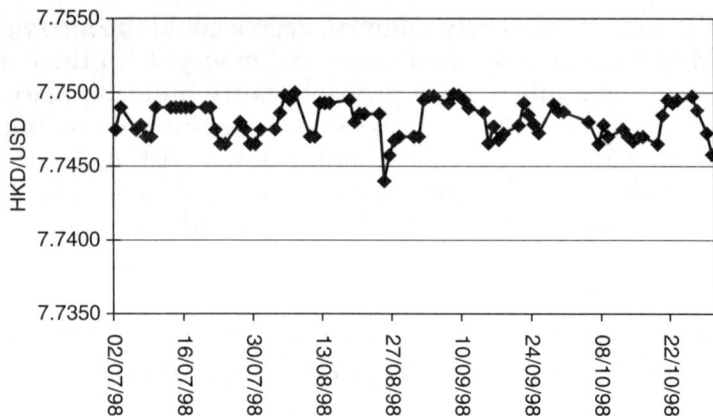

FIG. 6.1. Day-end spot exchange rate of Hong Kong dollar against US dollar (July–October 1998).

Hong Kong dollar spot and use the US dollar proceeds to invest in US riskless government assets, covering the US dollar exposure by buying back the now cheaper Hong Kong dollar forward. Such covered interest arbitrage then transfers the speculative pressure on the forwards back into the spot market.[9]

This combination of speculative pressure on the forwards, transmitted back to the spot foreign exchange market by covered interest arbitrage, can be met (unless the authorities surrender to the

[9] Using the assumed numbers (rates) in the preceding footnote, an arbitrageur can make a (risk-free) profit from adopting the following strategy:

1. Borrowing HK $1 million at 2 per cent for 3 months.
2. Sell HK $1 million spot at US $1 = HK $7.7500 for US $129,032.
3. Invest US $129,032 at 1.5 per cent for 3 months.
4. Make a forward contract to exchange US $130,967 for Hong Kong dollar in 3 months at the 3-month forward rate of 7.8000.

In 3 months the following occurs:

1. US dollar deposit matures, delivering US $129,032(1.015) = US $130,967
2. $130,967 are sold under the forward contract for US $130,967(7.8) = HK $1,021,543.
3. Pay back the bank loan of HK $1,000,000(1.02) = HK $1,020,000 and the net profit from this process is HK $1,543.

Whenever there is a large forward discount on Hong Kong dollar (F_t is particularly high), there is a chance for the arbitrageurs to make a profit by selling the Hong Kong dollar spot and buying it forward. Thus, the discount pressure on the forward exchange market can be easily transferred to the spot market.

pressure by a devaluation of the peg, the 'link' in the case of Hong Kong) either by raising Hong Kong interest rates, (to remove or even reverse the arbitrage margin), or by direct intervention to buy the Hong Kong dollar being sold by the arbitrageurs. On the occasion of previous speculative attacks, as will be shown in more detail in Section 6.3, the authorities had chosen the first route—interest rate defence–but this had unhinged the stock market. Now the speculators in their 'double-play' were betting that this would happen again. It was the authorities' aim, in turn, to undermine the speculators' position by taking the second route–direct intervention.

We have discussed the limited available data on the quantity of sales of US dollars and purchases of Hong Kong dollars, undertaken by the HKMA in Section 6.1. Here we note that the progress of the battle between the speculators and the government can be charted by the scale of the forward discount. Ever after the first speculative attack on the Hong Kong dollar, on 23 October 1997, there was a continuing perceived risk of further attacks and a possible readjustment of the 'link', possibly in the context of a simultaneous, or preceding, devaluation of the Chinese Renminbi, of which there was much talk at the time, some of which no doubt emanated from the speculators themselves, since it suited their book to spread concern about the future of both currencies.

Be that as it may, we show end-weekly figures for the 3-month forward discount on the Hong Kong dollar from the first week of October 1997 to the last week of December 1998 (Figure 6.2).

Figure 6.2 shows that the 3-month forward discount in July was about normal for the non-attack periods from October 1997 onwards. Thereafter, starting about the beginning of August, the evidence of increasing speculative pressure begins to build. We turn to higher frequency data, end-daily figures for the 3-month discount (not surprisingly, other period forward rates, e.g. one week to a year, show an entirely similar time path) for the period from 1 July to 30 October 1998. Observe the difference in the different vertical scales between Figures 6.2 and 6.3.

Figure 6.3 shows that the 3-month discount remained fairly constant in July, around 550 basis points, followed by a sharp rise in the week till Friday, 7 August. Although there was no further increase in the discount in the week till Friday, 14 August, the authorities apparently got wind of rumours that the speculators were planning to unleash their main attack on Monday, 17 August, which was a holiday in Hong Kong, but not in the US, UK, or

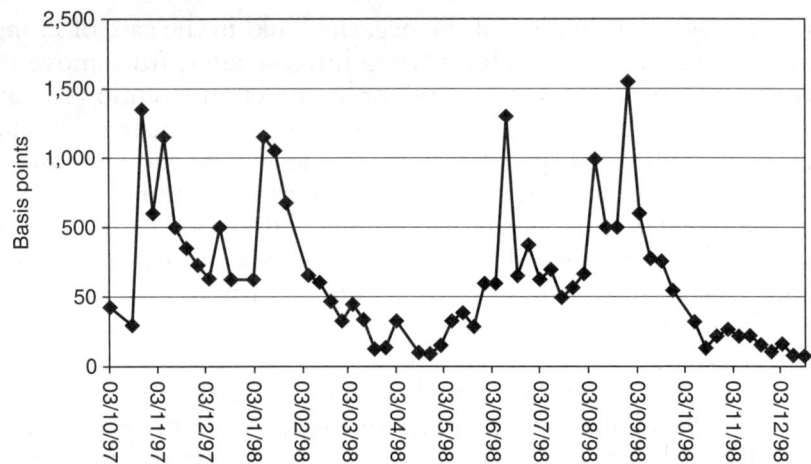

FIG. 6.2. Week-end 3-month forward discount on the Hong Kong dollar (October 1997–December 1998).

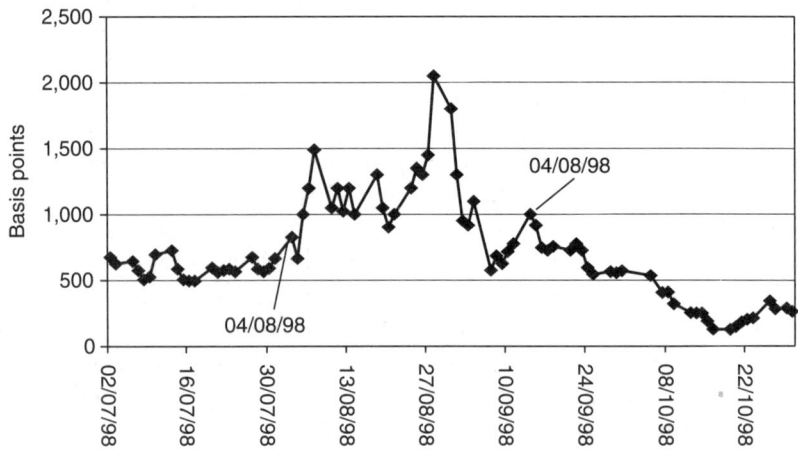

FIG. 6.3. Day-end 3-month forward discount on the Hong Kong dollar (July–October 1998).

Japan. They hoped to catch the Hong Kong authorities unaware. According to Anthony Ngai, Standard Chartered Bank Treasurer, 'Rumour suggested the institution had bought US $1 billion worth of six-month and one-year forwards in the morning and another US $500 million worth in the afternoon. The market's focus was now on the forthcoming local holiday on Monday, during which forwards could still be traded overseas but in much thinner volumes, making it easier for speculators to exaggerate movements and shake confidence with smaller bets (*South China Morning Post*, 12 Aug 1998). The government also believed that speculators had used rumours about a prospective Hong Kong dollar devaluation to destabilize the market. In an interview with *Euromoney* later in July 1999, Donald Tsang said: 'We have a totally free press, free phone calls. You can start a stampede just by rumour-mongering. In Hong Kong there was the rumour on Thursday (i.e. 13 August 1998), reappearing on the Friday, '"Donald Tsang is going to devalue on Monday"' or '"the Renminbi is going to be devalued in two weeks".'[10] It is very likely that this was the reason, as already noted in Chapter 2, why the government unleashed its unexpected interventional counter-attack on 14 August.

As Figure 6.3 demonstrates, the discount then remained high, averaging around 1,200 basis points over the intervention period from 14 to 27 August 1998, before reaching a climax of over 2,050/1,800 on the peak days of 28 and 31 August, as the battle between the speculators and the government reached its peak. Although the government stopped its intervention in the equity market on 28 August, it was not at all clear for some time thereafter that the Hong Kong dollar would survive the pressures without readjustment, and that the speculators had been worsted. Indeed the 3-month discount did not revert to its opening July level until mid-September. This, however, does not support some observers' idea that Hong Kong was rescued by the near-collapse of LTCM, causing hedge funds to withdraw. As the forward discount on the Hong Kong dollar had actually closed before the rescue of LTCM was announced on 23 September 1998, the HKMA's intervention would, almost certainly, have been successful even without LTCM.

As will be shown in more detail in Section 6.3, although the HKMA and the government chose to tackle much of the pressure of the speculative attack through (sterilised) intervention, they neither could, nor did they want to, hold interest rates in Hong Kong down to the pre-attack levels. Indeed the pressure of the attack, combined of course with hedging and supporting speculation by others mindful of the considerable likelihood that the speculators might 'win', meant that Hong Kong interest rates were continuously driven up to levels at which spot/forward arbitrage ceased to be profitable. We have calculated the notional Hong

---

[10] Donald Tsang, 'How I saw off the speculators, by Donald Tsang', *Euromoney*, July 1999.

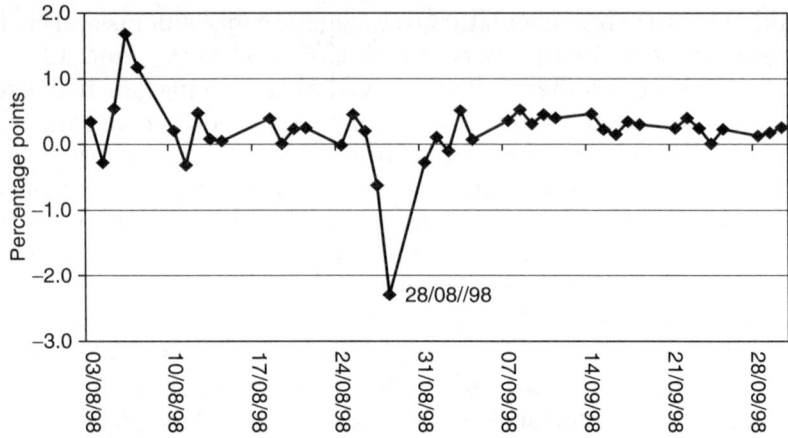

FIG. 6.4. Difference between the notional and actual Hong Kong 3-month interest rate (August–September 1998).

Kong 3-month interest rate that brings covered interest parity, and we compare that with the actual end-daily Hong Kong 3-month interest rate in Hong Kong, using daily figures from 3 August to 30 September.[11]

The results suggest that there were two periods when, after taking into account errors in data, observations occurring at different points of time, etc., there were signs of deviations from covered interest parity, sufficient to cause arbitrage flows. The first was early in August, from 4 to 6 August, when the discount on Hong Kong forwards increased more than Hong Kong interest rates, leading to possible arbitrage pressure to sell the Hong Kong dollar spot. This may have been the first wave of the speculative attack (with a second, and larger, wave planned for 17 August). As will be seen later (Table 6.13), longer-term rates reacted to the evidence of mounting pressure on the Hong Kong foreign exchange market (5–7 August), but short rates (overnight and one week), far from being jabbed upwards, rose more modestly, so that the yield curve

---

[11] The differences are calculated and shown as follows:
Difference = Notional Interest Rate − Actual Interest Rate
$\approx$ (Annualised depreciation of Hong Kong dollar $+ R_{us3m}) - R_{hk3m}$
$\approx [4^*(F_{3m} - S_0)/S_0 + R_{us3m}] - R_{hk3m}$

F_{3m} is the 3-month forward exchange rate of the Hong Kong dollar, S_0 is the spot exchange rate of the Hong Kong dollar, R_{us3m} and R_{hk3m} are the 3-month interbank middle rates (per annum) of the US and Hong Kong.

The calculation is, in essence, the same as that shown in footnote 9 of this chapter, but with annualised rates.

became upwards sloping. As we will show in the next sub-section, this was the reverse of what had happened during earlier attacks. A possible inference is that the Hong Kong authorities were already by then, i.e. the first week of August, making plans to switch from an interest rate to an intervention defence of the 'link' and of the equity market.

The second occasion when arbitrage flows may have been profitable occurred on 28 August and, perhaps, on 27 August. On these two days, Hong Kong interest rates rose so high, relative to the forward discount, that inward arbitrage, i.e. buying Hong Kong dollars spot and selling forward, may have been triggered. It is difficult to have a clear or simple picture about the event. The financial flows were so huge and the pressures so great on these days, that it must have been hard for the HKMA to control the money market with much precision. Given the uncertainties of the attendant crisis, the natural response of the HKMA would, surely, have been to keep money markets on the tight side. Whether they also consciously intended to raise rates sufficiently to generate inward arbitrage flows, i.e. adding an interest rate defence of the link to the reserve intervention defence, we cannot tell. It is arguable that with prices in the equity market directly protected by the intervention, there would be fewer damaging implications from once again using the interest rate defence in the foreign exchange market. But we do not rule out the possibility that the breach of covered interest parity was an inadvertent outcome of what was an extraordinarily disturbed day.

6.3 Money Market Developments

As already noted, the authorities had responded to the previous speculative attacks by raising interest rates sharply to try to defeat the speculators. The central banks' main instrument is the short-term interest rates, which they can control by means of utilizing their monopoly power to grant, or deny, access to cash reserves to the commercial banks. A good description of the normal working of the Hong Kong money markets, prior to the reforms of September 1998, can easily be found in the various volumes of the HKMA Quarterly Bulletin.[12] So, a clear indication of the

---

[12] See, for example, 'Of Pegs and Board' by Y.C. Jao (November 1997), and 'The Impact of Higher Interest Rates on Hong Kong: A Graphical Analysis' by Y.C. Jao and Andrew Sheng (February 1998).

authorities' interest rate response occurs when very short-term overnight rates are driven up sharply, with the upward pressure being translated to longer-period rates by market expectations about the likely future actions of both the speculators and of the authorities themselves. [A good account of how the term structure of interest rates is determined in money and longer-term debt markets is available in many textbooks, for example Campbell and Kracaw (pp.73–79, 1993).][13]

A rather extreme example of such a typical interest rate defence is provided by the events in the October 1997 speculative attack. Table 6.8 gives data for overnight and period interest rates from 20 to 30 October 1997.

Table 6.8 reveals that on the key day, 23 October, the overnight rate was driven up so sharply that the yield curve sloped sharply downwards. Although once the initial attack had been quickly staved off, and overnight rates reverted to their pre-attack levels by November, longer period rates remained buoyed up by fears both of renewed speculative attacks and of the authority's likely response to them.

There were, of course, solid grounds for such fears, and there were speculative attacks again, albeit perhaps less strong than on 23 October, observed on 12 January and 15 June. Again we observe that the authorities reactivated the interest rate defence, though less aggressively than in October, by jabbing overnight rates up. In June, the jump in short-term rates was sufficient, once again, to

TABLE 6.8. *Hong Kong interbank offered rates (20–30 October 1997) (Per cent per annum)*

As at end of	Overnight	1-week	1-month	3-month	6-month	9-month	12-month
20/10/97	5.1	6.6	7.4	7.5	7.5	7.4	7.6
21/10/97	5.9	7.8	9.0	9.0	9.0	9.0	9.0
22/10/97	6.3	8.5	9.3	9.3	9.3	9.3	9.3
23/10/97	100.0	175.0	30.0	25.0	20.0	20.0	20.0
24/10/97	12.0	14.5	14.5	14.5	14.5	14.5	14.5
27/10/97	11.0	14.5	14.5	14.0	14.0	14.0	14.0
28/10/97	10.0	13.5	14.0	13.0	13.0	13.0	13.0
29/10/97	6.5	9.5	11.5	10.5	10.5	9.5	9.5
30/10/97	5.6	12.0	12.0	12.0	12.0	11.5	11.5

Source: http://www.info.gov.hk /hkma/eng/statistics/index.htm

[13] 'Financial Risk Management: Fixed Income and Foreign Exchange', by Tim S. Campbell and William A. Kracaw, 1993.

TABLE 6.9. *Hong Kong interbank offered rates (5–23 January 1998)* *(Per cent per annum)*

As at end of	Overnight	1-week	1-month	3-month	6-month	9-month	12-month
05/01/98	4.9	6.4	8.0	9.8	11.1	11.3	11.3
06/01/98	5.0	7.3	9.0	10.3	11.3	11.8	11.8
07/01/98	4.8	7.3	9.5	11.0	11.8	12.0	12.0
08/01/98	5.5	9.0	10.5	11.5	12.0	12.5	12.5
09/01/98	8.5	11.0	12.5	12.5	12.5	12.5	12.5
12/01/98	12.0	12.0	13.5	13.5	13.5	13.5	13.5
13/01/98	9.5	13.0	13.0	13.0	13.0	13.0	13.0
14/01/98	9.5	11.0	12.0	12.0	12.0	12.0	12.0
15/01/98	10.0	11.5	12.8	12.5	12.5	12.5	12.5
16/01/98	9.5	10.5	12.5	12.5	12.5	12.5	12.5
19/01/98	8.5	10.0	11.8	11.8	11.8	11.8	11.8
20/01/98	8.0	11.0	11.8	11.8	11.8	11.8	11.8
21/01/98	6.5	9.0	11.5	11.5	11.5	11.5	11.5
22/01/98	5.5	6.5	10.0	11.0	11.5	12.0	12.0
23/01/98	5.0	6.0	8.5	11.0	11.8	12.0	12.0

Source: See Table 6.8.

TABLE 6.10. *Hong Kong interbank offered rates (8–19 June 1998)* *(Per cent per annum)*

As at end of	Overnight	1-week	1-month	3-month	6-month	9-month	12-month
08/06/98	5.5	7.3	8.5	8.9	9.4	9.5	9.9
09/06/98	6.0	7.3	8.5	8.8	9.3	9.5	9.9
10/06/98	6.1	9.6	10.1	10.5	10.5	10.3	10.5
11/06/98	7.4	10.3	10.3	10.3	10.3	10.0	10.0
12/06/98	8.3	12.0	12.0	12.0	11.5	11.5	11.5
15/06/98	12.5	18.5	17.0	14.0	12.0	12.0	12.0
16/06/98	9.5	11.5	11.0	11.0	10.5	10.5	10.5
17/06/98	8.0	9.5	9.8	10.0	10.0	10.0	10.3
18/06/98	7.0	7.8	8.3	8.5	8.8	9.0	9.6
19/06/98	7.5	8.1	8.9	8.9	9.6	9.4	9.8

Source: See Table 6.8.

import a downward slope to the yield curve. This is shown in Tables 6.9 and 6.10.

The problem, of course, with this interest rate defence was that the upwards ratchet in interest rates had a destabilizing effect both on the HSI and, just as importantly, on the vital Hong Kong housing and property markets. We illustrate this by comparing the increases in one-month interest rates with the decline in the

160   Intervention to Save Hong Kong

TABLE 6.11. *Currency attacks and HSI performances*

Date	Weekday	Interest rate change (%)	HSI fall from the previous day (%)
23/10/97	Thur	20.75	−10.41
12/01/98	Mon	1.00	−8.70
15/06/98	Mon	5.00	−5.72

stock market from the day before the main attack to the end of the day after, for the three attacks (Table 6.11).

As already noted in Chapter 2, the decline in property prices was perhaps even more damaging to Hong Kong's wealth and confidence, thereby weakening the economy and placing the political authorities under severe pressure. Table 6.12 gives the quarterly Hong Kong property price indices from beginning 1997 to end 1999.

TABLE 6.12. *Property price indices by type of premises in Hong Kong[14] (1997–99)*

(1989=100)

Year	Month	Private domestic*	Private retail	Private office[†]	Private flatted factories[‡]
1997	Q1	359	340	214	147
	Q2	429	379	217	145
	Q3	433	413	202	141
	Q4	422	395	191	135
1998	Q1	354	342	159	123
	Q2	321	294	145	118
	Q3	265	241	110	108
	Q4	258	220	105	95
1999	Q1	264	215	98	89
	Q2	264	218	98	83
	Q3	256	215	96	81
	Q4	245	206	94	79

*Classified by saleable floor area.
[†]The indices are not restricted to the main office district.
[‡]The indices are in respect of upper floor units only.
Source: Hong Kong Monthly Digest of Statistics.

[14] The above indices are based on an analysis made of the transactions scrutinized by the Rating and Valuation Department for stamp duty purposes. The number and location of transactions analysed may vary from quarter to quarter and, therefore, the price indices should be regarded as broad indicators of price trends only.

Table 6.12 shows that all indices tumbled quickly from the last quarter in 1997 onwards. This was largely due to the interest rate hikes caused by the currency attacks. By Q3 1998, the four indices had fallen by 38.8 per cent, 41.6 per cent, 45.5 per cent, and 23.4 per cent respectively. Following the intervention in Q3 1998, property prices continued to slide, but at a slower rate.

By midsummer 1998, the authorities felt that they could no longer afford, either economically or politically, the adverse effects that a repetition of the interest rate defence would bring on Hong Kong's wealth and confidence; neither could they ignore the huge rewards it would bring to the speculators, who, in the double-play attack, were banking on the government either abandoning the link or being forced into yet another interest rate defence.

The key give-away indication in the money market data is that, unlike the previous occasions of attack, the overnight rate is never jabbed up. Instead the yield curve remains upward sloping until the week beginning 24 August. Indeed from 3 till 21 August, the whole

TABLE 6.13. *Hong Kong interbank offered rates (3 August–4 September 1998) (Per cent per annum)*

As at end of	Overnight	1-week	1-month	3-month	6-month	9-month	12-month
03/08/98	6.8	9.1	9.3	9.6	10.2	10.0	10.3
04/08/98	6.7	8.1	8.9	9.4	10.1	10.0	10.3
05/08/98	7.1	9.6	10.2	10.3	10.8	10.9	10.9
06/08/98	6.4	10.0	10.3	10.3	11.1	11.0	11.0
07/08/98	7.4	12.3	12.8	12.3	12.0	11.8	11.8
10/08/98	7.1	10.3	10.6	10.9	10.9	10.6	10.9
11/08/98	7.6	11.0	12.0	12.3	12.3	12.3	12.3
12/08/98	7.5	9.9	10.0	10.5	11.3	11.1	11.3
13/08/98	8.0	10.8	11.5	11.8	12.3	12.0	12.1
14/08/98	8.3	10.3	10.6	10.8	11.3	11.1	11.3
18/08/98	8.6	11.0	11.9	12.0	12.1	11.9	12.0
19/08/98	8.6	10.5	10.9	11.1	11.5	11.4	11.8
20/08/98	8.8	9.4	9.6	10.1	10.9	10.8	10.9
21/08/98	9.1	9.8	10.4	10.6	11.4	11.1	11.3
24/08/98	10.1	11.5	11.9	11.9	12.1	11.9	12.0
25/08/98	12.8	14.3	12.8	12.3	12.4	12.1	12.1
26/08/98	13.3	14.8	13.0	12.3	12.3	12.0	12.1
27/08/98	15.8	16.8	15.5	13.8	13.5	12.8	12.8
28/08/98	19.3	23.0	19.5	18.5	17.5	14.5	14.0
31/08/98	17.8	20.8	19.0	15.3	14.8	13.5	13.4
01/09/98	16.3	12.8	12.8	12.3	12.0	12.0	12.0
02/09/98	5.8	8.0	9.4	10.6	11.0	10.8	11.0
03/09/98	4.4	5.0	8.3	9.8	10.8	10.9	11.1
04/09/98	4.6	7.8	10.3	11.3	12.1	12.0	12.1

Source: See Table 6.8.

TABLE 6.14. *Month-end 1-month interbank middle rate in Hong Kong and US markets (September 1998–December 1999)*

At the end of	HK1m	US1m
September 1998	7.0956	5.3750
October 1998	6.3688	5.2388
November 1998	5.4704	5.6206
December 1998	5.5699	5.0641
January 1999	6.3257	4.9391
February 1999	5.9821	4.9625
March 1999	5.6116	4.9372
April 1999	4.7299	4.9025
May 1999	5.1027	4.9438
June 1999	5.8080	5.2363
July 1999	6.0804	5.1938
August 1999	6.3438	5.3750
September 1999	5.4732	5.4000
October 1999	6.2656	5.4088
November 1999	6.0089	6.4825
December 1999	5.5647	5.8225

Source: Datastream.

term structure of interest rates moved up by almost exactly the same per cent, driven somewhat passively by the increasing discount on the forward Hong Kong dollar rather than by any aggressive defence by the HKMA. Table 6.13 tabulates the daily data.

The policy may have changed somewhat in the week beginning 24 August. From 25 August till 1 September the yield curve twists around in a more downwards sloping direction. Whether this was because of technical difficulties in handling the money market in the midst of such massive cash flows, or because with the titanic struggle with the speculators having been fully joined, the authorities by then felt that some support from the interest rate defence was justified, (since the HSI itself was being separately upheld by intervention), cannot be told until and unless the authorities themselves give a full report of this episode.

The fact that this episode was climactic and that the government had 'won' and the speculators 'lost' was, however, far from clear for quite some time. This is demonstrated by the fact that longer-period money market rates did not come back far from their August highs until towards the end of September. Thereafter, the cuts in the US interest rates, following the LTCM crisis, and the recovery in confidence in the Asian economies allowed Hong Kong rates to progressively fall back again, as shown in Table 6.14.

CHAPTER 7

Evaluation of the Intervention

7.1 *Controversy Aroused by the Intervention*

The Hong Kong government's stock market intervention was such an extraordinary and unexpected event that it at once became the focus of both local and international financial news. It immediately became controversial, and views were very divided. Supporters thought that the Hong Kong government had the right to fight back against the speculators and to protect the economy and financial markets. Opponents, on the other hand, thought that the government was risking public money to make up for loopholes in the currency board system, and that Hong Kong's financial management philosophy had been significantly changed. They argued that the government's role should be to maintain order in the market. By directly taking part in the market, it had confused its role; and this was a serious deviation from the non-interventionist rule. Some business executives in Hong Kong were of the opinion that what the government had gained in the short term by intervention would be lost over the long term, since the abrupt intervention would cause irreparable damage to Hong Kong's reputation among international investors. This, in turn, could be damaging to Hong Kong's open economy.[1]

Hong Kong government officials emphasized on several occasions that they believed that the speculators' double market play had distorted Hong Kong's financial markets and was causing serious damage to the whole economy. Even so, they admitted later that the intervention was definitely not a decision that they had enjoyed taking. 'Tsang agonized for 10 days: "I could do

---

[1] 'Business chiefs fear damage to free market', *South China Morning Post*, 7 September 1998.

nothing and thus uphold the free-market principle – and probably die with the economy." Intervention, though, was bound to cause outrage.'[2]

While most Hong Kong people understood the government's objectives and initiatives, they worried whether the government had a deeper pocket than the speculators—what if one day the government was to run out of ammunition and give up to the speculators, as the Bank of England did a few years ago during an attack on sterling? This question remained not only throughout the intervention period but continued to be posed long after the event. Since it is obviously hard, if not impossible, to assess the *ex ante* probability of the government's success, we have to make do with an *ex post* evaluation of the intervention result.

7.2 Overall Assessment

In this section, by looking at the intervention from different angles, we hope to give a reasonably comprehensive review of what the Hong Kong government has achieved and/or lost.

7.2.1 Propping up Asset Prices

Government officials in Hong Kong once mentioned that, if it had not been for the government intervention, the HSI would probably have been driven down to somewhere between the 2,000 and 3,000 points,[3] far below the likely 'fundamental' value of the market. Although nobody can tell exactly what the fundamental level of the HSI may then have been, we are interested in trying to assess what would have been the possible level of the HSI if the government had not taken the decision to intervene. Our efforts in this direction are outlined in the following sections.

7.2.1.1 Intervention Effects

A. Comparison with Singapore

To see to what extent the government intervention lifted up the local market, we have made a horizontal comparison between

---

[2] 'Donald Tsang vs. the hedge funds', *Asiaweek*, 23 October 1998.
[3] 'Intervention averted disaster, claims Tsang', *South China Morning Post*, 8 September 1998.

Hong Kong and another Asian market that has not known any intervention. In Chapter 4, we compared intervened stocks with local non-intervened stocks as well as similar stocks from other markets. Here we would like to show the relative performance of the stock indices of different markets. We chose Singapore as a comparator because it has many similarities with Hong Kong. Both of them are important financial centres and are fundamentally stronger than most other countries affected by the Asian Crisis. However, it is worth noting that Singapore does not have a currency peg with the US dollar. It allowed its currency to depreciate against the US dollar during the Asian Crisis when its market was under pressure. Figure 7.1 charts the performances of the stock indices of both markets from beginning July 1998 to the year-end.

Unsurprisingly, this comparison reveals a familiar picture. We can see from Figure 7.1 that the HSI experienced a sharper decline than the Singapore index from late July to mid-August. Then, during the intervention period, the HSI exhibited an initial recovery, while the Singapore index experienced a slight decline. In this context, the effect of the intervention appears quite clearly. Thereafter, the two markets tended to move up and down together again, while the gap opened by the Hong Kong government's purchases remained until late November, when the Singapore index caught up with the HSI.

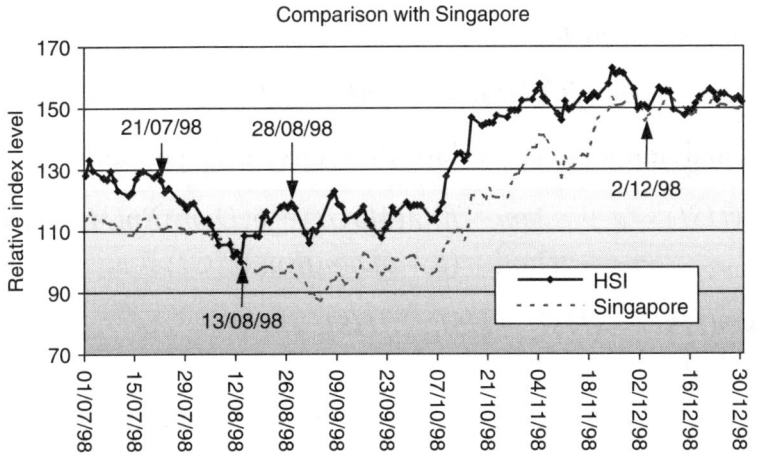

FIG. 7.1. HSI and Singapore Straits Times index (July–December 1998) (13 August 1998=100).

B. Regression test

Next, to statistically test the significance of the intervention in changing the market's behaviour, we carried out a simple regression test, whereby an international version of a market model was adopted. The original market model captures the relationship between the return on a common stock over a given time period and the return earned on a market index over the same period. The slope in a security's market model (β) measures the sensitivity of the security's returns to the market index's return. Here we suppose that the HSI is one of the 'stocks' in a portfolio of world market indices. The β of Hang Seng, like the β of a single stock in the domestic market model, measures the relative riskiness of the Hong Kong market to the global market portfolio. In this section, we will test whether the movement of the HSI significantly deviated from the world index during the intervention period and whether, as a consequence, the risk-and-return profile of the Hong Kong market changed.

We chose the Morgan Stanley Global Index (MSGI) as the proxy for the world markets' index. Daily data of the HSI and the MSGI were retrieved from Datastream. From 2 January to 13 August 1998 is the pre-intervention period; while from 14 to 28 August 1998 is the intervention period. We used data from both the pre-intervention and the intervention period to run the regression, but with dummies to control for both the intercept and slope changes. The regression model is given below:

The market model:

$$Rn(HSI) = \alpha + \beta Rn(MSGI) + \varepsilon \qquad (7.1)$$

Add in dummies to control for the intervention period:

$$Rn(HSI) = a + \gamma Dum + \beta Rn(MSGI) + \delta(Dum)Rn(MSGI) + \varepsilon$$
$$= a + \gamma Dum + (\beta + \delta Dum)Rn(MSGI) + \varepsilon \qquad (7.2)$$

$$Rtn(HSI) = (HSI_t - HSI_{t-1})/HSI_{t-1}$$
$$Rtn(MSGI) = (MSGI_t - MSGI_{t-1})/MSGI_{t-1}$$
$$Dum = 1 \text{ if the data is from the intervention period}$$
$$ = 0 \text{ if the data is from the pre-intervention period.}$$

The regression results are shown in Table 7.1.

Evaluation of the Intervention 167

TABLE 7.1. *Regression results for equation 7.2*

Variable	Parameter	Estimate	Prob > |T|
Intercept	α	−0.0036	0.0678
Rn(MSGI)	β	1.9314	0.0001
Dum	γ	0.0241	0.0053
(Dum)Rn(MSGI)	δ	−1.3256	0.0212
Adjusted R^2		0.2710	
Chow test	γ = δ = 0	Prob>F	0.0001

Since the return on the first intervention day is likely to have been large and positive because the intervention had been unexpected, and could possibly have had a strong influence on the regression, we also used a dummy variable for this single day. That gives the following regression:

$$Rn(HSI) = a + \gamma Dum + \omega First + \beta Rn(MSGI) \\ + \delta(Dum)Rn(MSGI) + \varepsilon \quad (7.3)$$

First = 1 if it is the first intervention day (14 August 1998) and 0 otherwise.

From the shown in Table 7.2 results, it appears that the intervention did indeed change the Hang Seng market's risk/return profile. Chow tests in both regressions are significant, denoting that adding the data from the intervention period to the pre-intervention significantly changed both the intercept term and the slope term (β) in the market model. The relatively low R-squares are normal in market model regressions, and adding a dummy to control for the first intervention day improved the R-square result slightly. Special notice should be given to δ, which indicates the change in the slope

TABLE 7.2. *Regression results for equation 7.3*

Variable	Parameter	Estimate	Prob > |T|
Intercept	α	−0.0036	0.0618
Rn(MSGI)	β	1.9314	0.0001
Dum	γ	0.0159	0.0714
Dum*Rn(MSGI)	δ	−1.4648	0.0096
First	ω	0.0732	0.0042
Adjusted R^2		0.3036	
Chow test	γ = δ = 0	Prob>F	0.0009

term β for the intervention period. During the pre-intervention period, β equals 1.9314, which by definition implies that whenever the world market has a 1 per cent change Hong Kong would have a 1.9314 per cent change in the same direction. However, during the intervention period β is largely reduced to 0.4666 (= 1.9314 − 1.4648), meaning that there was very little reaction from the HSI to movements in world markets during this period. This is consistent with the fact that the government was holding the Hong Kong market from going down along with other markets.

7.2.1.2 Forecast of the HSI Level Without the Intervention

Although we have used a market model to see the effect of the intervention in the above analysis, it is a very general model to explain the return on an individual asset or a market. The R-square is normally low because there are many other factors that could influence asset returns. It is almost impossible to list them all (and is totally beyond our scope here). However, we would still like to add a few Hong Kong-specific variables in the above market model, which might be able to improve the model to some extent. The factors included are the Hong Kong interest rate, and various economic announcements in Hong Kong. The exchange rate of the Japanese yen is also included, because we thought that this might be a critical factor for the regional economy, especially during the Asian Financial Crisis period, which could have influenced Hong Kong as well. Interest rates in Hong Kong were quite volatile before the intervention, and the local equity market was always sensitive to that. The 1-month interbank middle rate of Hong Kong and the yen/US dollar spot rate were retrieved from Datastream. The news announcement dates were acquired from the website of the government information centre: http://www.info.gov.hk.

Only the pre-intervention data are used (2 January–13 August 1998) to run the regression.

$$Rn(HSI) = \alpha + \beta Rn(MSGI) + \phi Chg(YEN) + \theta Chg(INT) \\ + d1(Unem) + d2(Rtail) + d3(Export) \\ + d4(CPI) + \varepsilon$$

(7.4)

$Chg(YEN)$ = daily change in yen/US dollar spot rate = $(YEN_t - YEN_{t-1})/YEN_{t-1}$

Evaluation of the Intervention 169

$Chg(INT)$ = daily change in Hong Kong interbank 1–month middle rate = $INT_t - INT_{t-1}$

$Unem = 1$ if it is the first trading day following the monthly announcement of the unemployment rate and 0 otherwise.

$Rtail = 1$ if it is the first trading day following the monthly announcement of the retail sales volume and 0 otherwise.

$Export = 1$ if it is the first trading day following the monthly announcement of the Hong Kong Export data and 0 otherwise.

$CPI = 1$ if it is the first trading day following the monthly announcement of the Consumer Price Index data and 0 otherwise.

The regression results showed that all the announcement factors, as well as the change in the yen/US dollar rate, were insignificant at any conventional significance level, while the change in the Hong Kong interbank one-month (middle) rate was significant even at the 0.01 level. Therefore, we excluded the non-significant factors and ran the regression again. The results are shown in Table 7.4, while results from the simple market model is shown in Table 7.3.

TABLE 7.3. *Regression results for equation 7.1*
$$Rn(HSI) = \alpha + \beta Rn(MSGI) + \varepsilon \qquad (7.1)$$

Variable	Parameter	Estimation	Prob > |T|
Intercept	α	−0.0036	0.0601
Rn(MSGI)	β	1.9314	0.0001
Adjusted R^2		0.2768	

TABLE 7.4. *Regression results for equation 7.5*
$$Rn(HSI) = \alpha + \beta Rn(MSGI) + \theta Chg(INT) + \varepsilon \qquad (7.1)$$

Variable	Parameter	Estimation	Prob > |T|
Intercept	α	−0.0031	0.0870
Rn(MSGI)	β	1.5731	0.0001
Chg(INT)	θ	−0.0097	0.0001
Adjusted R^2		0.3691	

170 Intervention to Save Hong Kong

It can be seen that the model, including the interest rate variable, was a considerable improvement over the simple market model, with the R-square rising from 0.2768 to 0.3691.

Next, we use the estimation from the above model to forecast the return on the HSI for the following day and then derive the level of the HSI day by day. The forecasting results are presented both in Table 7.5 and Figure 7.2.

The results give a picture of the extent to which the Hong Kong government lifted the market during the intervention period above its 'fundamental' level predicted, using the local interest rate

TABLE 7.5. *HSI forecast results*

Date	HSI	Forecasted	Difference
13/08/98	6660		
14/08/98	7225	6679	546
18/08/98	7211	6787	424
19/08/98	7623	6848	775
20/08/98	7743	6837	906
21/08/98	7528	6559	969
24/08/98	7845	6469	1376
25/08/98	7890	6491	1399
26/08/98	7834	6323	1511
27/08/98	7923	5793	2130
28/08/98	7830	5393	2437

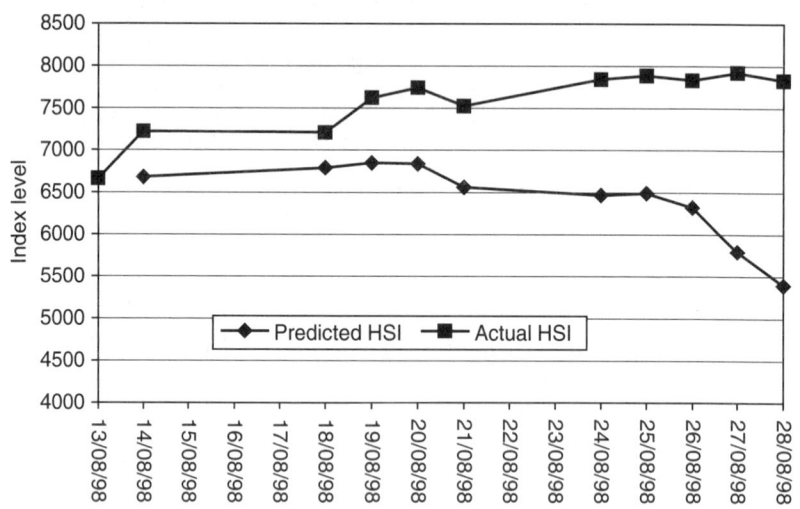

FIG. 7.2. Comparison between the actual and predicted HSI.

and the world market's performance. Of course, Hong Kong interest rates rose towards the end of the intervention period, but they may well have risen even higher if the Hong Kong government had continued to use an interest rate defence, as in October 1997, against the speculative attack. If so, the above calculations would underestimate, perhaps markedly, the effective support given to the market by the intervention.

We have to admit that the model that our predictions are based on may not be the best possible, but the idea conveyed here should be clear and succinct—the government did prop up the market against its falling trend. Another defect of the above analysis, however, is that it assumes that the market condition was normal, which was not the case. The Hong Kong market was under speculative attack, and it is clear from the comparison with the Singapore market (Figure 7.1) that the HSI was being driven down much faster than the Singapore index from 21 July. Although it would be hard to estimate quantitatively the destructive power of those attacks, we contend that they were likely to have made the situation even worse for Hong Kong.

7.2.2 Beating the Speculators

It is well known that the futures market played an important role in the government–speculator confrontation in August 1998. Since the government turned the market around successfully, we are interested to see how much the speculators lost in the futures market, or by how much their profit was reduced due to the unexpected intervention. However, since investors' positions and their identities are not released by the relevant futures exchange, the total profit or loss of any particular group of investors, say possibly identified speculators, is generally unknown and has to be indirectly estimated by making various assumptions and using some available market information, such as open interests, close/settlement prices, and trading volumes.

7.2.2.1 Total Profit/loss of all Short Positions in HSI Futures

First, we are going to use a formula derived by Lam and Mak (1997) to estimate an upper bound of the total profit/loss of all short positions in the HSI futures contracts over the intervention period. The total profit on all short positions means the sum of the profit (or loss if the profit is negative) cumulated over each position

172 Intervention to Save Hong Kong

taken in the market within a certain period of time. We have to note that this concept does not take into account the investor's individual identity, since any seller or buyer can close out their positions or even change to an opposite position within the time period. However, in sum, the total profit of all short positions should be the same as the total profit of all sellers under this assumption.

Lam and Mak (1997) gave different formulae to estimate the short sellers' profit/loss in the futures trading under different assumptions. Due to the limitations of our information, we chose the following two formulae to calculate the upper bound of all the short positions in different contracts as well as over different periods of time. (The derivation of these formulae can be found in Appendix III).

$$SPTP \leq OI_0(P_0 - P_c) + (AveP - P_c)(OI_c - OI_0) \quad (7.6)$$

$$SPTP \leq OI_0(P_0 - P_c) + \left(\frac{H+L}{2} - P_c\right)(OI_c - OI_0) \quad (7.7)$$

SPTP : short position total profit over day t,
OI_0 : the open interest at the end of day $t-1$,
P_0 : the closing price on day $t-1$
OI_c : the open interest at the end of day t,
P_c : the closing price on day t,
AveP : the average of the traded prices on day t, and
L and H : the daily low (high) price.

Although the above formulae hold for short positions taken from the end of day $t-1$ to the end of day t, it can be extended to any fixed period of time. We apply these two formulae to the government intervention and also to the post-intervention periods as follows:

Tables 7.6 and 7.7 show that during the 10 days of the intervention, the highest loss estimated of all short position holders in the August contract was over HK $5 billion. The September contract is a bit more complicated; as we have mentioned in Chapter 5, the HKMA's involvement in September contract trading was obscure. They were selling purposely at the end of August, but we do not know when they closed their short positions or even shifted to the buying side. But in total, short positions in the September contract suffered a loss of about HK $2 billion over the period from 31

TABLE 7.6. *Upper bound for the total profit of all short positions (August contract)*

	August contract							
Date	Open	High	Low	Close/Sett. Price	AveP	Gross O.I.	SPTP(7.6)	SPTP(7.5)
13/08/98	6880	6880	6505	6610	6622	93,490		
14/08/98	6550	7290	6510	7210	6983	92,838	−55,891,880	−55,945,996
18/08/98	7150	7300	7130	7215	7203	87,992	−464,190	−406,038
19/08/98	7400	7780	7360	7665	7618	75,142	−38,375,650	−38,992,450
20/08/98	7650	7960	7610	7790	7825	64,491	−9,339,495	−9,765,535
21/08/98	7620	7750	7390	7390	7655	57,808	24,593,460	24,025,405
24/08/98	7590	7820	7430	7820	7570	58,335	−24,960,205	−24,989,190
25/08/98	7820	7985	7770	7955	7890	56,930	−7,766,338	−7,783,900
26/08/98	7930	7950	7610	7910	7907	55,166	2,791,170	2,567,142
27/08/98	7830	7960	7830	7940	7906	46,435	−1,262,085	−1,358,126
28/08/98	7800	7990	7750	7851	7857	42,905	4,065,645	4,111,535
Total							−106,609,568	−108,537,153
Loss in dollars*							−5,330,478,375	−5,426,857,650

*Loss in dollars = HK \$50 × (total point loss), since the HSI contract is settled in cash and one index point is worth HK \$50.

TABLE 7.7. *Upper bound for the total profit of all short positions (September contract)*

Date	September contract						
	Open	High	Low	AveP	Gross O.I.	SPTP(7.6)	SPTP(7.5)
13/08/98	6910	6910	6550	6632	17,685		
14/08/98	6570	7295	6560	7046	18,031	−10,545,735	−10,504,734
18/08/98	7190	7300	7175	7233	23,217	283,430	260,093
19/08/98	7420	7760	7400	7636	31,402	−10,836,045	−10,377,685
20/08/98	7650	7940	7630	7820	38,808	−4,387,390	−4,128,180
21/08/98	7620	7750	7420	7640	45,629	16,066,545	16,441,700
24/08/98	7580	7740	7400	7548	57,496	−13,743,870	−14,004,944
25/08/98	7740	7895	7700	7783	73,277	−10,027,863	−10,256,687
26/08/98	7790	7800	7600	7745	91,267	9,166,210	9,975,760
27/08/98	7480	7720	7480	7594	102,442	9,927,620	9,860,570
28/08/98	7450	7610	7100	7375	107,085	41,650,035	41,742,895
Sub-total						27,552,938	29,008,788
Profit in dollars						1,377,646,875	1,450,439,400
31/08/98	7300	7310	6980	7098	103,074	21,906,255	22,094,772
01/09/98	6790	7180	6720	6944	96,242	18,627,580	18,668,572
02/09/98	7080	7210	6920	7088	91,973	−13,045,085	−13,143,272
03/09/98	6890	7150	6860	7026	88,818	−1,981,435	−2,047,690
04/09/98	6780	7180	6780	6977	86,539	−18,218,770	−18,211,933
07/09/98	7450	7980	7450	7771	82,053	−61,933,295	−62,184,511
08/09/98	7970	8195	7970	8097	75,916	−17,472,628	−17,561,614
09/09/98	8150	8150	7700	7892	74,829	30,506,840	30,542,711
10/09/98	7640	7820	7565	7715	74,336	2,607,923	2,596,830
11/09/98	7350	7475	7320	7392	75,058	21,570,075	21,566,104
14/09/98	7450	7570	7250	7419	72,341	−7,315,610	−7,340,063
15/09/98	7580	7688	7460	7592	70,532	−9,339,206	−9,371,768
16/09/98	7570	7830	7540	7746	68,081	−9,715,165	−9,864,676
17/09/98	7710	7710	7370	7511	66,596	23,287,470	23,330,535
18/09/98	7300	7380	7180	7291	65,922	5,687,620	5,680,206
21/09/98	7200	7220	7085	7130	63,409	13,102,728	13,159,270
22/09/98	7220	7440	7190	7378	54,385	−16,715,555	−17,284,067
23/09/98	7300	7560	7300	7469	48,225	−8,172,725	−8,412,965
24/09/98	7770	7950	7690	7857	34,662	−14,618,220	−15,120,051
25/09/98	7650	7785	7550	7674	32,359	4,696,058	4,681,088
28/09/98	7980	8035	7890	7963	26,412	−6,149,958	−6,152,931
29/09/98	7950	7950	7840	7903	24,000	744,480	725,184
Subtotal						−41,940,624	−43,650,269
Loss in dollars						−2,097,031,175	−2,182,513,450
Total loss in dollars (14 August–29 September)						−719,384,300	−732,074,050

August to 29 September 1998—the expiration day of the September contract.

Note that the above estimation made no differentiation among different groups of investors, of which speculators took only a portion, so the result cannot be totally ascribed to the speculators. In the next section, we will try to assess the loss incurred (or the reduction in profit) by the speculators alone, by taking into account the timing of their possible accumulations and settlement of positions.

7.2.2.2 Calibration of Speculators' Loss

Since there is no way of accurately calculating the speculators' profit/loss in the futures market from publicly available data, we can only give a calibration based on some pre-assumptions. We know that the speculators were accumulating the futures contracts long before the government intervened and were trying to close their positions and roll over to the September contract after the intervention started. Suppose that we did know the purchase and settlement prices as well as the amount of their positions in both August and September contracts, then we could work out their total gain or loss.

A. Position in the August Futures Contract

The HKMA Chief Executive, Joseph Yam, outlining the situation in August 1998, once said that the estimated short positions held by some large hedge funds totalled 80,000 contracts.[4] We assume that these positions were all in the August contract and this forms the basis of our estimation. However, in order to know the cost of this position, we need to know the accumulation layout, i.e. at what time and at what price they accumulated their position.

When we examine the daily transaction records of the August contract in July and August 1998 (Table 7.8), we notice that on 27 July 1998, the basis between the August futures and the HSI increased abruptly to –134, and on the same day the settlement price dropped 470 points and the trading volume also increased significantly. We, therefore, assume that this is the start of the speculators' accumulation, and we calculate the trading volume weighted average settlement price from 27 July to 13 August as the cost of the speculators' position in August futures contracts, which is equal to 7,343 index points. It needs to be stressed here that it is actually hard to determine the exact accumulation period of speculators

---

[4] 'Defending Hong Kong Monetary Stability', Joseph Yam's speech at the TDC Networking Luncheon, Singapore, 14 October 1998.

176   Intervention to Save Hong Kong

only from publicly available records, and the estimation of speculators' cost is rather sensitive to the assumption of the exact time that the speculators came in. For example, if we assume that most of the speculators' position was accumulated during the first two

TABLE 7.8. *Daily trading of August HSI futures contracts (1998)*

Data	Settlement price	Gross O.I.	Volume	HSI	Basis	Additional O.I.
02/07/98	8915	3	0	8866	49	
03/07/98	8630	3	0	8639	−9	0
06/07/98	8470	3	0	8484	−14	0
07/07/98	8460	3	0	8444	16	0
08/07/98	8670	7	4	8629	41	4
09/07/98	8355	225	238	8434	−79	218
10/07/98	8160	441	226	8206	−46	216
13/07/98	8070	444	5	8099	−29	3
14/07/98	8175	595	152	8179	−4	151
15/07/98	8475	1,366	1,047	8456	19	771
16/07/98	8595	2,071	815	8587	8	705
17/07/98	8650	2,539	911	8629	21	468
20/07/98	8515	10,085	8,433	8493	22	7,546
21/07/98	8515	17,863	9,206	8565	−50	7,778
22/07/98	8360	32,913	16,838	8421	−61	15,050
23/07/98	8105	41,944	11,558	8176	−71	9,031
24/07/98	8320	47,041	7,816	8257	63	5,097
27/07/98	7850	55,690	12,790	7984	−134	8,649
28/07/98	7830	68,088	22,623	7926	−96	12,398
29/07/98	7735	82,438	28,298	7809	−74	14,350
30/07/98	7830	86,873	22,441	7906	−76	4,435
31/07/98	7865	87,806	23,755	7936	−71	933
03/08/98	7495	92,161	23,000	7553	−58	4,355
04/08/98	7590	92,475	25,570	7581	9	314
05/08/98	7505	92,548	25,067	7466	39	73
06/08/98	7200	90,624	27,416	7254	−54	−1,924
07/08/98	6980	92,062	26,227	7018	−38	1,438
10/08/98	7010	92,823	18,627	7035	−25	761
11/08/98	6705	94,438	25,145	6780	−75	1,615
12/08/98	6840	92,869	23,413	6859	−19	−1,569
13/08/98	6610	93,490	25,066	6660	−50	621
14/08/98	7210	92,838	35,349	7225	−15	−652
18/08/98	7215	87,992	23,414	7211	4	−4,846
19/08/98	7665	75,142	43,364	7623	42	−12,850
20/08/98	7790	64,491	38,111	7743	47	−10,651
21/08/98	7390	57,808	26,808	7528	−138	−6,683
24/08/98	7820	58,335	42,264	7845	−25	527
25/08/98	7955	56,930	43,246	7890	65	−1,405
26/08/98	7910	55,166	38,038	7834	76	−1,764
27/08/98	7940	46,435	31,253	7923	17	−8,731
28/08/98	7851	42,905	7,444	7830	21	−3,530

Source: http://www.hkfe.com.

Evaluation of the Intervention 177

weeks in August 1998 before the intervention, the average settlement price would be much lower at 7,106 index points. But if we extend the accumulation period to one week before 27 July, the cost would equal 7,484 index points.

After the gross open interest reached its monthly highest of 93,490 contracts on 13 August, we see that the gross positions kept declining during the intervention period; about half of the contracts were closed out before the last trading day and half were left to expire. So, we think it is proper to use the average price weighted by the additional open interest as the average settlement price of the August contract. Therefore, for the August contract, we have the following computation:

Quantity of the contracts shorted = 80,000
Average purchase price = 7,343 (for accumulation from 27 July to 13 August)
Average settlement price = 7,759
Loss = 80,000 × (7,759 − 7,343) × 50 = HK $1,664 million ($50/point)

For the other two scenarios we did the same calculation and the results are summarized in Table 7.9.

B. The September futures contract

During the 10 intervention days, the September futures increased by 89,400 contracts. We assume that the speculators, either by rolling over their August contracts or by opening new contracts while letting the old ones expire, accumulated the same amount of 80,000 contracts in the September futures. We have mentioned in Chapter 5 that the government claimed that they had not bought any of the October futures or options. We further assume that there was very little rollover into October and that speculators'

TABLE 7.9. *Speculators' loss in the August futures contract (1998)*

Quantity	Average settlement price	Average accumulation price		
		27 July–13 August	20 July–13 August	3–13 August
80,000	7,759	7,343	7,106	7,484
Speculators' loss		1,664 m	2,612 m	1,100 m

positions were all closed out on, or before, the expiration date of the September contract—29 September 1998.

The purchase and settlement prices of the September contract are calculated in the same manner as for the August contract. The purchase price is the trading volume weighted average price from 14 to 28 August. The average settlement price is the average price weighted by the additional open interest calculated from 31 August to 29 September.

The calculation is as follows:-

Quantity of contracts = 80,000
Purchasing cost = 7,572
Settlement price = 7,480

therefore, the dollar gain on the September contracts is:

Gain = 80,000 × (7,572 − 7,480) × 50 = HK $368 million

To sum up, the overall loss over August and September 1998 under our assumption of August contract accumulation is
HK $(1,664 − 368) m = HK $1,296 million.

However, before we leave this calibration exercise, there is still one mystery that is left unexplained. Look at Figure 7.3. It displays the difference between the settlement price of September futures and the HSI during August and September 1998. (Many similar figures are included in Chapter 5). We observe that the September contract was kept way below the underlying index and did not

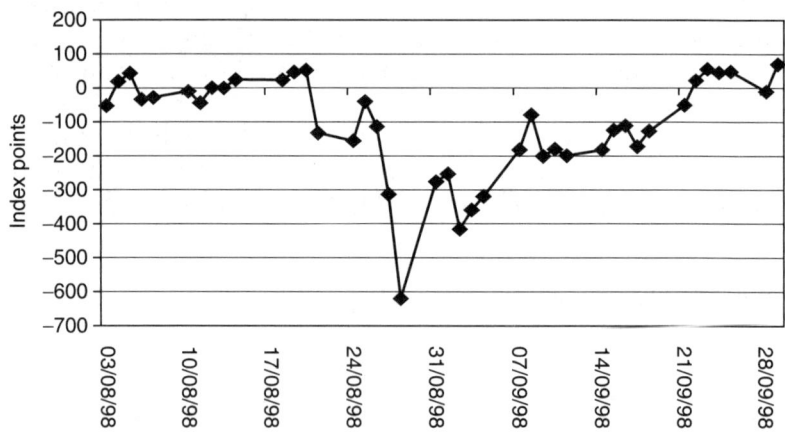

FIG. 7.3. September futures basis (3 August – 28 September 1998) (Basis = futures price-spot price)

come back in line until 21 September. From the 'news' review we know that the government was pushing the September contract price low during the last two days of the intervention because they wanted to increase the rollover cost for the speculators. But why, then, did the large negative basis continue into September? Especially for the first week, the bases were all larger than 200 points. If the speculators were trying to close their position by buying the September futures, who would be on the other side to take the short positions? We now outline our conjecture.

When entering September, the speculators wanted to fight back and they tried to depress the market in their direction. They deliberately kept the basis negatively large in order to attract more arbitrage activities and transfer the pressure to the cash market, even though it was much harder for them to do the short selling themselves, due to the additional restrictions on such short selling since the beginning of September. Nevertheless, the market did not move in their favour, and the whole international environment turned around from the second week of September.[5] So, they had little choice but to start closing their positions. If this guess is true, then the average settlement price should be calculated using the data starting from the second week of September, which is equal to 7,777 points. This settlement price would then imply a loss, instead of a gain, to the speculators' trading on September contracts as well. The calculation is as follows:

Purchasing cost = 7,572
Settlement price = 7,777
Speculators' loss = 80,000 × (7,777 − 7,572) × 50 = HK $820 million

The calculations in this section indicate that, due to the government intervention, the speculators suffered quite a sizeable loss. We have estimated the total loss of all short positions in both the August contract and the September contract over the intervention period and the following month. However, since we have no publicly available information on the identities of those position holders, and, therefore, no way to differentiate between hedgers, speculators, and other investors, we can only make a guess at the

---

[5] There is no hard evidence to show that hedge funds and other speculators cut their positions in Hong Kong due to the threatened failure of LTCM, as the sentiment of global markets, particularly of Hong Kong, started to improve even before the rescue of LTCM was announced on 23 September 1998.

loss incurred by those speculators under different assumed scenarios. As the results show, the estimates are quite sensitive to the assumptions made, which, we agree, has made our conclusion less persuasive. But as we have emphasized at the start of this book, we have only used information available in the public domain to carry out this exercise, and therefore have to content ourselves with these estimation results.

7.2.3 A Good Investment?

The Financial Secretary back at that time, Donald Tsang, during an interview on the radio once said, 'I've acquired them (33 intervened stocks) when (the) HSI was below 8,000, when the P/E ratio was in single digit. This is good investment. I am quite happy to hold them in the Exchange Fund, you know, long term.'[6] We will now evaluate the intervention as an investment.

Our estimation will use *one year* as the investment horizon. Close prices on 31 August 1999 are used as the end-of-period price.

From Table 7.10 we observe that, during the one-year period, there was a huge spurt in prices of most stocks that the government bought. The simple average of the percentage price change is about 78 per cent. Twelve stocks out of the 33 more than doubled in price, with the largest rise being in Wharf Holdings (00004)—a 178 per cent increase. The smallest changes were in the utility companies, such as CLP Holdings (00002) and Hong Kong Electric Holdings (00006). Table 7.10 also shows that, as an investment, the Hong Kong government clearly had a very good rate of return. Without considering the dividends, we will use only the capital gains as a proxy of return.

Investment rate of return = (End-of-period value)/Initial investment -1

$\quad = \sum [(P_{iT})^* Q_i]$/Initial investment -1

P_{iT} = End-of-period price of stock I

Q_i = Number of shares bought by the government for stock i.

The end-of-period value of the total 33 stocks is therefore HK$200,582 million. Compared to an initial investment of

---

[6] Transcript of the remarks made by Donald Tsang in an interview with RTHK Radio-3's programme 'HK Today' http://www.hknews.com.hk, 29 August 1998.

TABLE 7.10. *Price changes of Hang Seng stocks one year after the intervention*

Stock code	Name	Price on 31 August 1999	Average purchase price	Percentage change
1	CHEUNG KONG HDG.	67.50	33.53	101.31
2	CLP HOLDINGS LTD	36.80	35.02	5.08
3	HK.& CHINA GAS	9.91	9.00	10.11
4	WHARF HDG.	21.10	7.59	178.00
5	HSBC HDG.*	288.75	172.05	67.83
6	HONG KONG ELECTRIC	25.55	24.95	2.40
8	CABLE AND WIRELESS	17.65	15.24	15.81
10	HANG LUNG DEV.	8.95	6.62	35.20
11	HANG SENG BANK	87.75	43.75	100.57
12	HENDERSON LD.DEV.	41.10	23.77	72.91
13	HUTCHISON WHAMP.	68.86	38.06	80.92
14	HYSAN DEV.	10.10	5.22	93.49
16	SUN HUNG KAI PROPS.	66.50	25.77	158.05
17	NEW WORLD DEV.	18.70	8.93	109.41
19	SWIRE PACIFIC 'A'	40.10	24.00	67.08
20	WHEELOCK & CO.	10.10	4.16	142.79
23	BANK OF EAST ASIA	17.90	8.46	111.58
41	GREAT EAGLE HDG	11.40	6.56	73.78
45	HK & SHAI HOTEL	6.15	4.18	47.13
54	HOPEWELL HDG*	1.08	0.83	30.12
69	SHANGRI-LA ASIA LTD	8.80	5.03	74.95
83	SINO LAND	3.90	2.58	51.16
97	HENDERSON INV.	5.35	4.23	26.48
101	AMOY PROPERTIES	7.65	3.83	99.74
142	FIRST PACIFIC	6.00	2.59	131.66
267	CITIC PACIFIC	24.15	10.41	131.99
270	GUANGDONG INV.	1.59	1.40	13.57
291	CHINA RES.ENTREP.	12.75	5.68	124.47
293	CATHAY PACIFIC	13.20	6.25	111.20
363	SHANGHAI INDUSTRIAL HDG.	18.50	10.99	68.33
511	TV BROADCASTS	34.60	17.60	96.59
941	CHINA TELE (HK) LTD.	24.15	10.88	121.97
1038	CHEUNG KONG INFR.	15.65	14.33	9.21
			Average	77.72

*Price has been adjusted to later share changes: HSBC 1 to 3, Hopewell 5 to 1

HK$118,132 million, the gain is as large as 69.79 per cent, without even accounting for any dividends.

In order to evaluate the success of the investment, a comparison analysis can be done. What we are interested in knowing is what would have been its return if the government had not put the

Exchange Fund money into the stock market. The previous investment benchmark for the Exchange Fund is as follows:[7]

Instruments: 90 per cent bonds, 10 per cent equities.
Currencies: 70 per cent US $-bloc, 20 per cent European-bloc, 10 per cent Yen.

The benchmark does not give us any other distribution details of the Exchange Fund, and it is difficult for us to do a counterfactual calculation. However, we can offer the following figures, which would give a rough idea of the returns in comparison of a non-intervention investment.

For bond investment, the benchmark we can use is the 3-month United States Treasury Bill; and the average rate from 31 August 1998 through 31 August 1999 was 4.56 per cent.

The equity returns are calculated using the respective market indices changes over the period from 31 August 1998 to 31 August 1999. The Dow Jones Industrial Average is used for the US market, the Nikkei 300 is used for the Japanese market and the Dow Jones Euro Stoxx (price index) is used to proxy the European market. The returns are as follows (Table 7.11):

Suppose that the Exchange Fund did not invest money in the Hong Kong stock market, but instead invested 90 per cent in bond and 10 per cent in equity markets outside Hong Kong, the return would be about 8 per cent. This is much less than the 70 per cent return that the Exchange Fund achieved by buying and holding Hong Kong blue chips.

TABLE 7.11. *Equity returns in different areas (31 August 1998–31 August 1999)*

Area	Equity returns
US	34.49%
Europe	19.36%
Japan	25.30%

[7] 'The New Asset Allocation Strategy of the Exchange Fund', the HKMA's press release from http://www.info.gov.hk/hkma, 3 March 1999.

7.2.4 Impact on the Free-market Image

7.2.4.1 Criticisms After the Intervention

Immediately after the government initiated the intervention, there was much criticism that the unprecedented action had damaged Hong Kong's free-market reputation.

'Hong Kong investors will be frightened of touching the markets, and international investors won't touch us with a barge pole,' one local source said.[8]

'The manoeuvre has blemished Hong Kong's record of non-intervention in the stock market since 1987's global crash, when it halted trading.... It may scare off not only short sellers but other investors too.'[9]

'Interventionism is like any bad habit. Once a taste is developed, it is hard to forgo the pleasure... The cost of this is impossible to measure in dollars, but it is enormous...' said one Asian regional strategist of Santander Investment.[10]

In the face of all these worries and criticisms government officials sought to explain their motives to both the local people and the international community. To quote Financial Secretary Donald Tsang: 'I'm sure some will believe that we have tarred the reputation as a freest market in the world. But they must remember that there are some points when there are improper abrupt market movements, (they) would need to be removed, they (would) need to be addressed before you have an orderly system. I do also believe, therefore, international investors who want to invest in Hong Kong for a long term, they would look for stability.... So, I do not believe that what we have done in a long term is a bad thing. In fact, it is something for all financial administrations, all central banks to mull over very carefully what we are dealing with.'[11]

The reason why this reputation issue is important is that Hong Kong has always been proud of its image as the freest economy in the world and, in fact, Hong Kong's economic competitiveness may depend a great deal on this factor. The two most authoritative sources for evaluating economic freedom are: *The Economic*

---

[8] 'Intervention and peg under attack', *South China Morning Post*, 16 August 1998.

[9] 'Market Force', *The Economist*, pp.57, 22 August 1998.

[10] 'International trader: Stocks around the world get rattled by Russian instability and U.S. airstrikes', Barron's (Chicopee, Mass.), 24 August 1998.

[11] Transcript of the remarks by Donald Tsang in an interview with RTHK Radio-3's programme 'HK Today', http://www.hknews.com.hk, 29 August 1998.

Freedom of the World Report, published by the Fraser Institute in Canada, and the *Index of Economic Freedom*, published annually by the Washington-based Heritage Foundation. On 1 December 1998, the President of the Heritage Foundation, Edwin J. Feulner, sombrely declared that Hong Kong was no longer the freest economy in the world because of the government's US $15 billion intervention in the stock and futures market. Hong Kong stayed as number one on the Index only because the cut-off date for collecting data for the index fell before the intervention. Feulner told a Hong Kong press conference, 'It is my sad duty to report today that Hong Kong, on 1 December 1998, no longer has the freest economy in the world. All other factors remaining equal, this would give Singapore the top spot in next year's index.'[12] Moreover, Singapore aimed to displace Hong Kong as Asia's No. 2 financial centre after Tokyo. Besides trying to attract banks and other financial services from Hong Kong, Singapore also cut its margins and other costs on futures trading, while the Futures Exchange of Hong Kong then raised its margins.

Despite all these worries, the Hong Kong government insisted that the intervention was necessary to drive speculators from the market, and that it was only an exceptional move under very special circumstances. They did not seem to worry excessively about Hong Kong's free-market image. As the Financial Services Secretary, Rafael Hui, said, 'only time would tell'[13] whether Hong Kong's reputation as a non-interventionist economy had been affected.

7.2.4.2 Disposal of Shares

After the equity market intervention was completed, Financial Secretary, Donald Tsang, said: '...when we unload these stock and shares acquired during this period, (we) must not cause a disorder. So, we will do it in a very orderly manner over a long period of time.'[14]

The intervention took only 10 days, but its consequences took a longer time to handle. The problematic issue was how to feed the acquired stocks (which totalled almost 10 per cent of the HSI stocks) back into the market without having an adverse market

---

[12] 'Back to basics', *Far Eastern Economic Review*, 10 December 1998.
[13] 'Global bid to defend intervention', *South China Morning Post*, 17 August 1998.
[14] Transcript of the remarks by Donald Tsang in an interview with RTHK Radio-3's programme 'HK Today', http://www.hknews.com.hk, 29 August 1998.

impact. The partial solution was the creation of a Tracker Fund. On 11 October 1999, the government publicly announced its plans for the sale of part of its equity holdings in an index-tracking fund, the first security of this kind in Hong Kong.

The Tracker Fund, named TraHK, is similar to other index-tracking mutual funds. Its shares are technically units in a trust. The trust owns enough shares in all 33 HSI constituents to correspond to the amount of outstanding units. There are two other such mutual funds tracking the Hong Kong equity index, namely the Hang Seng Investment Management's Hang Seng Index Fund and the Manulife Fund Direct's Index Hong Kong Fund. But unlike these two, TraHK can be quoted and traded on the SEHK just like other companies' shares. This feature makes TraHK much more liquid than a regular index mutual fund. A 'tap structure' was adopted, whereby the government would release more shares through new fund units on a consistent and regular basis.

Before the IPO of the Tracker Fund occurred, many analysts expected a poor response from the investors, since they thought that Hong Kong investors were historically reluctant to buy index funds, as well as suspicious of new products. However, the market reaction was beyond anyone's expectations. A total value of HK $33.3 billion Tracker Fund was issued. More than two-thirds, or HK $23.3 billion of the issue, was allocated to retail investors, who submitted applications for units valued at HK $28 billion. Another HK $10 billion was issued to meet HK $20.3 billion in institutional demand.[15]

The success of the IPO of TraHK was not only because of the discount in its pricing, but also because investors had confidence in the Hong Kong market. It helped to appease concerns about the government's huge equity portfolio, and thereby helped to attract international investors back to Hong Kong. In fact, after the launch of TraHK, the market kept rising and more units were issued through the 'tap facility' in the following quarters. Concerns that liquidity would dry up because of the launch of TraHK were brushed aside by improving sentiment.

The Tracker Fund was the first attempt to dispose of the Hong Kong government's large equity holdings. However, the composition of the government's portfolio would enable disposal of only HK $70 billion shares out of the 200 billion via the Tracker Fund.

---

[15] 'Effect of Track Fund could be muted–analysts expect daily impact to be less dramatic than initial demand', *Asian Wall Street Journal*, 10 November 1999.

186 *Intervention to Save Hong Kong*

Besides an approximate HK $50 billion that might be held by the government as a long-term investment, the other HK $80 billion shares would have to be fed back into the market at some future time through other means. But according to the chief executive officer of the Exchange Fund Investment Limited (Efil), Mr Li Ka-Cheung, there was no concrete disposal plans for the rest of the shareholdings, and they would probably consider means, such as placement, convertible bond issue and corporate buy-backs, 'some time next year'.[16]

7.2.4.3 Updated Evaluation of Economic Freedom

On 30 November 1999, the Heritage Foundation published its *2000 Index of Economic Freedom*. Hong Kong retained its place at the top. But if we look at the report more closely we find that Hong Kong was penalized for the intervention but rewarded for having lower inflation. This is what the section on Hong Kong has to say: "In 1998, the Hong Kong government intervened in the country's stock market to counter speculative attacks. This raised concerns about the government's commitment to a free market. Recently announced plans for the disposal of the assets acquired in the intervention are encouraging. As a result of a decrease in inflation, Hong Kong's monetary policy score has improved over last year." Indeed, in the Executive Summary, the authors have included a special note on Hong Kong: "Hong Kong has achieved enviable economic growth without compulsory saving, industrial targeting, or other policies that not only impinge on economic freedom but also do nothing in the long run to foster growth." However, while they praise Hong Kong's laissez-faire policy, they point out that Hong Kong is moving away from its firm commitment to the rule of law in some aspects. Amongst all the other changes, only the government intervention in the stock market affected its index score. This indicates that the unprecedented intervention was really a big concern for the international community. Nevertheless, they applauded the government's decision to sell most of its holdings. Hopefully, this would enable Hong Kong to recover its score, as well as help retain confidence in its free-market policy. For that, we still need to wait and see.[17]

---

[16] '"Profit-making was never reason...for incursion" Portfolio launch date set', *Hong Kong Standard*, 12 October 1999.

[17] On 1 November 2000, the Heritage Foundation reported in their *2001 Index of Economic Freedom* that Hong Kong still held the top spot in the index. http://www.heritage.org.

7.2.5 Summary

We now attempt to evaluate the Hong Kong government's intervention from four aspects, namely, as propping up asset prices, as beating the speculators, as a long-term investment, and the impact on Hong Kong's free-market image.

From both our regression analyses, we concluded that the market-index level would have been much lower if the government had not intervened. Government officials have said that the HSI could have slid down to somewhere between 2,000 and 3,000, but our results did not go that far. However, our analyses did not take any possible panic reaction into consideration. What the speculators engaged in was not only a 'double market play', but also a psychological game. 'Local and investors' confidence was on the verge of collapse.'[18] We had less than enough information to simulate the possible situation if the market had fallen to a level low enough to trigger panic. Although government officials frequently stressed that their intention was not to prop up the securities market, we are prone to believe that this was one of the most important reasons for the intervention. Luckily, they were quite successful in doing so. The HSI closed on 28 August 1998 at 7,830, achieving a 1,170–point, or a 17.6 per cent increase over its 13 August level.

The most emphasized reason put forward by the government officials for the intervention is that they wanted to maintain a level playing field and avoid any serious distortions caused by market manipulation. Aiming to hit the speculators and frustrate their plan of 'double play', the HKMA had a very fierce battle with them on both the stock and the futures markets. Based on our assumptions, we made a rough guess at the extent of speculators' loss in the futures market. The loss, according to our previous calibration, in both August and September futures trading could be as high as HK $2,484 million (HK $1,664 million in August contract trading and HK $820 million in September). This may seem to be a small amount for those large hedge funds. However, compared to their predicted gains if the market had gone in their direction, which is HK $4 billion for every 1000-point index fall, the difference is huge. What is more, they also had to pay for the high interest rate on

---

[18] '"Profit-making was never reason...for incursion" Portfolio launch date set', *Hong Kong Standard*, 12 October 1999.

the large Hong Kong dollar position that they borrowed to sell, which as estimated by government officials was at about HK $4 million a day.[19]

As a long-term investment, the Exchange Fund obviously achieved a very high rate of return. Taking a one-year period after the end of the intervention as our evaluation horizon, the initial investment of HK $118 billion increased to over HK $200 billion, without considering dividend payments, implying an almost 70 per cent capital gain. This could be the best outcome in the history of government interventions.

However, at the outset of the mammoth intervention in August 1998, the government almost certainly did not expect that they would end up with such a big share in the market, and they themselves had recognized the danger of damage to Hong Kong's free-market image. Luckily the IPO of the Tracker fund was quite successful, which was a big relief to the government. Speaking on their behalf, Donald Tsang said, 'I cannot tell you how happy I am today to officiate at the launch of TraHK.'[20]

Donald Tsang had good reason to feel happy. The intervention, although it halted the decline of the stock market, had brought howls of protest from both local and international free marketeers. They warned that once the government entered the market, it would be hard for them to get out. But the Hong Kong government found a way of exiting by issuing a stock-index-tracking fund, which is the first collective investment fund of its kind in Hong Kong and in Asia (except for Japan). This attempt to dispose of the government's holdings was welcomed and thought partly to counter the intervention's damage to the free-market image. Hong Kong retained its top ranking in the *2000 Economic Freedom Index*, although this was largely due to the economy's low inflation rate. The Heritage Foundation also considered the Hong Kong government's decision to sell off the shares to be a good move. Even the IMF commented that: 'The Tracker Fund launch represented a very good start in this process (of divesting the bulk of authorities' holdings); further divestment should continue as market conditions permit, to eliminate the overhang of shares in an orderly and

---

[19] 'Defending Hong Kong's monetary stability', speech by Joseph Yam, http://www.info.gov.hk/hkma, 14 October 1998.

[20] '"Profit-making was never reason...for incursion" Portfolio launch date set', *Hong Kong Standard*, 12 October 1999.

transparent fashion.'[21] Furthermore, the timing of TraHK's launch was good. Economic conditions in the first two quarters of 1999 were dull, but, by the third quarter, GDP rose by 4.5 per cent, and the equity market rebounded sharply. On TraHK's first listing day, the HSI was as high as 14,189.67. The market reaction to the TraHK outperformed the best predictions, and the government had to issue many more units than planned to satisfy the large demand.

7.3 Conclusion

Overall, there is no doubt that official intervention is a very risky business, with many potential disadvantages (not least to the careers of those involved). It is extremely hard to predict the potential scale of the exercise into which the authorities may get sucked, if they are to achieve their objectives. We believe that the Hong Kong government did not appreciate in advance the massive volume of equity sales on 27 and 28 August. Even if the authorities have enough resources (to out-run the speculators), the final outcome may well depend on events elsewhere that will affect fundamentals, and over which the government involved will have no control. Failure is always possible, in some cases probable, and will bring down a hail of accusations and invective on those involved.

Moreover, intervention will inevitably distort markets, both during the intervention and also over a longer later period during which the intervention unwinds. Furthermore, intervention, as in this case, is often bolstered by added restrictions on market operations; in this case it was the extra September measures to constrain short selling. Against this, those advocating intervention will claim that the market has already been distorted by speculators, or by other factors driving the market away from 'fundamentals'. But how can one assess what the fundamental values may be, and may there not be several possible equilibria? So, any decision to intervene directly must be something of a leap in the dark, an act of faith.

Yet, the authorities in Hong Kong were prepared to take that leap, that decision, and, on the evidence presented in this chapter and in the book more widely, did achieve an outstanding success. Although counterfactuals are impossibly hard, we are confident

---

[21] 'IMF Concludes Article IV Consultation with People's Republic of China in Respect of the Hong Kong Special Administrative Region', International Monetary Fund, 6 March 2000.

that the Hong Kong economy with intervention was in a far better condition than it would have been without intervention.

After the intervention ended, there were several weeks during which judgement about its apparent success appeared to hang in the balance, until world markets began to improve. There is no doubt that the Hong Kong authorities were lucky in their timing (it is far more important to be lucky than to be good!). Nevertheless, we think that those who tend to dismiss this case of successful intervention as just a lucky break for the authorities (an exception) are overstating their case. We have heard, for example, several critics of intervention claiming that the authorities' victory was largely due to the LTCM collapse, and the subsequent and consequential withdrawal of hedge funds from their positions. At several stages of our analysis, notably in Chapter 5 on mispricings in the futures market and in Chapter 6 on the forward discount in the foreign exchange market, we have, however, demonstrated that market conditions had moved strongly in a favourable direction for the HKMA before the collapse of LTCM.

We certainly do not advocate such intervention as a regular instrument. It is far too dangerous and distorting for that. Nevertheless, speculators and markets left on their own can also precipitate dangerous and distorted outcomes. Fortune favours the brave.

APPENDIX I

The Basis and the Futures Return

According to the theory of behavioural finance, when investors are overly pessimistic about certain stocks, they drive the stock prices down to a level below their true fundamental value. They can then earn excess returns by buying these out-of-favour stocks, measured by low past returns, low price-earning ratios, or low market-to-book ratios. Fung and Lam (2000) have extended these studies to the futures market. They showed that the index basis could be used to identify occasions of overreaction in the index futures market. The rationale is as follows: when investors are overly pessimistic, the basis would go negative and when the pessimism is gone, the futures price would recover. Hence, when investors buy index futures after observing a negative basis, the returns should be higher than buying after a day that closed with a positive basis. Data from both the S&P 500 futures and the HSI futures confirmed this 'basis effect'. They also showed that the more negative the basis, the higher the return of buying index futures. The test period for HSI futures in this paper extended from September 1986 to the end of 1997. The authors purposely eliminated the days in the 1987 crash and cut off before 1998 because they thought that the turmoil might affect normal market behaviour. In contrast, we wanted to discover how differently the market behaved, as well as when normality was restored after the abnormal period of 1998.

We follow Fung and Lam's (2000) idea of testing the relationship between the return from buying index futures and the magnitude of the basis at the previous market close. Both the nominal basis and the standardized basis (SB) are adopted and the futures return is defined as the percentage daily price change.

$$R_{F,t+1} = 100(F_{t+1} - F_t)/F_t \qquad \text{(A-1)}$$

Appendix I

F_{t+1} and F_t are the futures price at market close on day t and $t+1$, respectively.

The tested relationship is given by the following equation:

$$R_{F,t+1} = a + bSB_t + \varepsilon_t$$
$$\text{where } SB_t = 100\,(F_t - S_t)/S_t \qquad \text{(A-2)}$$

Fung and Lam (2000) showed that b is significantly negative for the HSI futures data before 31 December 1997. In this context, we extended this test to 1998 and early 1999. We picked data for three periods: 1 May to 31 July 1998 the pre-intervention period; 14 August to 13 November 1998, the intervention period; and 1 December 1998 to 26 February 1999, the post-intervention period. The day immediately following the expiration day of the spot-month contracts was excluded from all the periods for two reasons. First, the calculation of basis on the futures expiration day is different from other days according to the 'Asian' style settlement of HSI futures. Second, after the expiration of one futures contract, the spot-month futures would change. For example, after the 1998 August contract expired on 28 August, the September contract became the spot-month contract on 31 August. Investors' behaviour may thus have little dependence on the previous basis of another contract and, therefore, we excluded these days from our regression test. As shown in Table A.1, before the intervention, no linear relationship existed between the basis and next day's futures returns; so the index basis at the previous market close could no longer be used to predict the magnitude of the future market's reversal. During the government's intervention, however, the relationship turned out to be marginally significant, at the 10 per cent significance level, but the R-square was less than 5 per cent. The post-intervention period saw a robust return to the negative relationship between the basis and the futures return. The b is significant at any conventional significance level with a value of -1.42. The R-square is as high as 28.31 per cent. This means that the basis at the previous market close resumed its role of an indicator of overreaction, which can be used to predict the next day's futures price reversal.

This simple test showed that, for the chosen pre-intervention period from May to July 1998, either the signalling effect of the basis was distorted or trading activities on the futures market were abnormal. We may not be able to test whether, or not, the abnormality was due to the speculators' activities, but at least we see that the normal relationship between the futures market return and the basis on the previous day was restored after the government's intervention.

TABLE A.1. *Regression results of equation (A-2)*

	Pre-intervention	Intervention	Post-intervention
Period	01/05/98–31/07/98	14/08/98–13/11/98	01/12/98–26/02/99
Observations	62	58	56
a	0.3937	0.4491	−0.1521
P-value	0.3572	0.4334	0.6208
b	−0.0173	−0.5908	−1.4473
P-value	0.9774	0.0961	0.0001
R^2	0.0000	0.0487	0.2879

APPENDIX II

Bases of Futures Contracts on Expiration Days

In our previous analyses on futures market, the expiration day was normally deleted from the daily data series since the settlement arrangement differs. However, it might be of some interest to examine the intra-day behaviour on these days, especially in August, September, and October. Minute-by-minute data of the HSI were acquired from the HSI Services Limited. Intra-day transaction data for the HSI futures were provided by the Futures Exchange of Hong Kong.

Both HSI spot and HSI futures prices are collected into five-minute groups and the last recorded price within each group is selected. The final settlement price of the futures contract is the average of quotations of the cash index taken at five-minute intervals during this last trading day. The cash index and the index futures, as well as the basis on three expiration days, are shown in Figure A.1 (a)-(c). The settlement price is included for reference.

As can be seen, the deviations of the basis from zero were all larger towards the end of these three trading days than during the day. However, the deviations in the afternoon trading are no longer an indication of mispricings because the futures prices have to converge to the settlement price, which is the average of the index level at five-minute intervals throughout the day. We know from the 'news' review in Chapter 5 that the government took part in futures trading in both August and September 1998. Here we see that the basis towards the market's close was positive on 28 August and 29 September 1998, while on 29 October 1998 the spot index went up in the afternoon and therefore left the basis negative at the close. At this point, we would like to know whether the day-end bases of futures contracts on expiration days have any signalling

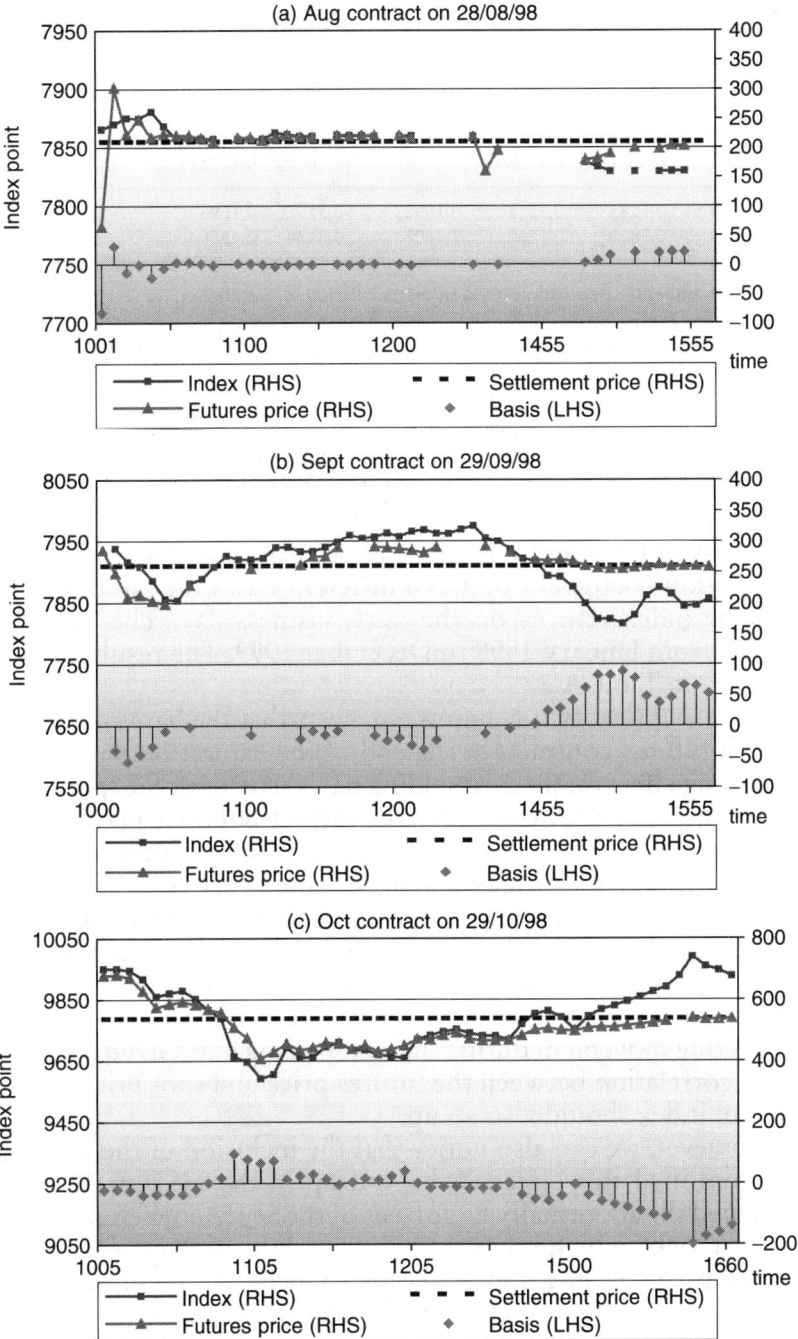

FIG. A.1. Price performances of the spot-month futures on expiration days.

TABLE A.2. *Correlation between different bases and index returns*

	Include all data N=24		Exclude 28/08/98 N=23		Exclude 28/08/98 and 29/09/98 N=22	
	SPOTBAS0	SECDBAS0	SPOTBAS0	SECDBAS0	SPOTBAS0	SECDBAS0
RTNIDX1	0.1183	0.3211	0.1690	−0.5107	0.1696	−0.5336
P-value	0.5820	0.1260	0.4407	0.0128	0.4506	0.0105

*N is the number of observations used in the calculation of correlation,
(Day) 0 is the expiration day of the spot-month futures,
(Day) 1 refers to the first business day after the expiration day of the spot-month futures, i.e. the last trading day of each month,
RTNIDX1 is the log return of the HSI on (day) 1, $(RTNIDX1 = Ln(HSI1/HSI0))$,
HSI1 and HSI0 are the close HSI levels on day 1 and day 0 respectively,
SPOTBAS0 is the basis of the spot-month futures contract on day 0,
SECDBAS0 is the basis of the second month futures contract on day 0.

effect or information content. For that purpose, we checked the correlation coefficient between different bases on expiration days and the index returns on the next business day. The data series extend from January 1998 to December 1999. The results are summarized in Table A.2.

Table A.2 (last two columns) suggests that the bases of the spot-month futures contracts at the end of the expiration days have no signalling effect on the next trading day's returns of the spot market, while the basis of the next month futures contract may show the direction of the next day's spot trading. For example, if the next month futures price shows a significant negative basis, the cash index would usually tend to go up during the next trading day. We can again use the 'basis effect' to account for this movement. That is to say, when the second month futures contract is pushed much lower than its theoretical price, the investors should expect a correcting movement during the next trading day. Given the normal close correlation between the futures price and spot price, the spot market index should also go up.

However, we can also notice that the inclusion of the 28 August data nullified this effect. A huge drop in the HSI on 31 August followed the abnormally large basis of the September contract on 28 August 1998, which might have been partly, perhaps even largely, caused by government intervention to increase the rollover cost of the speculators. The inclusion of 29 September data, on the other hand, did not exert much influence on the correlation coefficient between the *SECDBAS0* and *RTNIDX1*. So the question which follows is whether the distorted 'basis effect' at the end of August 1998 lasted long after the intervention. To answer this question, the following regression is adopted.

$$RTNIDX1_t = a + bSECDBAS0_t + cPOST_t + \varepsilon_t \qquad (A3)$$

RTNIDX1 and *SECDBAS0* are defined as before, *POST* is a dummy variable, which equals to 0 if the data is before 28 August 1998 and 1 if after it. (28 August 1998 is excluded from the regression.)

TABLE A.3. *Regression results of equation (A-3)*

Parameter	Estimate	*P*-value
a	0.00242	0.6827
b	−8.555E-05	0.0190
c	0.002351	0.7442

The results show that the relationship between the expiration day basis of the second month futures and the next day's cash index returns did not change after the intervention finished, although the futures prices were seriously distorted on 28 August 1998, the last intervention day.

APPENDIX III

Lam and Mak's (1997) Estimation of the Profit/Loss of all Short Positions in the Futures Market

1. Introduction

The purpose of Kin Lam and Billy S. C. Mak's (1997) paper, *Estimating the total profit of short positions in a futures market*, is to provide an upper bound and an estimate for the total profit of short positions, which can be further used to estimate the degree to which a drop in the spot market value has been hedged through taking short positions in futures trading.

For any participant in the futures market, taking either a long or a short position, he or she has to offset his or her position at a later time on or before the expiry of the contract. In doing so, a profit or a loss is derived. The total profit of all short positions is simply the sum of the profit (or loss if the profit is negative) cumulated over each short position taken in the market. However, the investor's identity is not taken into account in this process.

2. Estimations

OI_0 : the open interest at the end of day $t-1$,
P_0 : the closing price at day $t-1$
OI_c : the open interest at the end of day t,
P_c : the closing price at day t.

For each contract traded on day t, the buyer (or the seller) can either be establishing a new position or is offsetting an existing position which was established from the end of day $t-1$ to the end of day t.

$X_1 = OI_1 - OI_0$
 = 1, if neither the buyer nor the seller is offsetting an existing position (type 1),
 = 0, if either the buyer or the seller is offsetting an existing position (type 2),
 = −1, if both sides are offsetting some existing positions (type 3).

N_t: total number of contracts traded, $N_t = n_1 + n_2 + n_3$, (i = 1, 2, 3 type of the trading)

SPTP: short position total profit, which by assumption takes the value zero at the end of day $t - 1$,

P_j: the price of the jth contract traded.

Since the first contract is traded at price P_1, the change in the short positions' total profit after marking to market becomes:

$$\Delta SPTP_0 = OI_0[P_0 - P_1] \quad (A\text{-}4)$$

And

$$SPTP_1 = SPTP_0 + \Delta SPTP_0, \quad OI_1 = OI_0 + \Delta OI_0 \quad (A\text{-}5)$$

$$\Delta SPTP_{j-1} = OI_{j-1}[P_{j-1} - P_j] \quad (A\text{-}6)$$

When the second to the last contract is traded at price P_{n-1} and the last contract is traded at P_n, then the total profit after marking to market at the end of day t is given by

$$\begin{aligned}SPTP &= SPTP_{n-1} + \Delta SPTP_{n-1} = SPTP_{n-1} \\ &\quad + OI_{n-1}(P_{n-1} - P_n)\end{aligned} \quad (A\text{-}7)$$

$P_c = P_n$ (for any trading days before the expiration day)
 = Average of HSI taken at five-minute intervals (for the expiration day).

Combining (equations A-4, A-5, A-6, A-7) we have,

$$\begin{aligned}SPTP &= OI_0(P_0 - P_1) + OI_1(P_1 - P_2) + \ldots + OI_{n-1}(P_{n-1} - P_n) \\ &\quad + OI_n(P_n - P_c) \\ &= OI_0(P_0 - P_1) + (OI_0 + X_1)(P_0 - P_1) + \ldots + (OI_0 + X_1 + \ldots \\ &\quad + X_{n-1} + X_n)(P_c - P_n) \\ &= OI_0(P_0 - P_1) + X_1(P_1 - P_c) + X_2(P_2 - P_c) + \ldots + X_n(P_n - P_c)\end{aligned}$$

$$= OI_0(P_0-P_1) + n_1(AveP_1) - n_3(AveP_3)$$
$$- (X_1 + X_2 + \ldots + X_n)P_c$$
$$= OI_0(P_0-P_1) + n_1(AveP_1) - n_3(AveP_3) - (OI_c-OI_0)P_c \quad (A\text{-}8)$$

$AveP_1$ is the average traded price of the type 1 contracts and $AveP_3$ is the average traded price of the type 3 contracts.

However, since $n_1, n_3, AveP_1$, and $AveP_3$ are generally unknown, further work is necessary for the estimation of $SPTP$.

3. An Upper Bound for Short Positions' Overall Profit

While n_1, n_3 are unknown, they are subject to the following constraints:

$$n_1 + n_3 \leq N_t \text{ and } n_1 - n_3 = OI_c - OI_0$$

It is clear that $SPTP$ is maximized at the boundary of $n_1 + n_3 = N_t$. Thus $SPTP$ is maximized when $n_1 = (N_t + OI_c - OI_0)/2$, $n_3 = (N_t - OI_c + OI_0)/2$ (assuming that $(N_t + OI_c - OI_0)/2$ is an integer; if not, some rounding work is necessary), and when $AveP_1$ is the average of the highest n_1 transacted prices and $AveP_3$ is the average of the lowest n_3 transacted prices.

Let $P_{(1)}, P_{(2)}, \ldots, P_{(n)}$ be the trades prices arranged in order of magnitude, i.e. they satisfy

$$P_{(1)} \leq P_{(2)} \leq \ldots \leq P_{(n)}$$

Where $P_{(1)}$ denotes the lowest traded price and $P_{(n)}$ denotes the highest traded price, etc. Therefore,

$$SPTP \leq OI_0(P_0 - P_c) + \sum_{j=\frac{n-d}{2}-1}^{n} P_{(j)} - \sum_{j=1}^{(n-d)/2} P_{(j)} - dP_c \quad (A\text{-}9)$$

Where $d = OI_c - OI_0$.

In the case that the transaction prices are unknown, then it can be assumed that: (a) new positions are established at highest possible prices, i.e. $AveP_1 = H$, and (b) existing long positions are offset at lowest possible prices, i.e. $AveP_3 = L$. (L and H are respectively the daily low price and the daily high price). Thus,

$$SPTP \leq OI_0(P_0 - P_c) + (\frac{n+d)}{2})H - (\frac{n-d}{2})L - dP_c$$
$$= OI_0(P_0 - P_c) + (n/2)(H - L) + d(\frac{H+L}{2} - P_c) \quad \text{(A-10)}$$

Since the above (a) and (b) assumptions are too extreme to be realistic, a more reasonable assumption is $AveP_1 = AveP_3 = AveP$, which is the average of the traded prices on day t. Then,

$$SPTP \leq OI_0(P_0 - P_c) + (\frac{n+d}{2})AveP - (\frac{n-d}{2})AveP$$
$$- dP_c = OI_0(P_0 - P_c) + (AveP - P_c)(OI_c - OI_0) \quad \text{(A-11)}$$

(This is the formula 7.6 in Chapter 7)

If transaction prices are unknown, then we can estimate $AveP$ by $(H+L)/2$ and the upper bound can be estimated as

$$SPTP \leq OI_0(P_0 - P_c) + (\frac{H+L}{2} - P_c)(OI_c - OI_0) \quad \text{(A-12)}$$

(This is the formula 7.7 in Chapter 7)

REFERENCES

Ahn, Hee-Joon, and Yan-Leung Cheung (1999). 'The intra-day patterns of the spread and depth in a market without market-makers: The stock exchange of Hong Kong'. *Pacific-Basin Finance Journal*, 7 (December): 539–56.

Allen, F., and G. Gorton (1992). 'Stock price manipulation, market microstructure and asymmetric information'. *European Economic Review*, 36: 624–30.

Bae, Kee-Hong, Baekin Cha, and Yan-Leung Cheung (1999). 'The transmission of pricing information of dually-listed stocks'. *Journal of Business Finance & Accounting*, 26(5&6): 709–23.

Barro, Robert J., Eugene Fama, Daniel R. Fischel, Allan H. Meltzer, Richard Roll, and Lester G. Telser (1989). *Black Monday and the future of financial markets*. Homewood, Illinois: Dow Jones-Irwin.

Basset, G. W., V. G. France, and S. R. Pliska (1989). 'The MMI cash-futures spread on October 19, 1987'. *Review of Futures Markets*, 8(1): 118–46.

Biais, B., P. Hillion, and C. Spatt (1995). 'An empirical analysis of the limit order book and the order flow in the Paris Bourse'. *Journal of Finance*, 50(5): 1655–89.

Blume, M. E., A. C. Mackinlay, and B. Terker (1989). 'Order imbalances and stock price movements on October 19 and 20, 1987'. *Journal of Finance*, 44(4): 827–48.

Blume, M. E., and M. A. Goldstein (1997). 'Quotes, order flow, and price discovery'. *Journal of Finance*, 52(1): 221–44.

Brennan, M. J., and A. Subrahmanyam (1995). 'Investment analysis and price formation in securities markets'. *Journal of Financial Economics*, 38: 361–81.

Campbell, T. S., and W. A. Kracaw (1993). *Financial Risk Management: Fixed Income and Foreign Exchange*. New York: HarperCollins.

Chan, Kalok (1999). 'Does Hong Kong government's intervention increase stock market volatility?' Working Paper, Department of Finance, The Hong Kong University of Science and Technology, January.

Chan, Kalok, and Y. Peter Chung (1993). 'Intra-day relationships among index arbitrage, spot and futures price volatility, and spot market volume: A transactions data test'. *Journal of Banking and Finance*, 17: 663–87.

Chan, Y. C. (2000). 'The price impact of trading on the Stock Exchange of Hong Kong'. *Journal of Financial Markets* (March): 1–16.

Cheng, Louis T. W., Joseph K. W. Fung, and K. C. Chan (2000). 'Pricing dynamics of index options and index futures in Hong Kong before and during the Asian Financial Crisis'. *Journal of Futures Markets*, 20(2): 145–66.
Cheung, Y. L., P. Pope, R. Y. K. Ho, and P. Draper (1994). 'Intra-day stock return volatility: The Hong Kong evidence'. *Pacific-Basin Finance Journal*, 2: 261–76.
Chung, Y. Peter (1991). 'A transaction data test of stock index futures market efficiency and index arbitrage profitability'. *Journal of Finance*, 46(5): 1791–809.
Cornell, B., and E. R. Sirri (1992). 'The reaction of investors and stock prices to insider trading'. *Journal of Finance* 47(3): 1031–60.
Coughenour, J., and K. Shastri (1999). 'Symposium on market microstructure: A review of empirical research'. *The Financial Review*, 34: 1–28.
Datar, V. T., N. Y. Naik, and R. Radcliffe (1998). 'Liquidity and stock returns: An alternative test'. *Journal of Financial Markets*, 1: 203–19.
De Brouwer, Gordon (2001). *Hedge Funds in Emerging Markets*. Cambridge: Cambridge University Press.
Dwyer, Gerald P., Jr., Peter Locke, and Wei Yu (1996). 'Index arbitrage and nonlinear dynamics between the S&P 500 futures and cash'. *The Review of Financial Studies*, 9(1): 301–32.
Easley, D., N. M. Keiefer and M. O'Hara (1997). 'One day in the life of a very common stock'. *The Review of Financial Studies*, 10 (Fall): 805–35.
Easley, D., and M. O'Hara (1987). 'Price, trade size and information in securities markets'. *Journal of Financial Economics*, 19: 69–90.
Financial Stability Forum (2000). Report of the Working Group on Highly Leveraged Institutions, http://www.fsforum.org.
Foucault, Thierry (1999). 'Order flow composition and trading costs in a dynamic limit order market'. *Journal of Financial Markets*, 2: 99–134.
Fung, Alexander K. W. (1999). 'Overreaction in the Hong Kong stock market'. Working Paper, Hong Kong Baptist University (February).
Fung, Alexander K. W., and Kin Lam (2000). 'Effect of index basis at market closing on futures return in the US and Hong Kong markets: An overreaction perspective'. Working Paper, Hong Kong Baptist University (March).
Fung, Joseph K. W., and Paul Draper (2000). 'On screen trading of stocks and the mispricing of index futures during the Financial Crisis and government intervention'. Working Paper, Hong Kong Baptist University (August).
—— (1999). 'Mispricing of index futures contracts and short sales constraints'. *Journal of Futures Markets*, 19(6): 695–715.

Fung, Joseph K. W., and Li Jiang (1999). 'Restrictions on short-selling and spot-futures dynamics'. *Journal of Business Finance and Accounting*, 26 (1&2): 227–39.
Gerety, M. S., and J. H. Mulherin (1994). 'Price formation on stock exchanges: The evolution of trading within the day'. *Review of Financial Studies*, 7(3): 609–29.
Glosten, L. R. (1994). 'Is the electronic open limit order book inevitable?' *Journal of Finance*, 49: 1127–61.
Greenstein, M. M., and Heibatollah Sami (1994). 'The impact of the SEC's segment disclosure requirement on bid-ask spreads'. *Accounting Review*, 69(1): 179–99.
Harris, Lawrence (1989). 'The October 1987 S&P500 stock-futures basis'. *Journal of Finance*, 44(1): 77–90.
Harris, Lawrence, and J. Hasbrouck (1996). 'Market vs. limit orders: The SuperDOT evidence on order submission strategy'. *Journal of Financial and Quantitative Analysis*, 31(2): 213–31.
Hasbrouck, J. (1988). 'Trades, quotes, inventories, and information'. *Journal of Financial Economics*, 22: 229–52.
—— (1993). 'Assessing the quality of a security market: A new approach to transaction cost measurement'. *Review of Financial Studies*, 6: 191–212.
—— (1991). 'Measuring the information content of stock trades'. *Journal of Finance*, 46(1): 179–207.
Hausman, J. A., and A. W. Lo (1992). 'An ordered probit analysis of transaction stock prices'. *Journal of Financial Economics*, 31: 319–79.
Ho, Richard Y. K., Jimmy Fang, and C. K. Woo (1992). 'Intra-day arbitrage opportunities and price behaviour of the Hang Seng index-futures'. *The Review of Futures Market*, 11: 413–30.
Huang, Roger D., and R. Stoll Hans (1997). 'The components of the bid-ask spread: A general approach'. *Review of Financial Studies*, 10(4): 995–1034.
Huang, Yi-yi, and Da-jian Lin (1999). Guan E Da Zhan: Xiang Gang Zheng Fu Yu Guo Ji Chao Jia Dui Han Ji. Tong xin chu ban she.
Huque, Ahmed Shafiqul (1999). 'Hong Kong's policy of positive nonintervention: A critical appraisal of the 1998 stock market intervention'. *Issues & Studies*, 35: 152–73.
Jao, Y. C. (1997). 'Of pegs and board'. *HKMA Quarterly Bulletin* (November): 70–2.
—— (2001). *The Asian Financial Crisis and the Ordeal of Hong Kong*. Westport, Conn.: Quorum Books (Greenwood Publishing Group).
Jao, Y. C., and Andrew Sheng (1998). 'The impact of higher interest rates on Hong Kong: A graphical analysis'. *HKMA Quarterly Bulletin* (February): 10–14

Jones, C. M., G. Kaul, and M. L. Lipson (1994). 'Information, trading and volatility'. *Journal of Financial Economics*, 36: 127–54.

Kleidon, Allan W. (1992). 'Arbitrage, nontrading, and stale prices: October 1987'. *Journal of Business*, 65(4): 483–97.

Klemkosky, R. C., and J. H. Lee (1991). 'The intra-day ex post and ex ante profitability of index arbitrage'. *Journal of Futures Markets*, 11(3): 291–311.

Krugman, P. (1998). 'What Happened to Asia? For a conference in Japan, January 1998'. http://faculty.washington.edu/karyiu/Asia/papers/AsianGrowth.htm

Lam, Kin, and Billy S. C. Mak (1997). 'Estimating the total profit of short positions in a futures market'. Working Paper, Hong Kong Baptist University (December).

Li, Yong Sheng (1999). *Xiang Gang Jin Rong Bao Wei Zhan*. Liao Ning Chu Ban She.

Liang, Y. H. (1999). Guan E Zhi Zhan: Jiu Ba Nian Ba Yue Gang Fu Ru Shi Shi Jian Bu. *Hong Kong Economic Times*.

Lin, J. C., G. C. Sanger, and G. G. Booth (1995). 'Trade size and components of the bid-ask spread'. *Review of Financial Studies*, 8(4): 1153–84.

MacKinlay, A. C., and K. Ramaswamy (1988). 'Index futures arbitrage and the behaviour of stock index futures prices'. *Review of Financial Studies*, 1(2): 137–58.

Madhavan, Ananth (1992). 'Trading mechanisms in securities markets'. *Journal of Finance*, 50(2): 607–43.

McGuinness, Paul B. (1999). *A Guide to the Equity Market of Hong Kong*. Oxford: Oxford University Press.

McKinnon, R., and H. Pill (1996). 'Credible liberalizations and international capital flows: the overborrowing syndrome', in T. Ito (ed.), *Financial Deregulation and Integration in East Asia*. Krueger, A. O. Chicago: Chicago University Press.

Naranjo, Andy (2000). 'Government intervention and adverse selection costs in foreign exchange markets'. *The Review of Financial Studies*, 13 (Summer): 453–77.

Neal, Robert (1996). 'Direct tests of index arbitrage models'. *Journal of Financial and Quantitative Analysis*, 31(4) (December): 541–62.

Perry, Guillermo E., Guillermo Calvo, Corden W. Max, Stanley Fischer, Sir Alan Walters, and John Williamson (1997). *Currency Boards and External Shocks: How Much Pain, How Much Gain?* World Bank Latin American and Caribbean Studies.

Pope, P. F., and P. K. Yadav (1994). 'The impact of short sales constraints on stock index futures prices: Evidence from FT-SE 100 futures'. *Journal of Derivatives*, 1 (Summer): 15–26.

Puttonen, V. (1993). 'Short sales restrictions and the temporal relationship between stock index cash and derivatives markets'. *Journal of Futures Markets*, 13(6): 645–64.

Silk, R. (1986). 'Hong Kong index futures market'. *Asian Monetary Monitor*, 10(4): 1–13.

Sofianos, G. (1993). 'Index arbitrage profitability'. *Journal of Derivatives*, 1 (Fall): 6–20.

Sutcliffe, Charles M. S. (1997). *Stock Index Futures*: theories and international evidence. 2nd edn London, Boston: International Thomson Business Press. 2nd edn.

The Stock Exchange of Hong Kong (2000). *Rules of the Exchange*, Hong Kong.

Yadav, P. K., and P. F. Pope. (1994). 'Stock index-futures mispricing: profit opportunities or risk premia?' *Journal of Banking and Finance*, 18(5): 921–53.

Yam, Joseph (1998). *A Modern Day Currency Board System*. Hong Kong Monetary Authority.

—— (1998). *Coping with Financial Turmoil*. Hong Kong Monetary Authority.

Yau, J., T. Schneeweis, and K. Yung (1990). 'The behavior of stock index futures prices in Hong Kong: before and after the crash', in S. G. Rhee and R. P. Chang (eds.), *Pacific Basin Capital Markets Research*. 357–78. Amsterdam: North Holland.

Other main sources of news and information

Far East Economic Review, 1997–2000
Hong Kong Standard, 1997~1999
South China Morning Post, 1997~1999
http://www.freeconomy.org
http://www.heritage.org
http://www.hknews.com.hk
http://www.hksfc.org.hk
http://www.imf.org
http://www.info.gov.hk
http://www.info.gov.hk/hkma
http://www.londonstockexchange.com
http://www.sehk.com.hk
http://www.worldbank.org

INDEX

ADR *see* American Deposit Receipt
Aggregate Balance
   definition 22n
Ahn, Hee-Joon 42
American Deposit Receipt (ADR) 114, 116n
AMS *see* Automatic Order Matching and Execution System
Asian financial crisis 7–14
   impact on Hong Kong 4, 8, 11–20, 21–2, 32, 168
"The Asian Miracle" 8–12
Automatic Order Matching and Execution System (AMS) 41, 70–1

Bank of England 4, 164
Biais, B. 67n
Black Wednesday 4–5

Campbell, Tim S. 158
Certificate of Indebtedness 145n
Chan, K. C. 5
Chan, Kalok 6
Cheng, Louis T. W. 5
Cheung, Yan-Leung 42
Chinese Renminbi *see* Renminbi
covered interest arbitrage
   definition 151
Currency Board arrangements 3, 15, 16n, 20–2, 36n, 145n

De Brouwer, Gordon 5, 33n
"double market play" *see* speculators
Dow Jones Industrial Average Index 28–9, 63, 107, 182
Draper, Paul 6, 132, 134, 137, 138
Druckenmiller, Stanley 2

ERM *see* Exchange Rate Mechanism
The Economic Freedom of the World Report 183–4
Euro Stoxx (Price Index) 182
Exchange Fund 1, 141, 144–51, 182, 188
Exchange Fund Investment Ltd (Efil) 186
Exchange Rate Mechanism (ERM) 4

Federal Reserve Bank of New York 34
Federal Reserve System 114
Feulner, Edwin J. 184
Financial Stability Forum 33
   report on highly leveraged institutions 28, 33

Financial Times Stock Exchange 100 Share Index (FT- SE 100) 80–1, 107
FOMC 114
Footsie *see* Financial Times Stock Exchange 100 Share Index (FT-SE 100)
foreign exchange market intervention 48, 151–7
Fraser Institute (Canada) 184
FT-SE 100 *see* Financial Times Stock Exchange 100 Share Index (FT-SE 100)
Fung, Alexander K. W. 134, 191–2
Fung, Joseph K. W. 6, 132, 134, 137, 138
futures market (Hong Kong) *see* Hang Sang Index (HSI) futures
futures trading (Hong Kong) *see* Hang Sang Index (HSI) futures

Goldman Sachs 99
Greenspan, Alan 34n

Hang Seng Index (HSI) 1, 2, 5, 25–26, 29–30, 59, 63, 98, 104, 106–7, 112, 114, 117, 120, 123, 130, 133, 138, 141, 148, 159, 164–5, 167–78, 173, 178, 181, 189, 194, 196
Hang Seng Index Fund 185
Hang Seng Index (HSI) futures 50, 121–6
   arbitrage opportunities 6, 132–3
   futures contracts on expiration days 194–7
   futures return calculation method 191–3
   market behaviour during intervention 126–40
   price behaviour during intervention 130–40
   profit/loss during intervention 171–8, 198–201
Hang Seng Investment Management 185
Hong Seng London Reference Index (HSLRI) 78, 91–2
hedge funds 32–35
Heritage Foundation (Washington) 2, 184, 186, 188
HIBOR *see* Hong Kong interbank offered rate
highly leveraged institutions (HLIs) 5, 29, 32–5
   Report of the Working Group on 28, 33
Hillian, P. 67n
HKATS *see* Hong Kong Futures Automated Trading System
HKFE *see* Hong Kong Futures Exchange
HKMA *see* Hong Kong Monetary Authority
HLIs *see* highly leveraged institutions

208 Index

Hong Kong
  Asian financial crisis and 4, 8, 11–20, 21–2, 32, 168
  Currency Board arrangement 3, 15, 16n, 20–2, 36n, 145n
  Economic situation 14–28
  free-market image 2, 183–6, 188
  futures market 50, 121–40, 171–8, 191–201
  gross domestic product 16–18
  highly leveraged institutions 32–4
  monetary supply 149–51
  property price index 20, 157
  as Special Administrative Region of China 15, 17n, 189n
  stock exchange 40–3, 66, 69–72, 185
  tourism sector 18, 20
Hong Kong Association of Banks 11
Hong Kong Futures Automated Trading System (HKATS) 123
Hong Kong Interbank Offered Rate (HIBOR) 22–4, 26–7, 30, 158–9, 161–62
Hong Kong Futures Exchange (HKFE) 122, 124, 194
Hong Kong Jockey Club 2–3
Hong Kong Monetary Authority (HKMA) 1, 8, 15, 20–4, 27–30, 32–3, 35–6, 48, 59, 66n, 67, 92, 99, 100n, 104n, 106–7, 110, 124, 140–51, 153, 155, 157, 162, 172, 175, 187, 190
Hong Kong shares
  trading in London market 78–94
HSBC Holdings/stocks 29, 44–5, 69, 75, 78, 81, 87, 94, 96, 102, 135, 138, 181
  comparison with UK bank stocks 114–20
HSI see Hang Seng Index
HSI futures see Hang Seng Index (HSI) futures
HSLRI see Hang Seng London Reference Index 78, 91–2
Huang, Yi-yi 5
Hui, Rafel 30, 125, 184
Haque, Ahmed Shafiqul 5

Index of Economic Freedom 184
  position of Hong Kong 186, 188
International Federation of Stock Exchanges 122n
International Monetary Fund (IMF) 146n, 188, 189n

Jao, Y. C. 5, 157n

Kracaw, William A. 158
Krugman, P. 10n

LAF see liquid adjustment facility
Lam, Kin 171–2, 191–2, 198
LERS see linked exchange rate system
Li, Young, Sheng 5
Lin, Da-Jian 5
LIFFE 137
linked exchange rate system (LERS) 20–1, 36
liquid adjustment facility 16, 23–4, 30, 36
London Stock Exchange 1, 40, 43n, 92n
  trading of Hong Kong shares 43, 78–94, 97, 114–120
  Transaction Date Service (TDS) 81
London traded Hong Kong shares 78–94, 97
LTCM (hedge fund) 34–5, 114, 155, 162, 179n, 190

McDonough, William, J. 34
McKinnon, R. 10n
Mak, Billy S. C. 171–72, 198
Morgan Stanley Global Index (MSGI) 166–9

New York Stock Exchange 40
Ngai, Anthony 154
Nikkei 300 182

"order-driven" market 40–41

Paris Bourse 40–41, 67
Pill, H. 10n
Pope, P. F. 137n
Puttonen, V. 137n

"quote-driven" market 40

Real effective exchange rate (REFR) 16
REFR see real effective exchange rate
Renminbi 3, 23, 27, 31, 31n, 49, 153, 155
RMB see Renminbi

SEAQ see stock exchange automatic quotation
SEHK see Stock Exchange of Hong Kong
SETS see Stock Exchange Electronic Trading System
Sheng, Andrew 150n, 157n
Singapore Straits Times index 165
stock exchange automatic quotation (SEAQ) 80–1, 89, 91
Sofianos, G. 137n
Soros 2, 4
speculators 3–4, 7, 22, 24, 26–8, 121, 125n, 142, 145, 151–7, 163, 171, 175–80
Spatt, C. 67n
Standard Chartered Bank 114–16, 118–19, 154
Stock Exchange Electronic Trading System 80, 81
Stock Exchange of Hong Kong (SEHK) 66, 70, 185

definition of trading methods 71
trading mechanism 40–3
stock market intervention
 assessment of 163–90
 background 8–28
 disposal of purchased stocks 184–6
 financing of 141–62
 foreign exchange market intervention 48, 151–7
 intervened and non-intervened stocks 97–120
 literature survey 5–7
 an overview 28–38
 post-intervention stock price changes 181
 press coverage of 94–6, 123–6
 process of 43–96
 speculator's role 3–4, 6, 22, 24, 26–8, 121, 142, 145, 151–7, 163, 171, 175–80
 volume of purchased stocks 63–78, 76–7

Tokyo Stock Exchange 40
Tracker Fund Hong Kong (TraHK) 38, 185, 188–9
TraHK *see* Tracker Fund Hong Kong
Transaction Data Service (TDS) 81
Tsang, Donald 1, 3–4, 28n, 31, 35, 37, 141–2, 155, 164n, 180, 183, 184n, 188

Union Bank of Switzerland (UBS) 34
US Federal Reserve System *see* Federal Reserve System

Wells, Stephen 43n, 81n, 91n

Yadav, P. K. 137n
Yam, Joseph 8n, 21, 27–8, 30n, 106, 142, 150n, 175, 188n
yuan *see* Renminbi
yen 25, 31, 63, 114, 168